The Life Story
of a Little Boy Called
MIRACLE

My Life in the Valley of Snow

LEON DUMSTREY-SOOS

tellwell

Tellwell Talent
www.tellwell.ca

ISBN
978-0-2288-0586-1 (Hardcover)
978-0-2288-0584-7 (Paperback)
978-0-2288-0585-4 (eBook)

WHEN I WAS A BOY

*But as many as received Him, to them He gave
the right to become children of God.*

JOHN 1:12

Foreword

Birth to Immigration to Canada

To all those who will ever read this, I came to the conclusion that it is almost impossible to put a two-word title on eighty-six years of a life story. Therefore, I choose to put it into the format of a foreword.

This is the life account of my happy but interrupted childhood in the Kingdom of Yugoslavia (feudal system, fascism, post-war struggles with Tito's Yugoslavian Communism), my journey from my homeland to Germany and, finally, my immigration to Canada (democracy!).

Marshal Tito was a Communist Leader for the partisans, resisting German and Italian occupation on the territory of Yugoslavia (1941–'45). He ruled the country until his death in the early '80s. This was actually foretold to me when I was seven years old by an old gypsy woman who frequently visited my Grandma Baker by reading her palm and then mine, where a long road of adventure and a very hard but successful life began, filled with all the gifts and good friends that led to many rewarding enterprises and a beautiful family and home.

I was blessed and lucky: a community pioneer, active in sports, a member of community organizations, builder of the Catholic Church, married to a beautiful wife, father of two lovely daughters. And then, years later, tragedy struck my family. First, my wife and I separated and I became Mr. Mom. Then my older daughter Tania got mauled by a tiger and died, leaving two children, Adrienne and Nicholas. Nine years later, my younger daughter Vesna was murdered, and to top it all off I was diagnosed with terminal bone cancer three months before: 8–12 months to live.

I survived it all. Eight months later, my doctors, Dr. Kay and Dr. Miller, called me a miracle. I was born on November 9, 1931. This is where it all began, and the Gypsy woman did not miss very much.

The Life Story of the Little Boy Called Miracle, and My Life in the Valley of Snow

This is not only a story of that little boy, it is also a true struggle of a young immigrant and the hard-earned Canadian Citizenship that I am proud of, acquired after I had to give up my Yugoslav statehood. I served my Canada faithfully for over sixty years, worked hard building my country, my community (six subdivisions, church and a bridge across the Skeena River), and paid my taxes. Then the politics started to change, where peaceful democracy became a chaos of liberal-socialist-capitalist self-serving egoists. In my opinion, these liberal-socialist losers stripped me of my Canadian national pride and turned me into a second-class citizen, and took the nation apart by political correctness—giving special privileges to minorities, declaring the First Nations to be above all other citizenry in the country (the First Nations who have not in the past 10,000 years contributed anything to global civilization in science, technology, medicine, patents, literature, letters or language)—ignoring the fact that we all should be equal, thus imposing guilt on me and my children for generations that will have to satisfy their unrealistic demands on injustice caused not by me and my children but by the bad English colonial system.

The proof lies in the real difference between the U.S. and Canada. We agree that Canada and the U.S. are composed of the same ethnic groups, but the U.S. got rid of the British colonial powers and we and the other commonwealth countries have stayed under British colonial power.

Take a good look at what a tremendously powerful, wealthy, developed and rich country the U.S. became in past 250 years—a world power. Where is Canada?

This saga also illustrates many struggles with the incompetence of the local, provincial and federal authorities; the envy and deceit of local social organizations and some close friends and family members; and the kind consideration for my older daughter's demise by my lifelong bank: the Bank of Nova Scotia.

It is a story of a carefree childhood that was interrupted by cruel, savage and destructive war; a colourful education period; the difficult decision to leave my beautiful homeland of Yugoslavia and my life as a refugee; and my emigration to Canada, which was filled with considerable success, some disappointments and immense losses that make me cry rivers, just like now while I write this. My heart and soul are filled with a sea of sadness and pain.

It will go through the greatest tragedies in my life: the loss of my beautiful wife Babette from a fatal fall in 2002, the loss of my smart and beautiful older daughter Tania who was mauled and killed by a tiger in 2007, and the murder of my daughter and angel-child Vesna in 2016. Then I met a very charming lady, Leisl Kabery, a writer herself, wife, mom and local victim services officer. After many visits and conversations with her, she suggested I should write a book: my life story.

As I started these first pages it all felt so strange, remembering the Gypsy woman at Grandma Baker's place foretelling to the seven-year-old boy with the left-hand palm and making her prophecy ... shattering!

As I said recently, I was thinking about writing my life story: where I came from and what transpired from November 1931 till I was diagnosed with terminal bone cancer in 2015 and given eight months to a year to live—the dates have been reset by the hormone therapy, a gamble, an injection every three months for the rest of my life. It worked and I am still here. I survived; I am a miracle! So I started to seriously poke and wander through my mind's long hallways, knocking on and peeking in its many doors to see how much is there.

It feels like going through hundreds of rooms of an ancient castle, looking for old photos, pressing an ear to the walls hoping to hear live voices of the past, looking for answers. Family history tells me that the tribe was established in the 9th century as salt miners, through centuries of wars supporting the royal family, whoever was in power. So, on August

16, 1609, my great-great-grandfather, Valentine, was given the certificate of nobility by King Mathias II in Vienna, Austria, with all rights and privileges of the feudal aristocracy—together with complete armour, ring, helmet, sword, lance and family-crest shield—for all generations to come, for both males and females. It is registered in a museum of history. All these items are described in detail by king's order ... wow, we have blue blood! This certificate includes the names of all the nobility and dignitaries present on that occasion.

So, there I was in the 20th century, a noble rebel and perhaps God's gift to my family and relatives, who all loved me dearly (when/because I was cute, chubby, well-behaved little boy), and the childless ones competed for me. I was told that I always tortured everyone in a soft, innocent voice with hundreds of strange questions. This culminated in 1936 when we had our family reunion. Some three hundred of us gathered, of which fifty or seventy were children of all ages. New nobility of many different nationalities: Croatians, Hungarians and Austrians. Everyone spoke at least three languages. Can you imagine what kind of chatter it was?

Food was prepared for two weeks by supervised chefs; there was a large cellar with different kinds of booze offered. Hundreds of gifts on display. Ladies showing off their attire and jewellery. There were some beauties, I must say, but I silently thought that they had swollen noble heads. High noses and arrogance were always the order of the day. Children were separated from the adults under the supervision of governants.

In the beginning, everything went smoothly. Families were introduced to each other; some had never met before. One hundred years before travelling technology was developed and the first railroads were built, travel was mainly made by horse and carriage—fancy, custom-built ones. There were few cars. It was quite a sight to see all those carriages, horses, cars and drivers. It was my world to explore.

My father's side was the largest; there were sixteen of them: ten brothers and six sisters. (Many of them perished in WWI.) Two of my aunts were real beauties. They were not married, which was unusual for these times. I guess no suitor was good enough for their mother, who was a tiny, sinister woman. On that occasion, one of them fell instantly in love with me (it was mutual) and for the duration of the festivity I ended up by her side with my mom and brother.

My mom being an outsider (a wealthy baker's daughter), she was not received warmly, save for an aunt. I was really upset about it. It is worth noting that by that time the feudal system was in decline and many did not have much, they were just a show of the past.

My grandfather (this was the only time I ever saw him) was a big man. He was a bishop in the Greek Catholic community. His family was not lacking for anything.

Festivities went on for a week. Children were prepared for show. Those who played musical instruments did so (everyone had to learn to play the piano), others were to recite poems or history, or say a certain prayer. This show-off was mainly for the parents, so we knew we better perform well.

This lasted for hours, and finally came my turn. I had to recite the Rooster Song in Hungarian, which my aunt had taught me. I still remember it today. I was also the youngest amongst the children, so when five-year-old me stepped up, my mother was beaming with pride. The group went silent. Being an natural rebel and of my own mind, and perhaps an occasional shit-disturber, I stepped up onto the makeshift stage—cute, neat little boy—and looked at the crowd and my relatives. I was not liked by some of my cousins; many were making faces at me.

So I began: "Please may I ask a question after I recite my song?" I did not ask beforehand for permission from my father, which was a mortal sin, and before he could react one of my older uncles yelled, "Let him ask! There is no harm in it." So, when I finished my Rooster Song without a flaw, my father's eyes were sending me arrows and my mother had turned pale, probably thinking, *What is he up to now?*

I yelled loudly: "Why does Grandmother not like us? Why is my blood red when my nose bleeds yet everyone is talking about us as nobility and being blue-blooded. Is this because my mother is a baker's daughter?" This was like a bomb. Someone yelled, "Get this mis-birthed bastard away!" My mom was in tears and the crowd scattered. My father tried to get me, but his sister prevented that. We—my mother, brother and

I—immediately departed to Grandmother Baker's. I stayed there for a month till the storm settled. I am not sure how my mother fared, as later in life I slowly discovered that my father treated her very poorly, and me as well. I hated him for that.

I didn't see any of them till WWII ended.

LEON DUMSTREY-SOOS

6

Oh yes, my mom. She was a very beautiful, tall, dark-haired woman. She had beautiful, glacier-blue, cold, penetrating eyes. Rich baker's daughter. She had one brother. If someone ticked her off, she would just give them the long stare. I am sure their souls felt it. She used to do the same thing with my father. In my teens I started to understand that their relationship was under severe stress, yet life demanded they stick together, no matter what. At the time, divorce or separation was not an easy thing. It was considered shameful. There were no ministries of children and families to look after your mistakes.

Our original bake oven was part of a huge Franciscan monastery build in the 11th century. A bake oven with a bread-preparation room was outside of the gate of the monastery. It was a huge brick structure my great-great-grandfather and his crew slept on (just like I did centuries later while visiting my grandparents. It was a warm and cozy place, always full of the smell of fresh-baked goodies. Grandma used to wake me and my brother and feed us with fresh milk and honey croissants), then made the bread for the monks and fed them from their kitchen.

The monastery was a huge property of some fifty rooms: a large church, rectory and historically famous library and pharmacy (from where my godfather benefited, being a private local pharmacist), with the stables, huge green garden, catacombs and long escape tunnel all surrounded with a seven-metre wall to keep away robbers, and later to protect them from the Turks, who began the invasion and occupation of the Balkan Peninsula and advanced towards Central Europe: Budapest, Zagreb and Vienna.

In time, the monks gifted the bakery to one of my great-grandfathers, who started to add more rooms to the old structure. By the beginning of the 19th century, it had become a beautiful six-hundred-year-old, four-bedroom home on a large property as a result of a reputable and profitable bakery business.

Over time, the family acquired more land to grow their own wheat and they built a small mill for making flour for their bakery. Naturally, there was a vineyard. Without it, life would have been a poor go.

In the early 19th century, my grandfather married a girl from a rich landowner not too far away. They had two children, my mom and my uncle. They both went to school. My mother finished agricultural administration and my uncle studied at University of Z's faculty of forestry. He got his diploma in '36 or '37, and served in various location as a state forester. At the outbreak of WWII, he was recalled to the army, and when the Germans invaded the country he became a POW. He was freed through the Red Cross in 1942. My grandmother was ecstatic, as she loved him so dearly. That mother/son thing, you know.

My mom and dad met in the same school. She must have been seventeen or eighteen when they married, and he was eight years older. May he rest in peace. He was the youngest of sixteen.

After their marriage, his mother disowned him. All family members put us on the outside. My mother's background—the middle class—was not good enough for them. My brother and I were considered bastards.

I remember an attempted visit to Grandmother's—Father's mom—by Mom and two of us. My mom was refused entry into the house by one of the aunts. My mother was crying very hard. Two of us were already in the house, and were led by one of the servants to a reception room. We were told to be quiet unless asked to speak. That will never happen, I said to myself, remembering my family-reunion performance.

Finally, we were allowed to enter into the room. It was very large, with lots of furniture and heavy drapes on the windows, and it was dark. The large fireplace was burning, and there were two large chairs in front of it. I could not see Grandmother. Suddenly, she got up and walked towards us, stopping halfway and starring at us for a moment, and then saying: "Go away, you are not wanted here!" We left. My other grandmother went bananas upon hearing that. My father was in great discomfort.

Grandmother was a small, skinny woman with grey hair, very large and dark eyebrows, black glowing eyes, sunken cheeks and pale skin. She gave birth to sixteen kids. She died at ninety-nine.

I never forgot that moment in my life, the insult and the injury to my mom.

We spent the next few days with my beautiful aunt, who was also ousted because she had a daughter out of wedlock. That cousin and I became soulmates. She passed away in 2015. I miss her dearly. She had two kids, and we still keep in touch. My cousin and I kept in touch after I immigrated to Canada.

I lived in a feudal system where marriages were arranged to preserve the wealth (I think) and perhaps the "blue blood"—crap!

9

In my parent's case, my grandmother (Mother's mom) must have been impressed by having a "blue-blood" in the family, not knowing that my father was disowned and broke. Yet he had seen a good chunk of wealth from the baker's daughter. His dowry after the marriage was quite impressive. Complete furnishing for a five-bedroom home from kitchen to bedrooms, with all the necessities and some cash.

Women and children were always second to men. I remember my father was always served first, and sometimes he was in a bad mood, hungover, or he had found something wrong with the food and would throw everything off the table. My poor mother would cry. We kids were petrified and stayed hungry.

There were always big parties that lasted two to three days. Lots of food and booze was consumed and most men ended up behaving badly, getting sick, messing up the place and suffering horrible hangovers. Participants were dignitaries (oh boy, some crowd), bureaucrats, teachers, priests, lawyers ... anyone who was someone. They brought their wives if they were married, and others brought "housekeepers," most of whom were attractive women. As I was snoopy, I found out they were more than just housekeepers.

My brother was a year older than me. We almost never played together, and when that did happen we always argued and fought. I could never understand—he would go to the extreme sometimes, grabbing a fork or shovel to try to stab or hit me. I was usually very quick, but twice he succeeded in stabbing me in the hand, and another time he hit me on the back with a shovel. I think he was very dangerous, like my father. From then on I stayed away from him. We slept in the same bedroom, but we never talked or played very much.

I was relieved when he started school. There were none where we lived. Father was in the process of building one (it still stands today) so my brother went to Grandmother Baker's. I followed, and when Father completed the school we finished the elementary courses at home, then we went to a boarding school run by the Catholic order of Don Bosco to continue our high school in the city.

Our farm was surrounded by six small villages where the labour for the farm came from. They were all very poor. The houses consisted of one large room with a large stove oven made out of clay and heated by wood, which served for cooking and baking and as a bed for the children and elderly in cold winters. There was a meat smoker in the attic. Smoke was derived from the stove; the roof cover was made of straw. People mostly walked barefoot year round (except in the winter), save for church on Sundays and special occasions. Shoes were precious and expensive belongings. The cheap footwear called "opanak"—a strapped, boat-shaped, soft-soled shoe made out of home-produced leather—was worn by many female workers.

Other beds were placed along and against the perimeter wall. They were made of wood with twin-size mattresses on them filled with straw. Bedding was made from flax and burlap from hemp. Duvets and pillows were filled with the goose feathers or flax "wool." It was a tedious process. When the trees of flax and hemp reached full growth, they were cleaned of branches, which were tied into bundles then submerged into the pond where water could run through them. In about a month they were taken out, dried and beaten. Inner-core material came as wool, which the women treaded into various thicknesses of string. This was put on a simple weaving table and turned into cloth that was boiled/washed with the soap made of slaughtered pig-lard residue and then bleached in very acid stone. Cloth pieces were than rinsed and hung in the sun for several days, from which women made rough skirts and blouses. Covers, men's pants and bags of different sizes were made as well. Many had a cow or two, some chickens and pigs. Some were sold or traded at area fairs.

As the farm was prospering, Father decided to build the school with a chapel, where a young priest came by bicycle every month to give services. Thus, the walk to it was cut in half for us, and the same for the school children, as the closest school was six kilometres away.

It was very hard for children in grades one to four to walk that far, particularly in the winter's deep snow and cold. Most of the time, adults made the path and escorted them. The school was well built, and when it was finished my brother and I attended it. My brother went in the fourth grade and I went between three and four. Before this, we were at Grandmother Baker's and went to school there. She always treated us with fresh milk and honey croissants. Mostly we only ate the corners and the rest we stuffed into the mattress. When it was discovered, everyone laughed and a whole bunch of bread crumbs were made.

My Grandmother Baker was a super cook like all the ladies of the time. She made wonderful cabbage rolls that I enjoyed. I ate four to five eggs for breakfast; my lunch was garlic sausage with a loaf of white bread.

I was a wanderer; sometimes during the lunch break I just went off into nowhere. As there was always someone in the fields, somebody would notice the little boy wandering, carefree. Sometimes I spent the nights in the hay heaps. When I ran into workers in the fields, they would offer me milk, water, bread and cheese. When I was found, my grandmother was very upset. I had to kneel on the corn seeds for ten minutes. Ouch!

I loved noodles in the baking pan. I always checked with the neighbours to scrape their burned noodles.

I was not a very social boy, but, being a cute and chubby little rascal, childless family members and relatives competed for me (my godfather and godmother particularly) to stay in their homes. It was wonderful, and I think it did a lot for me as I was growing up. So, I spent a lot of time during school breaks in many different places in the city and the country.

My godfather and godmother lived in the same place as Grandmother Baker. They bought me a bike, and a sled that crashed one winter sledding through the small town. We had four or six sleds tied together; twenty kids were screaming. The run was down Main Street, a fairly steep two- to three-kilometre run. There was sharp turn on the intersection, and we ended up in the snow pile. Sadly, my sled collapsed. I went the next day to my godfather, crying and apologizing. He gave me a big hug. "It is only a sled, my boy. The important thing is that you are OK." Two days later, I got a new, bigger and stronger sled

My bike was a beautiful one, but it was a challenge to learn how to ride. When I was good on it, my brother and I went for a six-kilometre ride, and downhill on the way back I went full blast and could not negotiate a sharp turn. I crashed, bending the pedals and steering and scraping my right leg and arm. My brother took off and I pushed my bike the three kilometres home. Oh yes, my father then came into the picture ... nothing to talk about. The bike was taken away and fixed. In the end it was ruined by my father's mailman and it finally disappeared.

Sometime later, my godfather and godmother came to visit in a beautiful black Mercedes convertible. The next day after he heard the story, he confronted my father and, after a heated exchange, he left with his wife. It took a long time for them to reconcile. My father was furious with me for speaking to my godfather. Later in life they became good friends.

There was one occasion when my godparents visited that I should write out in full.

I must admit that my father was a great prankster. My godmother on the other side was extremely afraid of ghosts. I mentioned before that the castle belonged to the wealthy landowner, well, he also had the sawmill, and as the story goes, he murdered his wife in the kitchen with a shotgun. So while Godmother was visiting my father, he slowly built the ghost case by telling her about unusual occurrences during the night-time. Like noises in the attic, or that you could hear the saw motor going, or on occasion ghosts were seen around the castle sawing wood after midnight. Here was the poor woman, slowly becoming so petrified that my mother or father had to go with her to the bathroom or to her bedroom. Distances through the dark rooms and hallways are always longer and the areas were not illuminated, so one had to have a lit candle or an oil lamp. The walk to the toilet was the longest from the dining room, and there were a number of doors on one side.

Everybody stayed up late. One night, when my father guided the poor thing past the kitchen, all the doors were closed. All was prearranged. My father and godmother just happened to stop at the kitchen door, when suddenly there was the scream of a woman coming from the kitchen. As my godmother grabbed my father, the candle went out and then there was a shotgun blast, and my godmother peed herself. Suddenly there were lamps lit and everyone was consoling her.

Her bedroom was next to my parents'. Her door was open (my godfather slept in a separate room because of his snoring). Her window was on the back-garden side. So, a few nights after the kitchen episode she was OK. Everybody laughed at the episode.

That particular night there was a horrible shriek and we were woken up. My godmother ended up in my parents' bed, muttering that there were ghosts outside her window sawing wood. Father had gotten two workers to dress in white with an old oil lamp, saw, sawhorse and a piece of wood. My father took his time lighting the lamp, so at the first flash the workers retreated. By the time Father brought my godmother to the window there was nothing to be seen.

My father, I never liked him. In my opinion he was a selfish, insecure despot. He tended to be a horseman (this was from his army experience); he always dressed in riding pants and high riding boots. He rode every day, checking the activities on the farm. He had a bullwhip stuck in his boot. He always had a pistol on him, and when going away he would strap a short-barreled shotgun on his shoulder and slide a hunting gun with scope into the saddle boot. He was a short, skinny man, very temperamental but very smart and clever. He could not stand the sight of blood and he was afraid of bad people. I think he lived in self-inflicted fear.

Both Mom and Dad completed farm-management school. Mom specialized in farm management; she also had first aid and training in animal birth. Father completed farm agriculture administration and specialized in vineyard development and orchards. When he graduated, he got an offer to work for his brother-in-law—a German national, very rich—who had a huge pig farm not too far away. He was a huge man and very handsome; he wanted to adopt me. He bought an old rundown farm which had a sawmill.

When the owner shot his wife in the kitchen he went to jail and the farm went on the block. He proposed that my father restore it and make it profitable, and he would get part ownership of it. My father and mom agreed and went to work. They started in 1928, and by 1937 the project was completed and it became the jewel of the farm: two thousand acres of forest, fields, meadows, vineyards, orchards, beautiful gardens and a large green garden. The farm became completely self-sustaining; there were stables with horses and cows, chicken coops and pig pens. Cows produced milk, butter, cheese and meat. Horses did the work in the fields. Chicken, geese, ducks and turkeys provided a lot of eggs and meat and so did the pigs. Geese and ducks also provided feathers for bed coverings and pillows.

I think that the three primary fields were grain and corn, the vineyard and the plum orchard. Bread was an important part of our diet—the poor had nothing but corn bread. White flour was a luxury. Grapes of various kinds—mostly for wine making—were my father's specialty. There were wines for sale. He went to wine exhibitions in good years. The vineyard had large vine stems growing on wire and were cut about one metre in length and grafted with other species, then put into the ground to root. In about a year, seedlings were dug out and bundled. Maybe thirty to forty plants were dipped in manure mix, wrapped in burlap and shipped to the market.

Pulp from pressed grapes was burned in a special still for brandy. It was a lot of fun being around the grape press and drinking the sweet juice.

Plums were used for yummy jams and, most importantly, for making a famous national spirit, Slivovitz, which supersedes any other brandy at any time in that part of the world. It's very potent stuff. Wine brandy and plum Slivovitz are really a cultural art and the pride of the people.

The green garden was huge, many veggies grew there, and in the orchard a variety of fruits. Much of it was preserved for winter. Hard work never stopped...

Fall harvest was an exciting time. It began in summer with hay storage, then later corn, pumpkins, special feeding of the poultry for Christmas and the slaughtering of the pigs. Making sausage and smoking the meat was done by an aging villager who was a master at smoking meat. And yes, there was the making of the sauerkraut.

The farm—our new home—was a three-hundred-year-old small castle that used to have a sawmill. Before I describe our new home, I'd like to tell a few things about me. Aside from being a smart, clever, well-behaved boy, I was at times a real brat. One month after we moved into our new home I knew every part of it. There was not a corner that I did not check out. That included the worker's quarters, stables, pig pens, storage magazine ... I was everywhere.

My mother broke a few cooking spoons on me, as I was always a mess coming back from my explorations.

The old structure was built with baked clay bricks. It had a sloped roof covered with clay tile. The walls were one metre thick. It had eleven large rooms with high ceilings. The front half was a long hallway with a main entry, with heavy oak doors on the outside and a heavy iron gate on the inside that gave access on one end to toilets and staff quarters (one chef and three maids), pantry, kitchen, family room and first-aid room. All the windows had heavy iron gates.

On the other end was a large utility/storage/access room. On each side was a large cubicle for the wood storage and access to three ceramic tile stoves in each room that provided heat. There were stored dishes, cutlery and extra chairs for large dining parties adjacent to it. The entrance to the family sleeping quarters (two bedrooms) had a large two-tub bathroom with a double sink and a large steel stove that also heated the water. Adults had a bath twice a week, we the kids once a week, other days we were washed in the family room in small tub. The family room had a round steel stove. On winter mornings it was red hot; the staff kept the fires going 24/7. One morning, a maid was dressing my brother; he was very restless and ended up pressing his butt against the red-hot stove. The rest I leave to your imagination.

From the bathroom was the access to the guest dining room, four bedrooms and Father's large office with his safe. All the workers received their pay there; some monthly, others semi-monthly.

The basement was divided into three sections. A heavy steel door guarded the hallway. On the left was a tool crib and the repair shop, on the right was a large room used as a laundry room and slaughter room, and later I concluded it was a torture room. At the end of the hallway was another steel door (it was not locked anymore) that led into the dungeon. The last part was a huge wine cellar with the cool storage.

There was no electricity, running water or proper toilets. Kerosene and petroleum were used in lamps for light and candles. It was dangerous to use it in the attics and stables. Toilets were very simple; today I can describe them as indoor outhouses.

Water was brought in pails and the small tanks were filled in the kitchen and the bathroom. The same water was intended for fire protection. There was actually little to burn as all the walls were made from brick and the ceiling was covered with heavy plaster. The only danger was in the attic, because of the large roof structure.

Drinking water was brought from some distance in the forest, where there was a small stream running out of the hillside. I will never forget its taste. In 1936, my father build a concrete holding tank. In 1966, I returned for the first time to my country. The first thing I did was drive my parents and Mom's brother there. We had a nice picnic and a good drink of water. We shared many moments of our lives and cried. We took some water home and put it into a cooler. That was fifty-one years ago; what a memorable day that was.

After that day I came to the conclusion that we are all people, good and not so good, regardless of colour, blood and legal relationships. Amongst the not so good, maybe we are lucky to find a few that could pass.

There was a blacksmith shop, stables and a coach garage. There was a silo space built by my father, where greens of various kinds were shredded and preserved for cows in the winter, stimulating their milk production. All these together with the pig pens were in one long building. The attic throughout was filled with prime hay.

There were another four buildings in the yard. One for machines (grain thrasher and tractor); another was a huge carport for various carriages, the attic filled with straw which was used on the stable floors; a corn silo; and a honey beehive shed, attached to which was a large chicken coop. There were three large lime trees in an open area next to it. Behind it was a fenced passage leading to the livestock watering tub that was filled with water by buckets from the cistern nearby. Below was a beautiful green slope full of hazelnut shrubs. Lime-tree flowers were used for a very tasty tea.

On the other end of the main yard was a large building attached to the breezeway to the main structure. It housed the foreman and farm staff. There was a schoolroom, a room for visiting tradesmen, a large fruit-storage room and the room for my uncle when he came to study before exams.

In the old schoolroom there were two large maps of the world. I used to sit in front of them and fantasize about what all was out there. Look where I am now. Who could tell then, some eighty-one years ago, that I would write about them. It was those two maps that perhaps planted the seeds of my long voyage in 1955...

Nights were very black there—in summer and winter you could not see your hand in front of your face.

Sundays we always went to church, six kilometres away. Father seldom joined us. Mom and Dad were of different faiths. She was Roman Catholic and he was Greek Catholic. They had to have the cardinal's permission for their marriage. Perhaps that was the reason my father did not participate. Who knows?

As I mentioned before, I was a curious kid—a real rat. My curiosity to observe, to listen and to investigate was fanatical. I simply had to find out and understand everything. I had the tendency to quietly and as unobserved as possible snoop around. The dungeon was one of the places that fascinated me for many reasons, like the spookiness of the place—dark and damp with rusty old chains and iron rings hanging on the walls. Some of the chains had shackles indicating that it had been a horrible place for anyone who ended up in it. It was intended for thieves, bandits and not-well-behaving peasants. To keep places like that showed me how cruel humanity can be/is. This, in my opinion, included my father.

The dungeon was divided into three parts. On one side of a short hallway was a smaller room, about four by five metres without windows or air holes. Next to it were three one-by-one-metre cells, probably for solitary confinement. I used to sit there for hours in complete darkness listening for the sounds in the walls, fantasizing about the horrors that occurred there. Who knows what transpired, who was tortured, molested or killed there? It was petrifying sitting in the total darkness and dead silence. The place was soundproof.

It was also a place where, during laundry days or pig-slaughter days, there were many women and young girls working. I used to hide in the solitary cells and listen to the noise created by the screwing that went on by the workers who snuck in. Sometimes it was noisier when boys dragged in the young girls. Goodbye virginity!

Peasant women and girls did not have any underwear, just skirts and blouses. When they were sweaty from working they would show nipples, their clothes nicely sticking to them. Men were aggressive and the climate assisted their human nature, of which I must admit I become victim to later in my youth. Today, when I think about it ... it's too bad recorders were not available. I also found condoms on the floor, but peasants did not use them. Who then? My father always had some on his night table. My uncle? There were many pretty young peasant girls needing jobs, so "use and perhaps abuse" kept them in good company. Today I fantasize about how many I missed.

Later in life, it appeared to me that my father lived in fear and insecurity. He was very temperamental, short and skinny. He would hide this by being aggressive with his subordinates, his family and his dog. He was furious with me as he could not make me cry no matter how hard he beat me. I am not sure if he was a happy person. As life went on,

I learned about his character. He was a Gemini, and today this answers all my questions.

He was very meticulous and demanded the same from the others. Mother was not much different.

He rarely talked to us, even at meals, unless it was a demand or command. His friendliness came out only with the guests, especially dignitaries. I am not sure if he was a happy man unless he was boozed-up. But when he came amongst us in such a state, it was better to stay away from him as he was aggressive and mean.

I remember the episode of a visit of a high inspector from government. Oh boy, a stuck-up aristocrat. One morning he wanted to walk on the grass with patent leather shoes. As there was dew on the grass, he demanded it be wiped off. Sure thing, my father complied; he got a bunch of peasant workers to sweep a path on the grass and wipe it off with towels.

My brother was one year older. He started elementary at the age of six. He went to Grandmother Baker's for the first three years, I followed the year after as the school on our farm that was being built by my father was not completed. So, for one year I was the king of the castle.

In the feudal-system family, sons were very important, as well as healthy daughters to be able to give many kids. The first son, on the other hand, had to be a doctor, the second a priest (guess who was second) and the third a lawyer. Others were trained for farming and the army. So it's no wonder my brother and I ended up in a highly regarded boarding school run by the Catholic order of Don Bosco.

We were exposed to the same abuse that I am today paying Canadian aboriginals for. The world has really gone nuts, and I do not have a place to make claims for it. Maybe a tax credit?

The castle had two beautiful yards created by my father while restoring the neglected property. The front yard, some two acres, was turned into a real botanical garden by a professional gardener employed by my father who wanted the best and nicest. It took almost a year to finish. All this I watched intently every day, asking the gardener questions, learning the names of flowers, shrubs and trees. Would you believe that all this enhanced my employment as a student and led to a very profitable business later in a life when I immigrated to Canada? I received a reward for the best commercial garden in my community.

The grounds consisted of many flower beds. The place was always in bloom. There was a variety of ornamental shrubbery and a stone-paved walkway, with the flower beds on each side. It was all contained with a six-foot wooden fence, and on the inside was planted a hedge of jasmine and lilac. In one corner was a very deep cistern and next to it was a huge spruce tree. On the other side there were two beautiful silver spruces, very dense, and very noisy as masses of sparrows nestled in them. Then the shady rest area created by the semicircle of six huge spruces with four hammocks hanging between them. A clearing was made of fine gravel with a table and four benches. And on the side was my sandbox to play in. There were three gates; one led to a green garden and orchard through the breezeway created when the worker's quarters were built. This building was attached to the castle. There was also a second entrance with a heavy steel door leading to Father's office.

Before I continue into the huge green garden...

The roof on both structures was made of baked clay tile. The attic was spacious and the floor was made of clay, and during the night there was always noise and I feared it, not knowing what it was until Mom told me that a bunch of wild cats lived there, playing and chasing mice and rats.

On the end of the breezeway was the gate where a vegetable-garden path began. The path was about one hundred feet and covered with stepping stones. On each side was a ten-foot beech hedge, very thick and trimmed; I used to sneak there after lunch for a poop. I was never discovered; I think the garden was about ten acres in size. It was a beauty. There were two shaded areas. All was fenced in.

One section was close to the entrance of the vine cellar, for a good reason. There was a large gate with road access to the vegetable garden for workers and carriages. A shaded area was created by eight huge spruces; I used to climb them regularly and Mom again broke many cooking spoons on my butt. In the clearing there was a long table with benches for about forty people, and away from this in an open area was a fire pit for roasting the piglets or lamb. Roast piglet is a delicacy in my home country, and it has to be seven to eight weeks old.

The area was separated from the rest of the garden by two beautiful hedges, one was deep purple lilac and the other was my favorite: jasmine. They were quite tall and free-growing, but they were pruned as required. The jasmine was my tent where I played by myself.

The rest of the area was divided into three sections. A large potato field lay along the road all the way to the end of the garden, where a gate gave access to the vineyard. A bit away from the road was a row of all the possible berries that our climate afforded.

The vegetable garden was next, with all the species that would grow there. Mom made sure there was plenty of it. Her enemies were bugs, crows, blue jays and hail. On the end was a beech grove, Mom's favorite place to rest. Nearby was a large pond that was used for watering. As there were no pumps, all the water had to be carried in the pails—quite a chore—and also the same water was used for mixing with copper vitriol and lime—spray for the fruit trees, vineyard, vegetable garden and potato field.

The rest of the area was a large orchard with many varieties of fruit, mostly apples as they were kept through the winter. There were cherries, peaches, apricots and plums. Mom made fantastic jams and other fruit preserves for long winters. The shelves in the pantry probably had two hundred jars or more. Grass growing among the fruit trees was cut by a horse-pulled grass-cutting tool—the same that was used in the hay fields. The bases of the trees were trimmed by scythe. A scythe was sometimes used in the vineyards, but weeds were controlled with the hand hoe. Workers would simply scrape it off.

Areas were guarded with scarecrow puppets and clappers. In addition, there were two guards patrolling the area with shotguns, protecting it from crows and blue jays. They used to shoot a few and then hang them high. Birds surely stayed away.

Oh yes, the pond, another favourite spot of mine. In summers I would watch the frogs hopping and being hunted and eaten by different snakes.

We had a poisonous species of which I do not know the name in English. I was petrified and stayed clear of the tall grass around the pond.

There was a large log floating in the pond that I used to push with a long stick. When the winter came it was very cold and the snow was very deep. There was a path made by the hunter (an employee) who regularly checked the rabbit and fox traps. Foxes were always sneaking around the poultry, as were the hawks and eagles.

So, one winter, when I came to check out the pond, I noticed part of the log sticking out—it was close to the edge and iced in. I tried to push it with my cane (I always carried a cane going into the backyard or bush on the advice of our hunter). As the log did not move—a kid is a kid—I decided to step on it. Well, what happened next occurred like a flash. As I stepped on the log I went with it under the ice, and I was just as fast coming out of the pond. Perhaps it was the log that pushed me or my angel guardian who saved me. And then I ran home, which was couple of hundred metres away. I was running soaking wet, slowly turning into an icicle. I was freezing up and slowing down—halfway there it became real slow motion. I could barely move, and there was my mom coming with one of the maids. She was worried about me. I was already on the ground and they picked me up and carried me into the laundry room. My lucky day, it was the laundry day and warm inside. Mom took a knife and started to cut the buttons on my jacket and pants while maids poured lukewarm water on me. When I was naked and shivering, Mother said, "This is for good measure and to warm you up," and there was a whack with the large wooden spoon. Then she hugged me with tears in her eyes, saying, "You lucky little rascal." She turned to the staff and told them, "Not a word of this, understand!" My father never found out.

I mentioned before that Mom and Dad got married when Mom was seventeen (born October 1910). Father was seven years older (born June 1903). According to all the documents, they were married in November 1927 in Zagreb. This I do not understand, as the city was not family territory, but my Father wanted to get married in the Greek Catholic Church. My mother could also have been pregnant with my sister, who died at the age of two (in 1929, I never found out from what). She was probably pregnant at that time with my brother, who was born in 1930, and I followed In 1931—not much rest for my mom. She told me once that I almost died when I was two. I had a huge boil under my left armpit that needed serious medical attention.

(I guess I was destined to live for a long time, no matter what. I went through WWII, I was shot once, bombed twice and machine-gunned from a German plane (summer of '43 or '44). It was a two-seat patrol plane that appeared from nowhere; ten of us had just marched from the forest into an open field. It came low over us and we dropped to the ground; I could see the face of the gunner in the back seat. Suddenly, there was an unusually strong wind gust that shook the plane violently at the moment he started to fire on us. Bullets were flying everywhere, but missing us. The two men with the rifles took a few shots; the plane staggered and disappeared and we ran back into the forest. Today, seventy-three years later, I have survived terminal bone cancer so far. More on this later...)

My father must have been a very demanding and inconsiderate man, as he turned Mother into a chicken-egg incubator. I remember staying many times with Grandmother Baker while Mother had to recover from some internal issues. There were women who understood the problems, even more than the doctors of the time, and helped her.

As I grew older, I could slowly understand what the issues were and what had transpired.

In the beginning in our new home, we all slept in one bedroom. Brother and I were small so we had a large playpen to play and sleep in. Many times we were awoken by the noise our parents created; not understanding what was going on and afraid to utter a sound because Father would simply give us a licking. The noise was particularly louder when he had a drink or was drunk after having guests or after a party. He was very aggressive; all I know is that mother was not well the next day.

As the rooms were remodeled we got our own room with separate beds. There was no more fighting and throwing each other out of the crib.

Father had a large office with a safe and a gun rack. He was an early riser. He was on his riding horse just as early, pistol in holster (the pistol was always on his night table during the night) and the short-barrelled shotgun hanging on his neck. A large shell belt was strapped around his waist. Not a very friendly appearance. Then he went off to check the work in the fields and the farm in general, and to see if there were any improprieties caused by neighbours grazing, stealing wood or poaching. Once a month he was accompanied by our forest guard, who was always armed, and they rode together late into the evening. Father was a restless and very tense person.

There was on the north side of the garden in the forest a designed Hirsh hunting ground. It was a large area, one hundred metres by three hundred metres. The perimeter consisted of two rows of spruce about six metres apart. The centre was brush and grass, so Hirsh would be seen crossing into the grassy area to feed. When they had their fill they would go back to the water, crossing the area where hunters were waiting to shoot them.

Father was particular about the horses. Besides four pairs of working horses, there were two white Lipizzaner to pull the *fijaker* (coach). He did not like cars. For riding he also used a Lipizzaner. That male horse was twenty years old and he was used as a stud. He had quite a pedigree. His great-grandfather was a riding horse of the Austro-Hungarian Emperor Franz Josef.

Our farm was surrounded by six small villages approximately three to five kilometres away. There were two elementary schools in the area outside the six kilometre perimeter. One was located in a place with the municipal administration, federal police (gendarmerie), doctor's office, grocery store with the local fuel pump, two taverns and a regional rectory and large Catholic parish. Also there was the only cemetery in the area.

Adjacent to the community was a coal mine that closed due to the poor quality of its coal.

The parish had probably three to five thousand parishioners who donated weekly—Sundays, holy days, weddings, births and deaths—in goods and cash. The head of the parish was a young priest with a young chaplain as his assistant. There was a housekeeper and the priest's young attractive sister. She had quite a set of boobs to which I was helplessly attracted, so regardless of the consequences I used to ambush her and chase her to fondle those beauties with great pleasure (I was six or seven). I was very lucky she never complained to my parents; she probably enjoyed the fooling around as she always giggled, so I kept on doing it every time we came to visit or when I had my chance. She got married to a Taylor and they moved to the city. He was very good at his trade and they survived the war. It was common that all good suits were handmade. After the war all of us who survived reconnected. He also made a few suits for our family. When I came to his store for the first time after WWII, his beauty-breasted wife was there. She gave me a look (by then I was a girls' target) and afterwards asked me to help her carry some of the stuff home, which I gladly did. This was the beginning of an occasional and steamy relationship. She said, "I was often thinking of you and wondering how you were going to turn out ... not too bad, I see!"

I must confess it was my hobby do the same thing with peasant girls, sometimes grabbing them from behind. There were a lot of shrieks. Girls, particularly older ones—twenty-four to thirty—had a yen for me. War gave me an older, mature look and I was a handsome, athletic and very sexy boy.

The other school was located some distance to the south of the farm, serving a bunch of villages of a different district. A young teacher couple was stationed there. My father must have met them by checking the neighbourhood around the farm and, being a very social animal, introduced himself. Later, when he completed his school, he managed to bring them over—including three young female freshmen teachers. They had a couple of kids, a boy and a girl a year younger than me, so I had finally some company.

Before we visited as a family, Father went alone many times. I think he was having an affair with the lady, and any other, I discovered later, that he could lay hands on. That was his weak/bad side. I could never understand his motives; was it insecurity or was it to intimidate my mother and her family? I found out later that there was a local boy who became a veterinarian and wanted to marry my mom; he was not a blue-blood. I saw him twice—once he appeared on the farm to check animals. I am not sure how that all happened. All I remember is that when he was leaving, Mom, with me off to the side, escorted him some distance from the house. What they were talking about, I didn't stay close enough to hear. Life, life...

For my mom, life on the farm must have been difficult—having three children in four years, losing one, having a not-upstanding husband ... yet she managed the household to perfection. Also, she was some cook.

My brother was away to school at Grandmother Baker's. I was one year behind, roaming around on the farm. One day, I befriended an old neighbour who had come back from America. He was homesick so he returned with some money and bought the small farm adjacent to ours. He told me a lot of his emigration stories. He also knew a lot of fairy tales. He told me many of them. When I think of him today, his American experiences impressed me greatly ... perhaps these stories were the reason I am here in Canada.

Harvest was coming and I was taken by one of the relatives into the city. There was a whole bunch of kids in the small high-rise. We were playing in the inner court. There were kids of various ages; some I had met after WWII in high school and university. My aunt took me many times to the city to go to the cinema and the theatre. The high-rise was close to Main Street. I stood there many times watching the cars and street trams.

There are two memorable occasions. One was at the King's Parade. I watched it one day, fascinated by its floats—particularly the military segment, which was followed by many floats of city groups. Finally, the last person in the parade came. It was a clown made up as a hobo. He was pushing a small buggy with a hurdy-gurdy on it, stopping occasionally and playing music by cranking it. I was ecstatic. So when he stopped at our intersection I ran over to him and asked if I could turn the crank. He showed me how to do it and I made some music. Then he said, "I have to move on, son."

"Please," I said, "can I walk with you a while and listen to the music?"

"You should go home, boy," he said.

"Just a short distance, please?" So we went slowly; I was in a fantasy land thinking about becoming a clown one day. Suddenly, I snapped out of my dream when I heard my name being called. My relatives had found me; they were very upset. They took me home, where I was given a lecture about not leaving without permission. For the next little while I was good little boy.

My aunt and uncle were both working. Because they would get up early in the morning and come home early in the afternoon, they would always have a nap and then make love. I was told to take a nap at the same time on the couch. Naturally, most of the time I could not sleep, so I would get up and mope around the house. So one day I ended up bored in the large dining room and there was a large table covered with a beautifully knitted table cloth. It happened like I was in a trance: I picked up the scissors from the mending basket and started to dismember the table cloth bit by bit till it was gone. My aunt got up, and upon seeing the table cloth gone, fainted. I called my uncle, who brought her back. I was punished by being made to kneel on the corn for half an hour.

There were no kids around to play with, so besides the old American (as I called him) there were a few girls watching while the cows grazed, but they didn't trespass onto our hayfields. I used to walk to them, but most were shy and afraid. I think it was because of my father. Some of their parents worked on our farm. When I approached, they just turned their backs on me. It was sad that we could not meet them on the same level. I had a crush on two pretty ones, but I was also shy. So I always said a polite goodbye and walked away on my own into the forest looking for fox or badger holes.

Having a crush on some pretty girl or lady was some experience. Some strong emotions would overcome me, and for a short time I would be quite taken by them, and then it would all disappear. I think that my sexual development started very early without being able to understand what was going on, till my uncle—Mom's brother—stepped into my life after the end of WWII and became my tutor, my mentor and my friend. He opened many doors to me into life's mysteries. He also told me many stories when we took our breaks. He would ask me many questions about my inner feelings, and commented on my answers. It was awesome to be with him. He offered me everything that my father was short of.

A lot was going on at the farm: big barbeque parties with lots of wine and Slivovitz in winter. We started to ski, which was introduced to my brother and me by my uncle. We also skated on the ponds. Winters had been harsh with lots of snow. Travelling had been restricted as there were no snowplows save those pulled by horses; progress was very slow.

Horse-pulled sled riding was the only transportation. One time, returning from a visit late in the night, I think Dad had had a few drinks and was using the whip on the horses to go faster. We were asleep—my brother and I were zipped up in fur bags and ended up in the snowbank. By the time they arrived home, they discovered the kids were missing. There was a general panic, workers were woken up and a search party with torches was organized, and off they went into the snowy night, searching the snowbanks on both sides of the road. How they spotted us I have no idea, all I remember is hearing the voices: "Here they are, here they are!" We slept through the whole episode as it was nice and warm inside the fur bags. How they found us, nobody ever explained. Mom was ecstatic to see us later in the morning.

My adventures were sure stacking up. Once I was left alone with the farm foreman and a babysitter; Mom and Dad went to the city for a few days and my brother was at Grandmother Baker's. During the day I sold Father's cards to the workers. My father used to cheat at cards while pouring wine for his victims. It was my revenge. The babysitter was cute—an eighteen-year-old peasant girl. I was seven or eight. At bedtime I slept in the parents' room and she was in the access room next door. I was fantasizing about her so I started to pretend I was cold and crying. She came into the room bare naked and simply crawled into my bed, hugged me and started to calm me down. I was also naked, and as she was rubbing my body I got "excited;" noticing this she gently took my hand and placed it between her legs and started to rub her... After a while I started to help her and then she went into flame. I did not quite understand what was going on, all I remember is the door suddenly opened, the foreman burst into the room, yanked the poor girl out of bed and spanked her. Upon the return of my parents, the poor girl lost her job and I got the royal treatment with the belt from my father.

Today, I think I was a horny little bum; every time I got near a pretty female I got a you-know-what. At that time it was all a mystery to me, until, like I said before, my uncle came into my life.

The case of a small black lamb was one of the most impressive tragic incidents of my childhood. Perhaps this was the reason that I developed a deep-seated suspicion of human motives, and this made a loner out of me; I would come in or out of human circles whenever I chose.

One day out of nowhere my parents came to me with a large covered basket and said, "As you've been a good little boy for a long time this is your reward." They took the cover off the basket and there was a beautiful little black baby lamb. "It is your pet from now on," my father said, "to play with." I was ecstatic and jumped for joy. I named it Mila.

As the days passed, the little lamb and I got very attached to each other. I fed her with milk and porridge. She followed me everywhere. She slept in a bed made from straw. It must have been four or five weeks later when the preparation started for a national holiday. As usual, thirty to forty guests arrived with their families—dignitaries, priests, teachers, the police commander and others.

On that day Father asked me to go with the coachman, to whom he gave money and a list of items to be brought back from the store six kilometres away. I asked to take my pet with me, but I was told not to worry as they would look after it till I got back. It took us almost three hours to get back. Upon our return, people were mingling in the yard next to the wine cellar; smoke and the smell of burned meat was coming from the pit nearby. I asked my parents where my pet was. My mom looked at my dad, and he said, "It was wandering around here a while ago, go look for it." So I went, and one of the kids joined me to look for my Mila but she was nowhere to be found. No one had seen or heard her. At the dinner I got a few small pieces of meat on my plate. I did not eat very much with Mila on my mind.

We the kids sat on small tables near the main table, listening to the toast to my parents for a great evening and for great roasts, particularly the woolly one. At that moment it did not dawn on me. I excused myself and continued to look for my pet, and one of the boys joined me again.

The farm was very tidy and organized. In the middle of the yard was a large concrete basin for manure and next to it, buried in the ground, was a large piss container. All manure was used for fertilizing the fields.

As we walked by, my companion climbed on the manure-basin wall and suddenly yelled, "Leon, come up here and look!"

As I came up he said that there was a skin with curly black hair on it. I looked at it in shock, recognized it as belonging to my Mila, and started to scream, cry and vomit at the same time. I ran back to the party, screaming, "Who killed my Mila?" There was a dead silence and I yelled again, "Mom and Dad, you lied to me! You killed my Mila and you ate it! I hate you all!" I kept running into the garden and on into the forest. It took them two days to find me. My father beat me up with a willow twig; I never shed a tear. Nobody asked me how I felt, I was a heartbroken little boy in serious shock. Still today, if I smell lamb meat I get violently sick.

I mentioned before that the farm did not have running water or electricity. We also did not have a phone or a radio till Dad acquired one in 1940. So, the world news was only in the daily newspaper that was delivered through the mail service, and for the parents there was more hearsay during their semi-monthly visit to city. At dinner, Dad would comment on the events while my brother and I could hardly wait to look at the Mandrake cartoon.

I remember my mom and dad talking about the Germans marching into Italy, Czechoslovakia, Poland and Italy, and into Libya and Abyssinia (which I believe is today's Somalia). Then the drums of war got very loud; in 1941 Germany and Italy attacked the Kingdom of Yugoslavia and it was split accordingly. Croatia together with Bosnia and Herzegovina became an independent Fascist state, while Serbia became a German protectorate. It was probably a worse political situation than the one created by U.S. President Wilson after WWI. Then the resistance to the occupation started, and at the same time the ugly conflict between Croats and Serbs.

When the war started, both Brother and I were in boarding school, which for me was a lifelong experience. We also had tutoring there and regularly went to public school.

Every day I got up early, about 5:30 a.m. There were about forty of us sleeping in a dormitory with open wash basins. There was also a young student priest sleeping with us. He made sure there was a goodnight prayer and a reading of some holy person (we took turns reading these passages), and that everyone got up on time in the morning.

After I got up, I had to wash, brush my teeth and make my bed. A young supervisor would check us all out, then I went to the chapel to be an altar boy for a different priest who served a half-hour Mass. By 6:30 we all had bleak black coffee with corn polenta. Our bread ration was an eight-inch hard cornbread for the whole week. It was a challenge to eat it. Naturally, there was a short prayer before and after every meal. For those who were not selected for altar boy (ministrant) service there was service in the chapel. On top of it all was the Sunday service with us in the chorus, and at the same time, one after the other, we went into confession. There were many questions in regard to our sins.

To note, every time I got up early there were always two or three empty beds. When I asked what was going on, I was told that these boys were dedicated and praying. Later they appeared at breakfast washed and dressed up. I always wondered why; I got my answer later.

At mealtime I noticed that the head chef was always giving me a smile. One day while we were at study, I was told to report to him in the kitchen. When I arrived there he asked me to come up with him into the attic to help him sort some old stuff. When we were going up the staircase he put his arm on me. When we got there I could not see any old things to be sorted out. There was a counter with a light on above it and a chair with a bunch of fresh cherries on it. He sat in the chair and said, "Let us eat the cherries first." I said OK. I came over to stand next to him, leaned on the counter and started to eat cherries. He said, "There is no chair, you can sit on my lap." I was hungry and kind of suspicious, but I sat on his lap and he pulled me higher on his leg. Suddenly, I could feel that he was aroused. I jumped up and took off; I was upset and afraid. By the time I arrived in the study, no one looked up save the young supervisor to ask me to sit down. I realized later that I had escaped rape by a pedophile. The empty beds in the dormitory came to my mind. The place must have had a few homosexuals.

After breakfast, off to the public school, always two or more going together. I am sure that some of it ended up in confessionary, as there was always someone going to "Father Inspector for a briefing," and there were many extra sideline prayers and dishwashing in the main kitchen as punishment for your sins.

In the beginning I was a promising candidate, so after several months I was promoted as a server into the administrative dining room. Wow, what a different menu in there. I was serving food on the third floor that came up the elevator from the kitchen; I cleaned up the tables and was allowed to eat leftovers. This did not last very long, as I ended up in Father Inspector's office one day by being naive and trusting a couple of friends who also worked with me in the privileged dining room. I asked them why they eat all the goods that our parents send for us. That was the last of them and a big mark in my memory about the human race.

We returned from the public school after 2 p.m. and the whole thing started all over again.

The discipline was strictly enforced. For example, going to excursion was another experience—we had to be in a column of twos and march looking at the heels of the two in front of you. In the city we were not allowed to look into windows. We visited mostly the other Catholic orders. We could leave the institution only once a month and then only upon the request of parents or close relatives. On one occasion, I was picked up by relatives and we went for a picnic. I got a sunburn by taking my shirt off, which was a no-no and punishable.

The institution was run by the Father Director, and others were in charge of various departments pertaining to our lives. This order was also a parish, so it had a lot to do with the public of the surrounding area.

After that weekend I went to school for math. For a professor we had an high-ranking Fascist officer. When he entered and exited from the class, we had to stand up and salute him with the old Roman salute that the Nazis and Fascists later adopted. That day, at the end of the class, I did not get up on time to salute him, but I did get up and salute him when everyone else sat down. The professor was about to exit but spotted me and went ape. I was lucky to not end up in a concentration camp. I was immediately dismissed from my class and evicted from the school and all the other schools in the city.

When I returned to the boarding school I was approached in the hallway by the Father Confessor, who told me to report to the Father Administrator. "By the way," he said, "why are you so red?" So I told him the picnic story, he smiled and we parted.

I continued to administrator's office. When I came in, I greeted him and he asked me to sit down, then he told me a story of a phone call he received from the public school administration telling him that I was expelled from all the schools in the city. While he was talking to me, the phone rang. He said hello and listened for a minute, then said, "Thank you, Father Confessor." He turned to me and said, "I just received the report from Father Confessor. I think your conduct is inexcusable and I am evicting you from this institution. I will report to your parents." Without a word I left his office, went to the dormitory, picked up my suitcase and left the institution. I kept on marching to my relatives in the city. They all panicked, including my brother. There was no way my parents could be notified. So the next morning I continued the sixty kilometre walk to my Grandmother Baker's. When I arrived late the next day she was overjoyed.

It is worth noting that by that time, the territory where we lived was already insecure, as all Yugoslavia had become a war zone because of growing resistance, so mail and other communication out of and into the country was very slow to inform my parents of my situation.

When I left, I first went to relatives in the city. Everyone panicked, nobody wanted me, no one wanted to get involved in my affairs, particularly because of the incident with the math professor. Perhaps they thought I might be politically dangerous. It was the beginning of very uncertain times. Human life was worthless if you were of the wrong political colours, religion or ethnic origin. As I said, off I went to Grandmother Baker's. I was lucky, as I hitched a ride part way. The rest I did on foot. Late on the next night I arrived at my Grandmother Baker's home. She was all alone and happy to see me. There were several roadblocks and I had only my student card with a picture.

She told me that the farm was destroyed, burned down. Nobody knows what happened to my parents. She also told me that her son was a POW. Next thing, I went to my godfather's and told him what had transpired. He was very upset—not with me but with the situation. He told me to come back in two days and he would see what could be done, which I did. It was late in the evening and there was a stranger with him in the room. "You will go with this man," he said. "Good luck, I will be in touch. By the way, your parents are OK, they are with us." I looked at him, not quite understanding what he had in mind. At that time I did not know that he was already part of the growing resistance led by Tito, of which, without being aware, I became a part of when I left his place with that stranger that evening. So began a very dark side of my life. It is a nightmare that lasts a lifetime. In its place and for that period I will type a poem that was probably born in an old schoolroom when I sat on the floor looking at the old maps of the world:

> My home of long time ago—to all the dear ones that forever will stay in my heart!
>
> When I was a child, I seldom played other children's games
>
> I rather sat alone, stayed at home or in the forest,
>
> Reading many books, dreaming the dreams
>
> About so many things, without names.
>
> I remember seeing large maps of the world
>
> On the classroom wall,
>
> Fascinated by the huge bodies of water,
>
> Faraway lands, its people and mysteries beyond,
>
> That made my mind stall.
>
> It was the place so beautiful and tranquil, with the small castle on the hill
>
> Beautiful green meadows, orchards, wine-yards, forests full of trees,
>
> Sunshine in the fields, happy people working with the song
>
> A thousand different flowers swarming with the bees.

Then the war came with horror death and destruction,

I remember screams, pain and grief, lives: total reduction.

Suddenly all was gone, my home, people

Orchards, flowers with the bees, songs died in the fields

And so did many of my dreams.

The Yugoslavia that Tito has created after WWII was, for better or worse, the country that most of my generation and those up to his death cherished. I was neither Fascist nor did I later become Communist, yet I will state that we—all ethnic groups—were given the opportunity to live in peace and reasonable harmony. The proof is in the many inter-ethnic marriages. We, or at least most of us, supported him and his concept for our beautiful country. There were many demons inside the country and more enemies on the outside that were, I think, envious of his success and were working hard to destroy it. Finally, after his death (and, honestly, not following the constitution), they succeeded in creating the gruesome and horrible civil war in the late '80s, which, in my opinion, was won only by those who feared a strong Yugoslavia with the help of the losers / idiots / primitive nationalists in all the former republics who today live in enclaves, not having had enough of the catastrophe they helped to create and continuously rattling their sabers while others are kissing the rear end of the E.U. and the other political and religious ivory towers of the world. It's a shame what they have done.

By the end of the summer of 1945, most of us young ones were readied to go back to school. Some lost three to four years. I went back to my godmother's bakery; there she told me that my parents were with my father's older sister in the city. My uncle (Mom's brother) was again reenlisted in the Croatian army after he returned from a German POW camp. He survived and came home, and my brother was with Mom and Dad. I was not interested in this story. Sadly, when we got together we were all strangers to one another.

My godfather called me and told me that my continuum of schooling has been arranged by the state, and that I should return to the city and report to the special school in order to recover my four years of loss. It was hard work. By the end of 1947, I was back to normal, and by 1951 I graduated and entered university.

So here I am back with the family; it was a strange feeling seeing them all after such a long time. My mother hugged me for a long time, others were indifferent. It was OK with me. Like I said, we were all strangers to each other.

Father got a job with the government and we moved to another location in the city. The neighbourhood was loaded with kids of my age. The party was implanting its policy for everyone, including the youth. We were organized and had meetings for party propaganda, community watch for enemies of the state, work parties, sports and socials. It was way out of the people's control. At that time the Soviet system was imposed until 1948, then political resolution. Stalin expelled Tito form the communist bloc. This was a huge change and things slowly turned better.

There were a few kids who talked me into participating on their team, which I did. I accepted the invitation and joined their field hockey team: United. In high school we also played chess, handball and soccer. I really developed a liking for field hockey and I became very good at it. We took all the championships: city, republic and Yugoslavia. We also played international games between Italy, Austria and Germany.

(Note: In my high school all the educators were professors (not teachers) with diplomas. The curriculum was a requirement, not a choice. Regardless of which subject you failed, you repeated the year. For example, I had six languages: Serbo-Croatian, English, Russian, Latin, Greek and French or German. Our schooling and medical was tuition-free.)

A few months later my father was relocated to manage a large wine farm on the outskirts of the city, so we all moved out there. My friends stayed behind as I also had to change schools. We got together only for trainings and games. It was a very demanding time as I had to walk a distance of four kilometres to the city tram, sometimes twice a day.

Weekends, when there was not a game, I went to Grandmother Baker's to get some food, as times were hard. I would walk back and forth regardless of the weather. Then Father was relocated again to another vineyard, this time very close to the city. Ever since we got back together, the tensions between my father and me had gotten worse. When we were still in the city, he exposed me to some of his indiscretions that had been carried on for quite some time. Mom was very much abused by his behavior. That angered me; he was embarrassed and mad at me. It was a real challenge.

One night, he got drunk and his true feelings for me came to the fore. Mom was petrified that I might fight him, so I just left, walked to the city and spent a few days with friends so I did not miss school. When I returned home, no apologies were given.

In school I was doing pretty good. I was one of those kids that never did homework. I was doing well on my team—I became a member of the national team. I was a very good, reliable player, extremely well-conditioned from all the walking, running and other sports. Because of that I was fortunate to obtain certain privileges, like a pass to the special store (this was not for average citizens) where I could buy what was needed for my family. This was accepted by all but not acknowledged by my father and brother. I was careful not to abuse my privileges.

I also worked in a tailor shop and sometimes in an electrical shop for my teammate's father. This was my pocket money. Once I started to play internationally, my family did not look favourably upon it. I should also mention that I lost contact with my cousin Melika. These were exciting times in all aspects of my life.

Every year, we (the capable citizens) had to give the state one month of free labour on various state projects, highways, mines, railroads, etc., as this was your passport to go to school next year, or to keep your job if you were in the trades or a professional.

In 1948, I was called by the federal athletic administration to participate with five thousand other young people in exercises to prepare our representation for an all-Slavic competition in Prague. Practices were held at night in addition to all the other stuff. At the end of three months, we were rated. The failures were only medical cases. Then all the teams were moved to Slovenia. It was selection by a high standard: height, weight, looks and performance.

We continued to practise all day, every day for the next several weeks. In the end, only four thousand and seven hundred survived the rigorous working (a whole day) of just over an hour of program. Three hundred failed. There were many tears at their departure. Then we left for Prague by two trains. There we met the teams from all the other Slavic countries. As we were crossing the Hungarian-Czechoslovak border, Stalin, by resolution of the *informburo*, expelled Tito from Communist International. When we arrived in Prague, all the other nation's athletes (particularly the Russians) were forbidden to talk to us. Everywhere we went in the city we were followed by plain-clothed police. We always went in groups. We were there for eight days. Yugoslavia won first place. On the way home, we performed in Belgrade for Marshal Tito. Then we were allowed to go home.

After the state annual work, those who performed well were given a pass for fourteen days in designated all-inclusive hostels of your choice anywhere in the country. I did not get one, as I committed a sin. I was in charge of a hundred and forty students working on the Shamac-Sarajevo railroad. It was a very hot July, and a water tank that was to bring in water was late because the driver and my commandeer were drinking in some tavern while the tanker was parked in the sun. A few of my people got sick. Two girls passed out; we revived them, and I told everyone to stop working and sit down, and that I was taking the responsibility. We were all very thirsty. When the idiot came back with the water, which was warm so no one could drink it, he got out and asked who had stopped the work. I said, "You did, comrade, as you failed in your duty to supply us with fresh water." He started to yell at me and at the same time he also yelled at my people to get back to work. "No one gets up until you bring in fresh water," I said. Then he ordered me to go with him to the HQ to see the commandeer of our brigade. He gave his report and I gave mine. I asked to be dismissed if he did not smarten up and perform his duty responsibly, or if he wasn't replaced. My unit had performed well, but I was not risking their lives because of this individual's negligence. So the officer went out back to the work site and told him to get the bucket of water from the tanker. He had a drink and then he vomited. In the meantime, fresh water arrived. I was dismissed, and water-boy lost his position.

Afterward, I always went to my uncle's, where I had lot of fun. He knew many beautiful women. One time I met a beautiful Slavonian girl. A Platonic love!

I was progressing well in high school. In the last two years I was president of my class; there were fifty-four of us. It was all very political, the communist party propaganda until 1948 was always first. It reminded me of the boarding school I was at years before, when the religious aspect was the number-one aspect of our daily life. Everyone was expected, if qualified, to be a party member. I was not engaged as expected, so after one and a half years I was replaced.

Home was not a happy place; we were apart on all sort of things, in many ideas and outlooks on the world. Times were extremely politically correct. People were afraid of what they might say, even within the families. Wrong words or actions may have serious consequences.

My brother and I were in different schools, but he was not into sports. We shared the same bedroom. I was always on the go with school, sports, part-time work and, naturally, dates, so I was always very late coming home. My father tried to stop this, but as he was speaking through my mom, I ignored him. My mom always let me sleep late. My activities required a lot of energy. She understood me.

It was very seldom that I did homework. I was very attentive during the lectures and my memory was always working overtime. It worked for me and I passed the exams. It was a bit different as a university student. I was growing older and my world was changing.

By playing sports internationally my views were changing, and I had to be careful not to express them. I perceived my future there to not be a great success until I made serious changes in my life. My home climate was not supportive, and I did not want to be a party member. So, I started to think of not returning from one of the international outings. It happened in June 1953. We were going to Germany, two nights before a state security official asked me to officially keep an eye on two of my teammates. That was the moment of the crucial decision for me not to return.

I was very independent through working, and also by the opportunities from travelling in and out of the country. That in itself had many opportunities, but you had to be careful as customs were very much in search of anything and were very clever; also, there were many inquisitive people asking, "What did you bring." We had our ways of simple concealment. Once I took some diamonds for a person to Austria. On the way, we were playing cards and had a bottle of water on the table and two half-full glasses. When we came to the border everyone had to leave the train (there were police with dogs on both sides) for a body search. Just before I left the compartment, I took the pouch with the stones and divided them between the glasses and the bottle and said a small prayer.

In the strip room, I thought that if they touched the bottle and glasses that they would interrogate me. Nothing happened, and we all returned to our places. By a miracle, nothing was discovered. Other stuff, like currency and gold, was packed in the fake equipment. We were lucky, as there was no scanning technology in those days. Customs was tough, but many times blind to the obvious. I profited on these trips, and my family benefited as well.

It was coming close to graduation; the graduating class had fifty-four students. No one failed. There were some close bonds that lasted for a lifetime. Every year, even after I left the country, we had a class reunion. All my friends received university degrees but me. I was short two semesters when I left for Germany. During winters, my group of seven was always going on skiing trips. They were a kind of picnic fun.

On one occasion, returning from a skiing trip, we boarded the narrow-track train. We were standing in the doorway area when suddenly Branko, my dear friend, came back from snooping around the coach all excited, and said, "Boys, Leon's girlfriend is sitting inside, and look out, there is a ten-litre container full of wine. Must be hers; she loves wine."

"What gives? My girlfriend who?" I asked him.

"Our biology professor, you dummkopf."

"Oh my god," I said. The charming lady had a crush on me and everybody was talking about it.

"Look," Branko said, "the container has a tag with her name on it. You better get inside and entertain her so we can have some wine."

At that moment, our professor walked out and said, "Hello, boys, come in and sit with me."

"Thank you," said Branko. "We will stay out here."

Then she spotted me blushing and said, "Maybe you will and the rest of you can guard my container." So, I went in with her for the next two hours. Boys were coming in and out checking on us and smiling. I realized that they were drinking the professor's wine. She had another two-litre bottle with her, so she and I had a few glasses as well. By the time we got to the city, she asked me to help her with the container. The boys quickly disappeared, saying "see you!" She and I picked up the container—she was very tipsy—and she said, "This sure feels light." I said it was because two of us were holding it. My friends had drunk half of the container. We went to her home, and I deposited her and the leftover wine.

Next week in biology class she said: "Shame on the guilty ones!" They know who they are...

Many years later, when I came from Canada to visit my parents, I was driving home from visiting my friends and I spotted my old professor at the bus station. I stopped and asked her if she would like to have a ride. "Please do not be afraid, I am your old pupil. Remember Samobor and the lost wine?" She started to laugh and she came with me. We had a pleasant two hours in a local restaurant sharing memories.

In the sporting season, sometimes I would help my Grandmother Baker. On the home front things never changed, we had all run out of inner warmth. Everlasting tensions were like cancer eating everyone away. My mom was not well, she struggled and tried hard to cover up all her pains. Father's indiscretions of all kinds never stopped. A selfish, insecure world is the only thing he lived in.

I stayed away from all the conflicts after many provocations came my way from my brother and father. I had my sports and my friends and, yes, I fell in love with the beautiful Marica. It was a total saturation of body and soul by *amor*, multiplied by the beautiful country, its music and climate and my romantic character. In summer when I was working on a state project, she went with her mother to a city in the southern Adriatic. When we met two months later it was the end; she told me that her heart belonged to someone else. I considered it a personal tragedy, and I think I also became dangerous. I was sick in my soul, and I asked my mom to get in touch with my uncle. I knew he was the only one to whom I could confess my problem. He saved me with his wisdom.

My uncle worked in a beautiful serene provincial town in Slavonia. When I arrived there, he introduced me to a bunch of local students, a real happy bunch. My uncle had a charming companion, the owner of a local tavern. On Saturdays, boys played music in the tavern's garden. There was dancing in the beautiful summer nights. I met a very pretty girl, Slavica ... ah, what a summer that was.

When I left to go back to the city, the boys prepared a small party where I got hammered on plum brandy. My uncle's apartment was next to his office, so they brought me to bed early in the morning. From the bedroom you walked into a bathroom; the washroom was on the right side, and a large tub filled with the water (for cooling purposes) was just past the washroom. All I remember is getting up and wanting to go to the toilet. I was still pretty stoned, and I ended up in the tub. Fortunately for me, the custodian come early in the morning. He must have heard the big splash, and he simply saved me from drowning ... olé! Uncle and I made peace.

The next day, Slavica and I said so long, and I boarded the train that night and left. We exchanged many a letter, but I have never her seen again. It was long journey and it was late. I stepped out of my compartment into the hallway to stretch my legs, and it was fairly dark. Two doors down there was a pretty lady with beautiful curly black hair and a white dress, leaning on the window. I did not recognize her right away. I came closer and said good evening. She turned, and we both said at the same time, "Oh my god!" It was my cousin Melika. She motioned to keep my voice low. Then she quickly told me that she had gotten married to an older man, who was sleeping and was very jealous. I felt I should leave, so we hugged and said goodbye. I didn't see her again until I came back from Canada. But we did write while I was away. I cannot remember how I got her address.

Another time, my uncle was located in a North Adriatic city. I came for the summer; I was seventeen or eighteen, although I looked much older. He was dating a charming widow where I was staying who had another two sisters. They had a three-story villa on shore. One evening after I arrived, we went to a night club. There were four of us; Uncle's date brought her younger sister. She was twenty-five, and some looker.

He never told me anything, he had set me up. We were introduced. That is the night I learned how to dance. On the way back, they suggested that I should move with the younger sister, and the rest is a beautiful story. Late one night, she came to my bed complaining about chill, so I recreated summer and lost my virginity ... ole! I am forever thankful to my uncle.

Life after the war was moving slowly, but was also in a sense carefree and full of fun. I caught up with my schooling. One has to fulfill a number of requirements at school, and medical and public transportation for students was free. All your grades must be completed, your conduct in and outside the school must be correct, your appearance must correspond to the requirements of the school and absentia must be supported by a doctor or parent's note. Your participation in state projects was your passport to all the above.

Those who were not material for academic advancement were directed into industrial schools. Others who did not graduate or those with serious discipline problems were required to serve in the army. The former was for eighteen months and the latter served in working battalions for three to five years, and these were automatically under martial law. No escape! In some instances, this was worse than regular jail. If you were totally stupid you could get shot.

Those that finished university also had to serve eighteen months.

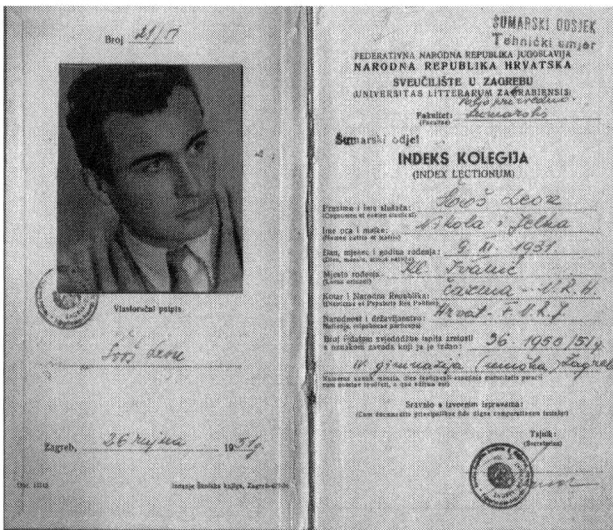

My aggressive and temperamental nature was a great part of my character. It interestingly showed more when I was/am active, at sports and work. Otherwise, I was mostly withdrawn. I channelled my energies into physical action. I was always eager to win, to score the goal. In work I could outlast most others who were aiming to produce quality results. This attitude helped me later in life in my business. Certainly, intensive training helped a lot.

You would not believe, but my coach at times was angry with me for playing rough. One day at halftime he called me out in front of everybody and said, "Listen, you calm down, either find a lover or masturbate before the game." The whole team was laughing. I was lucky, so I took the former route. We also had a young ladies' team in the club. I connected well with one of them; she was nineteen and a firecracker like me. This turned into a marathon sex affair. We just could not get enough of each other. It happens in life, but not often. My coach was happy because my play became very good. We parted after my family relocated to a different city. I truly suffered...

Sometime after training, I went to the city's Olympic pool. There I was introduced to a twenty-seven-year-old swimmer by my teammate. We were playing mini water polo; he approached me by telling that a young friend of his was interested in me. I accepted the invitation, and it turned into a beautiful friendship. We were dating very discreetly due to the age difference; later she told me she was engaged. She left the country a few months later to go to South America.

At home, it was always tense. I think the situation deep inside of me never changed after my parents disposed of my pet lamb. We always had dogs. My father mistreated them, I could never understand why. He controlled them—so he thought—by beating them. I always got so angry with him and he knew it. The we got a new Lab. He was not quite a year old. Kids are kids. One day, upon returning from school, I had lunch in the kitchen and I heard my mother outside in the hallway scolding the pup for peeing on the ceramic-tile floor. Father's office was down the hallway next to the kitchen, so he must have heard Mother talking to the pup. My dad and I walked out at same time. I was halfway between them; the dogs were under the staircase at the other end. My father was very angry as he went by, holding his bullwhip in his hand. I knew his intentions, so I asked him, "What are you mad about? For peeing on the floor? I can clean it up."

He stopped and looked at me. "How dare you talk to me? I will teach him a lesson." I thought he was going to strike me, but he turned for the pup and I quickly grabbed his arm with the whip.

He stopped dead in the tracks and went pale, and I said, "If you do not stop and go back to your office, I will break your arm." He must have been in shock; he dropped the whip as Mom was pleading with me and went back into his office. As he slammed the door behind him, he went into a rage, a tantrum, by making a mess out of his office. I opened the door and yelled, "If you touch Mom again it will be the last time. Enough of the crap you've given us in the past twenty years!"

I think this was in the second semester. I picked up a few of my things and left. I stayed with my friends, and after a week my mom asked me to come back, which I did.

Sorry, I kind of went ahead of myself. Let me finish high-school graduation. It was not with flying colors, but I graduated with "good." After graduation, my class took a photo outside the school. My mom and her brother were waiting for me. There were congratulatory hugs.

Most of us took different paths in life. Everyone but me ended up with a university degree. I was two semesters short because I had left the country. During that time, I participated in the student dances performed in our musical auditorium. My buddy could not participate. He was a good piano player; he played in a small band every weekend for some extra cash. All the best jazz bands in the city played there.

I managed to get a ticket every weekend (they were not cheap), and as I was working it was all good. I was dressed well—a real handsome boy, a member of the national team. Everybody knew me. I had many encounters there. One was with the pretty Ksenija. Life was carefree, beautiful and generous to me, somewhat parallel with my difficulties.

I was not keen to serve in the army, so I entered the university faculty of forestry. Perhaps I should have studied law, as I was good in political economics. I was good at understanding socialist utopias. The life of a university student is very different from all the other life norms, I can say. I remember that the daily forty-minute trips on the tram across the city to the university with my buddy Kruno were the funniest moments of my life. I usually boarded the tram three stops before Kruno came on. Then the humour riot started, entertaining everyone on the tram. Most of the daily passengers were the same people every day. Should one of us miss a day, there was a general sadness and silence among the travelers. Those were the days, my friend. When I left, Kruno graduated and became a court specialist on traffic issues. He unfortunately died from a heart attack.

Kruno and I spent most of the day together save the time for a training. He was a rower on the eight-team boat. We were natural-born clowns. We won first prize in musical auditorium. It was a very memorable evening, especially our costumes.

I was not a party animal at the time. I was dedicated to my sport and seriously looking into my future, which was appearing bleaker every day as some ugly demons within as well as those enemies outside the country started to lift their ugly heads. I felt that Tito's end would be the end of my beautiful Yugoslavia.

At the university, I was in charge of our army unit for a short time. This was part of the system. However, I received additional privileges for the state institutions.

While in university it was a different free life, yet you were responsible for regular participation in lectures and practicums. I believe it was the period that was preparing us for life's realities.

All records of your activity were recorded in your student index, together with your exam scores and professor's initials and signatures. I tremendously enjoyed practicums. I attended them in factories in different locations of Yugoslavia related to various forest products.

Out in the field, we were introduced to the building of narrow railroads, forestry roads and bridges. This part of my studies was the largest contributor to many successful projects later in my Canadian immigrant life.

On one of these practicums, we happened to go to the local railroad station to check the train schedule. As I was looking at the table, out of administration office came an attractive, very curvy, sexy dark blonde. She was twenty-seven, with the most beautiful green eyes I have ever seen. I greeted her, and she replied back with a smile. I then introduced myself and told her my purpose at the station, that I was a student from far away on practicum in a local factory (boy, oh boy, at the same time I could feel those green eyes X-raying me). She was listening, and casually said, "I am Olga! It is my lunch hour; would you like to join me?" Naturally, I was surprised. I blushed and thanked her, accepting the invitation.

This was a small provincial town, full of beautiful taverns with simple homemade food. Strangers were not an everyday event. I also came from a small town. I knew it was showtime for her amongst her friends. Sure enough, when we arrived at the tavern there were four girls and two boys sitting in one corner, and everyone jumped up: "Olga! Olga! Olga!" She went over to them and they exchanged hugs, then she waved me over and I was introduced. I was twenty at the time, tall, athletic, very handsome and I looked much older. I politely smiled and shook their hands and they asked us to sit down. She thanked them, but said, "Today I have a guest and I will sit with him in the garden." I guess this was a message that she wanted to be alone with me. She took my hand and led me outside into the tavern's pretty garden. In the shade there was a table for two. The owner led us there. We sat down, and she thanked him.

I looked at her and, looking straight into her beautiful green eyes, said, "Did you arrange this?"

She just smiled, reached for my hand and, squeezing it gently, she softly said, "Isn't it beautiful that we met?"

We had a small lunch; she had some wine. I did not, as I had to train for the soccer game that we were playing next day against factory workers. "Ah," she said, "I was thinking of taking the afternoon off and we could go for walk."

"I am really sorry, but we have to get our team tuned up. Perhaps after the training you can come with me and watch."

Excitingly, she said, "Cool!"

Two hours later we were done. It was a hot, sweaty summer day. There were no showers next to the pitch, unless I went all the way back to our quarters. Suddenly, she said, "We could go to my place, it's not far from here." I just looked at her and smiled, and off we went. She was also perspiring and had such a beastly scent about her. There was something going on (there sure was, I got horny as hell from that beastly scent), so we started to walk faster and faster. The moment the door closed behind us after reaching her small house, we both stripped our clothes off without a word and down we went on the bare floor. She was shaking and opened her legs so I could see the sex juice flowing out of her. I was also excited before I kneeled. She grabbed me and pulled me down, and while inserting me she said, "Boy, it has been a long time for both of us." And then the two cats started to make wild love. It lasted for the duration of my stay there, some ten days.

While on the practicum, we also had midterm exams in organic chemistry. Our young professor Marko had not seen much of me in class lecture, yet I spent my full time in the factory every day—about five to six hours. The rest of the time was consumed with my green-eyed lover.

On the day of exam, it was about thirty minutes long, aside from what I learned at practicum. I had a lot of stuff I'd learned from the high school. My answers were correct but short; the professor noted that I should have elaborated more. So I passed, but he also added, "Leon, you should sleep more." He knew more about my whereabouts than I thought, thanks to the gossip of my colleagues. In addition to this, we had to give a month of voluntary work on state projects.

The camps we stayed in were simple wooden barracks, with the two open sleeping levels. A straw mattress, two blankets and no pillow. About two hundred slept in one barrack. Fleas, bedbugs and lice were prevented by powdering everything with DDT. Powdering with DDT also included all your personal belongings and your clothing of the day. There was no running water. There was a simple long sheet-metal sink mounted on wooden legs, with many water taps above it mounted on the wall.

All water was heavily chlorinated. Typhoid was our greatest danger. Toilets were the latrines out in the field about two hundred metres away. They were heavily limed. We took baths in the nearby river.

I stayed with my garlic regimen that I maintained during wartime, which always afforded me free sleeping space and good health. I also recommended the garlic to all the girls in my unit, so they had the choice of DDT or garlic to save them from cutting their hair and having to shave underarms and private parts. Once you get used to its scent, everybody was normal. We the garlic people kept together. Have you ever smelled garlic p—? Garlic also prevented diarrhea.

Those who had experience with arms had to perform guard duty around the camp, and handle the heavy-duty equipment that provided the soil for the railroad that was stripped from the surrounding area. Stripping sometimes encroached on villager's land, which was not much appreciated by them, so they tried to retaliate by sabotaging the equipment—U.S. Army trucks, excavators, Cat loaders and fuel containers. Because of the tensions with villagers, the guard at night was called the "dead guard." Nights were very dark. There was no call of "halt, who goes there?" You just shoot.

There were also funny instances. One night at about 2 a.m., a beautiful moonlit night, I was camp guard, standing under a tree on the edge of the muster field; I could not be seen. Sometimes I moved up to the railroad as the finished section was by our camp, and I would lie between the rails and listen to hear if anyone was walking on them. Suddenly, there was noise in the barrack; a window burst open and a person started to run across the muster ground. I was standing in the shadow of a tree and it was so funny to watch—I recognized him; he only had shorts on and he was holding his behind with one hand. I yelled, "Halt!" He just kept on running, so again I yelled: "Halt or I will shoot!" There was the strange sound of a long fart, and he removed his hand from the shorts and kept on running, yelling back, "Diarrhea!" Later he returned from the latrine some two hundred metres away holding the shorts in one hand. I remembered what that strange sound was, he had messed up his shorts. He must have washed them in a river. I laughed so hard I had to sit down on the ground. There were quite a few in that condition, unfortunately.

When our month was up, we all returned to our homes. I went to my uncle's for a good time.

Autumn came, and a new semester started with hard training preparing for the next season, which was to include a trip to Germany. As the date of our departure, June, '53, was nearing, I had many sleepless nights in making the decision to not return from Germany. In fact, I had a lucky break in doing this. A few days before our departure I was visited by the authorities and asked to keep an eye on two of my teammates (what a nerve, it was actually blackmail). I went to my Grandmother Baker to say goodbye. That was the final nail in my decision not to return; I also went to her garden to kiss the soil of my homeland knowing that I was not coming back.

On the departure day, during the usual goodbye, she was crying and she gave me her cold stare. I wondered if she knew what I was up to? Off I went. At the border crossing there was no problem, it passed without excitement. I was in a different frame of mind, wondering what my future would be.

It is worth noting that, at the time, all the teams from Yugoslavia traveled on group passports for security reasons; without ID you were lost. Individual members of the team just got a small card with their name, birthday, address, the number of the group passport, stamp and signature of the official of the country's embassy they were traveling to.

My team arrived the next day in Munich. Representatives of the German team picked us up in their private cars and took us to our *Gasthaus* (not a hotel, perhaps a motel with a restaurant). My English and German at the time were sufficient for basic conversation, thanks to our schooling where grammar, reading and spelling was emphasized. Taking into consideration that in my childhood our family members communicated in four languages—Croatian, German, Hungarian and some French—my ear was already tuned to foreign sounds. So, with little conversation exercises my skills improved rapidly. Also, I think I had quite a knack for foreign languages.

The German player who picked me and one of my teammates up was assigned to us as a guide, and he also drove us to and from games. He was a nice young man, an engineer. I was cautious due to my experience with the Germans during their occupation of my country; nevertheless, the war was over and life was going on. He was my opponent on the pitch, a right fullback and I was left wing. We were equal but fair rivals and that was perhaps the reason the two of us developed a friendly atmosphere between us. I think we were good people. We talked about many things during the team meals. On the third day of the tournament, he asked me about my country. I looked at him and simply asked him, "Can you, would you, help me?"

He was evidently surprised, and said, "What do you mean? What kind of help you need?"

"I do not need any material assistance, just get me to the U.S. embassy on the day we return. I have decided to stay in Germany, this is my answer to your original question."

After the tournament, we had a kind of friendship banquet as there was also an Italian and Austrian team present. It was a lot of fun, and we took third place. There were a few older Germans present—managers and coaches, perhaps—they kept their distance and talked only with our officials. One or two looked very sinister; I wondered if they were old SS or Gestapo members.

On the day of our departure, he brought with him his girlfriend and his dog, so my teammate might go with someone else. Most departed while we were stalling the situation, then my teammate Mladen said, "I am not going back!"

I looked at him and asked, "Are you serious?"

"Dead serious!" he said. Now my German friend came into the conversation and asked me what was going on.

"He is also not going back," I said. "Let us go!" So off we went to the U.S. embassy. The guard asked us what the purpose of our arrival was. I told him we were seeking political asylum, and he advised us to go to the German police HQ. We said goodbye to the German and thanked him for his assistance.

Without much formality, the police took all the information from us then took us back to our hotel, made a booking for us and told us to be ready in the morning, and that they would pick us up.

The next morning, we sat in the lobby, and an officer came in and asked us to follow him to the back of the motel. When we went outside, there was only a police car and a medium-sized furniture van. He led us to the van, and there was a civilian standing by the back door. Without further ado, he opened the door and asked us to go in. As the door opened, I looked up and saw about fifteen people sitting inside. I could see right away that they were also runaways. As we boarded the van, the door closed and we started to roll, and about forty minutes later we stopped. The door opened, and two different people were waiting for us and led us all out. It was the side track of a railroad station in Munich. There was a parked coach and they led us to it and asked us to board it. The group was made up of different Eastern European individuals. Fifteen minutes later, the locomotive came and took us to the main compartment. We all got police IDs to Nürnberg.

It was night when we arrived at Nürnberg, three hours later. Same procedure: moving van, one-hour ride. The van stopped, and three people were waiting outside. There was a big sign that read: "Valka-Lager." I could see a lot of lights, many small bungalows, long barracks and a camp office building, and there was a barbed-wire section that we were led to, then given our rooms and told to report to the camp office in the morning.

That night, Mladen and I had a long talk; we had been good friends for a long time yet the world of suspicion we lived in did not afford us the ability to confide in each other. We had a long hug and cried like babies.

The next morning as we got up in that miserable place where the Germans kept two million Russian POWs, we came to the gate where the administration official was waiting for us (he was Bosnian, probably an agent; we called him Aga) to take us to the registration/interrogation office. Not too far from the gate was a small cantina for basic necessities. We asked the official if we could get a sandwich and some milk before we went to the administration, he said it was no problem. On the way, he told us that the proprietors were also from Yugoslavia. Mladen and I just looked at each other. As we entered the cantina, we saw there were three people there. One man and one woman were the owners. The man was a typical-looking salesman: medium height, chubby and wearing a mustache. She was quite attractive, with pure Slavic features. A round face with high cheekbones; beautiful dark-blonde hair; large, green inquisitive eyes; sexy kissable lips; a pretty smile that showed a set of nice white teeth, the two front teeth slightly separated. All that on a nice, curvy body. She was slightly taller than her man. I was not comfortable with this person.

The third person was turned with his back to us. He was a tall, very handsome Bosnian; I immediately recognized him. Zeljko, he was the right defenceman on the team. He was the second person I was to spy on. I yelled out his nickname: "Hey, Majmune (Monkey)!" He turned around and his mouth dropped open, and the next thing we knew the three of us were all over each other, hugging and crying. I noticed the owner of cantina was closely observing what was going on between the three of us. And here we were, of all the places in the world, meeting in a former German POW Camp. We went to the administration building.

Upon entering the administration building, we were immediately separated and assigned to different rooms, where the interrogators were waiting for us. My investigator/interrogator was an attractive German officer; she introduced herself as Jo and she spoke several languages, including Croatian. She was very pleasant. My purpose was to apply for political asylum. I spent four hours being asked political, non-political, economic and personal-nature questions. In the end, I was told to be back at the same time the next day.

My friends went through the same routine and were also told to report the next day.

Month later, I was browsing through Nürnberg one Sunday and I ran into Jo. I greeted her and she smiled; she was surprisingly friendly. Mind you, I was neat and well-dressed, so I asked her if she would like to have coffee and pastry, which was popular at the time. She accepted, and afterwards we went to the movies, then to the park. We went from holding hands to kissing to lovemaking. It was late and we had to catch the last tram, and she asked me to arrive separately. I thought it was because I was a refugee, she said, "No, I have lover in the camp. I will get in touch with you." Before I departed from Nürnberg we had a few more encounters in the city.

When I came the next day, I was ushered into a different office. When I entered, I politely said good morning, and there behind the desk sat a sinister-looking, skinny, bald, pale-faced man in civilian clothing. He had cold blue eyes and coke-bottle glasses. He just stared at me when I entered, never saying a word. He was going over my statement from the day before. Suddenly, he asked me in Croatian, "If approved, do you intend to stay in Germany?"

"No, sir," I said. "I would like to emigrate to the U.S. or Canada."

"I see," he said. "OK, for now you are free to go, and you will receive further instructions at the duty desk."

And so it went for the next ten days, our Bosnian guide took me from one agent to another. Boy, I met some strange people. Some were really scary. I stuck to my story. Two weeks later, he appeared with two young Germans who introduced themselves as the reps from two local field hockey teams, explaining that they had heard the news of three members of a Yugoslav field hockey team staying in Munich and who were now in the Valka-Lager camp near Nürnberg. Karl was from Schwabach, near Nürnberg, and Fritz was from Nürnberg. I asked if they would be able to do anything for me, like offering me any kind of job. They said they would be in touch, so we parted. A few days later, our Bosnian guide came and said he got a call from Karl to bring me to Schwabach, and that I should bring my hockey stick. When we arrived at the club house, the team was already gathered for the training time. I was surprised; they wanted to see if I was any good. Clever. Well, I was good. They were all pleasantly surprised. It was Thursday, and after practise they asked me if I could stay till Sunday and practice, and on Sunday there was to be a league game. I had two days to get myself together. Sunday came and off we went Nürnberg. (Most were OK teammates, but two were really different. They would never pass the ball.) In the dressing room, I happened to notice Fritz—he was the captain of the Nürnberg team. He never answered my hello. He was right midfielder for his team.

The game started fast and a bit rough; I was playing left wing. Fritz slashed me a couple of times. It was intentional; I got the feeling he did not like me. He was a chubby, older, nondescript German. I waited for my opportunity. It did not take long, he was always two or three paces behind me. I lunged backward to receive a pass and flipped the ball over both of us for my teammate, and at the same time I turned and started to sprint after the ball towards their goal. Fritz stepped in and tried to stop me. We collided and he headbutted me, but he knocked himself down, and as he was falling, he said, "You Balkan Swine." He had to leave the game with a bleeding head. I continued to play with my teammate and we scored. We won the game. After the game we all shook hands and I went to Fritz and apologized. I had to be careful not to engage in a fight as I could be deported.

My two friends were not interested. One pursued the position of sidekick to a former Yugoslav tennis champion who now played for the Germans. Zeljko pursued a possibility of finishing his studies, with help from his uncle who lived in South America. I was just getting in with my new club when, two month later, I received notice from the authorities that I was transferred to a camp located in Munster, Westfalia.

Note: By the end of July '53 we were granted our political asylum. We got our refugee passports and had no more fear of being deported, unless we committed a serious crime.

Like I said, Mladen stayed in Nürnberg and we communicated for a long time, including after my emigration to Canada. The last time we saw each other was in 1966 when I went to visit my parents in Yugoslavia. We kept in touch for another few years. He got married to Nürnberger

Leb-Kuchen Heires. In the early '70s we lost contact. The last time I talked to Zeljko was in the '90s; he was in Chicago.

In late August I packed for my relocation to Münster. A few days before departure, my team in Schwabach had a farewell party for me. Sadly, nothing happened about my future. I left one broken heart there—Inge. She was a real sweetie. It appears everyone was sad and at the same time happy to see me leave. It was not to be.

On the morning of the departure, a furniture van arrived, as usual. There were eight of us. Others were from Eastern Europe. The van took us to the side track at the railroad station and two hours later we left Nürnberg. The next day we arrived in Münster in the morning. After another furniture-van episode, we ended up in the camp. This one was an old German "*Funk Kaserne*," consisting of many two-story brick buildings. There were many different quarters. A few buildings housed refugees from Eastern Europe and the Balkans. There were a few emigration offices for the U.S., Australia and Canada. Some of their personnel housed there.

The camp was a very eroded-looking place. It was damaged in WWII by Allied bombing. I was designated to a room of forty individuals from all over. I was not impressed; I thought I had to get the hell out of there. There were a few hard-looking characters. Some of the others were not healthy. It was a concerning and depressing situation. There were many older Serbs from the Kingdom of Yugoslavia. I was from Tito's, which was not very compatible, and on top of that I was from Croatia. Everyone had an axe to grind.

There was one big Russian. We struck kind of a Slavic bond (he could not speak German). On the day the authorities came and asked for the labourers on the farms, railroad, construction etc., I was getting low on funds, so I asked what the best-paid job was. He said the cleaning of the sewer tanks at the farms, depending on the sizes. The standard size was 2.5m x 2.5m x 3m deep. "Is this negotiable here, or at the site? I'd like to see the job, and if I/we agree, you supply the rubber clothing and the farmers provide food." So, I talked to the Russian and he agreed, and off we went with the official from the employment office to check it out. When we came to the first farm, there were two standard-size shit-holes full to the brim; the solids were two-thirds. There was a tank for liquid and a big container for solid shit. Water hose, pails, rope ladder and pump. There were rungs on the wall. I looked at the holes and said, "We will do it if I am in charge. The cost will be 500 Deutsche Marks. They agreed. I had a good idea how to do it. On Tito's state projects we had to do the same thing many times. It took us about twelve hours to do it. What a stench. When we finished, we hosed ourselves down, had a shower and collected our money. We did this several times, plus the work on the railroad ballast, and by the end of September we had some money. Then my Russian disappeared.

My life in Munster was very colourful. Now that I had money, I bought some new clothing. In the fall there were many festivities. I always had a job when I needed one. I was pumping gas, checking oil, cleaning windshields and smiling at pretty ladies. Some were generous, probably well-off, particularly the older ones. Some even asked me for a date. There were many lonely women and not enough young men. Finally, I was offered a single room in the camp. What a relief. Three weeks into September I met an official in-camp, he was a Serbian married to a Russian woman working for the U.S. immigration. He was younger and there were no ethnic tensions between us. I went on a few outings with them; he had an official vehicle, a VW Bug. I also learned to drive.

My social life was very busy. During evenings I went to the city. There were many festivities in the fall with a lot of beautiful girls and women to dance with.

One evening, I ended up in a night club called Kaiserhoff. It was near the main railroad station. It was recommended to me as a place to meet nice women. It was *the* place in the city. As I went in, a nice lady took me to one of the tables. It was early; the place had just started to fill in. The band was good. By about 11:00, the place filled up. Three tables away sat a man with two ladies; one was very attractive and the other was very young and beautiful. So, as I was looking around our eyes met a few times. I had a feeling she was watching me. Suddenly, the man at their table got up and came to my side, saying, "I see you are alone. Please join us, as I have two beautiful women and always have to let one sit while I dance with other. Truly, the young lady asked me to invite you!" I got up and went over to their table. After formal introductions, the ladies turned out to be two sisters—Ingrid was the older one and Elke the younger (later she told me she was only sixteen and her sister was thirty-three). The man was the Ingrid's date, and Elke was visiting her sister.

Ingrid and her escort went dancing; Elke and I just kept on looking at each other. Then came a romantic tune and I got up and asked her, "Should we try?" She stood up, blushing. I was mesmerized—she was a tall and beautiful, particularly her arms and hands.

We went to the dancing area. I think they played an English waltz. I took her in my arms—oh, boy, we were shivering like two leaves on the breeze. There were not many words exchanged, just strange vibrations that took over all our senses as we started to dance closer and closer together. I was six years older yet lost for words. When the band stopped for a pause, we just stood there as everybody was leaving, holding each other. A moment I will never forget.

I guess her sister noticed our unusual connection, and being a woman of experience, she asked me for a dance. She was very inquisitive about me after she complimented me on my behaviour and looks. There was nothing to hide, so I told her my story in a short version. She was apparently satisfied, and we returned to the table.

Everyone was relaxed and smiling. She was quite taken aback when I explained the conditions in the camp that I lived in, yet I was very presentable, clean, well dressed and good-looking. For the next song, Elke asked me to dance. We danced even closer, speechless.

We continued until the last dance. It was 2 a.m.: closing time. Everyone was leaving. I offered to walk them home and they accepted, but Max had a car, so we drove to Ingrid's home.

Ingrid and her friend sat in the front, Elke and I sat in the back. There was all kinds of small talk during the short drive. At one point, Elke took my hand and slid a bit closer to me. Her beautiful soft hand was more than warm. I could see that her cheeks were aglow. Then she leaned on me and put her head on my shoulder. I am not sure if her sister was watching us in the rearview mirror, but as her friend drove with one hand and I observed that she was sitting very close to him, I did not think so. I put my arm around Elke's waist and pulled her gently to me.

She squished my hand and started to shiver, kissing me gently on the cheek. I knew this beautiful young lady was ready to surrender, and that this encounter would lead to something serious.

Thousands of thoughts went through my mind, and as much as I was excited I decided to wait. I had no papers, no job, I was a *flüchtling* and had my eyes on my emigration to Canada. Also, from my few other encounters with young German ladies, I knew they certainly opposed integration/marriage.

Finally, we arrived at Ingrid's parents' home. I said goodnight to Ingrid and her friend while Elke asked to stay out a bit. Elke and I stayed in a hallway exchanging some tender feelings. She was ready to give herself. For a gentleman's reason, I just did not want to take advantage of her. She was such an upright young lady, a virgin if I ever met one. I respected her. We made a date for the next day and I said goodnight. Elke was disappointed and crying. I left, and so began a lifelong relationship.

The next day we met and went for a long walk in the city. She had to return home some distance from her town: Münster-Letmathe. We parted, and the exchange of long letters began.

A week later, Dushan, a Yugoslav that worked for some Americans, called me and his buddy—to whom he had talked about me with—from wartime to come and talk to him about a job with the British Army. I was very excited, as I was desperate to get out of that miserable camp. So, the day came when Dushan's friend arrived, and he introduced himself. I believe he was a sergeant in the MSO (Mixed Service Organization) working for the British occupational forces in Germany. He was stationed in Osnabrück with the 10th Armoured Division ambulance group. He was a nice intelligent man from Vojvodina. He explained to me what the job was all about, and as I did not have many options I accepted the offer, which was to undergo six weeks of military training not far from Bremen, and after completion of my training he would make sure I joined his unit in Osnabrück.

When I informed Elke of my intentions, she was very sad. While I was in training, we exchanged long letters every week. We were looking forward to my coming to Osnabrück.

And so it went: a very hard training in an old German U-boat barracks outside Bremerhaven. The instructor was a member of General Anderson's Polish army, formed from Polish exiles during WWII in Great Britain. He survived the invasion in June '44. He was some character. He sure drilled us. (He was a real robo-soldier. He landed as a paratrooper in a glider behind German lines in Normandy. I thought I went through hell.) In my unit there were men from various Eastern European nationalities. There were two more Yugoslavs beside me. By the fourth week, after the pre-exam drill, they were not there anymore and a few more were rejected in the fifth week.

On weekends, we ended in the local bar outside Bremerhaven. It was hard drills in the underground of the U-boat barracks. Above ground there was a huge cow pasture and dairy, while below the surface were many canals that made it possible for U-boats to come in from the open North Atlantic Ocean, some eight kilometres away, to refit, resupply, rest and exchange U-boat personnel. It was a clever and well-designed German Navy installation.

In the last week, in order to finish my course we had to serve as parade guards for twenty-four hours at the main gate. Everything had to be perfect: your appearance, from top to the bottom; you shaved twice in twenty-four hours with your haircut. We had to re-polish our boots, belt, gun strap and ankle sleeves, and re-press our uniform and shirt. The guard officers in charge were Germans, so that tells you the whole story. Outside the guard house was a twenty-five-yard-long by four-foot-wide strip for the guard to march on back and forth, parade style, smartly, with the U-turn to be properly executed. When you got bored with the marching, you stopped at one end or the other, and by proper drill you took your rifle off your shoulder and put it next to your foot, slightly spread your legs, raised your chin up, looked straight forward and stood totally still. Should a high-ranking officer enter the compound, you had to perform an honour-guard salute. All this under the watchful eyes of the guard commander, who was watching your every move and rating you. In the end, we had a small reception where we got our papers with our assignments. I got the fare for Osnabrück. My new friends kept their promise.

That night, we went to town and got a bit wild. There was also a girl, I remember. The next day at 11 a.m., I was on the train to Osnabrück. Four hours later, I was picked up at the station by a Jeep that took me to the barracks on Sedan Street.

When I was still in Munster Camp, I was thinking, my god, here I am again surrounded by members of warring factions from WWII Yugoslavia. What will my outcome be? During WWII there were seven different factions fighting two main enemies, the Germans and Italians—the occupiers—and also amongst themselves in absence of these occupiers. These thoughts were on my mind again that morning leaving Bremerhaven on the way to Osnabrück—how will I be received by the others who I have not met yet?

It is worth noting that Tito's secret service kept a close eye on all military and others who had successfully left Yugoslavia, particularly those who were politically organized and laboured against his government.

When the jeep stopped at the gate on 44 Sedan Street, a corporal of the British Army came with an older sergeant in the same black uniform that I wore to check our papers. He checked mine and gave them to the MSO officer, who said to me, "Private Soos, I am Sgt. Nikolic, step out of the jeep, take your belongings and follow me." As I stepped out and took my suitcase, he came and shook my hand and said, "Welcome to the MSO." I thanked him and saluted. "Now, follow me to the office of the commanding officer of this unit, Captain Smyth [doctor]." We went to the first floor, and he knocked at the captain's door and we entered. The captain was sitting behind the desk smoking his pipe; as we stepped in, we saluted him and stayed at attention. He casually returned our salute. Sgt. Nikolic then introduced me.

The captain looked at me and said, "Do you speak English?" I told him I could communicate well. "Quite right, quite right," said the captain. Nikolic appeared surprised at my answer. Then the English officer checked my papers and welcomed me to the unit, and we were dismissed.

Nikolic then took me to his office for a further briefing.

"I see you came from Croatia."

"I was born there, sir. I came from Yugoslavia." Surprised, he looked at me and smiled.

"Thank you," he said. I had a good feeling. He pointed out to me that I should stay politically neutral, as this is not a good place for the subject. I thanked him and then he took me to the second floor to show me my room. When we stepped inside, he pointed to an empty bed for six right beside the door. I put my suitcase under the bed. He stepped in front of me and said, "The other five are older men of various sensitivities, be careful." I thanked him again. Then he told me that the person who contacted me in Münster would be back the following day (his name was Ostojic), when I would also be introduced to the MSO commander. We went to the mess hall. There I was introduced to Cook, a nice older man with whom I kept a good relationship for my duration there.

The barracks had huge grounds. Half was the assembly area and the other half was parking for many different types of ambulance vehicles. There were about forty of us MSO operators/drivers. There was a mess hall for British soldiers, a large repair garage, and the mechanics were Germans. In the main building, the fourth and the fifth floor were sleeping quarters for the Brits.

British and the best MSO drivers transported British personnel daily—mostly medical staff and some high-ranking officers—to and from their private homes and other local destinations, or to Germany or Europe as required. Some high-ranking officers had their private cars—we were drivers—and would visit NATO officer's clubs in European capitals for various reasons.

At 5 p.m.— dinner time—Nikolic introduced me to the whole group. Surprisingly, there were three young Slovenians. The reception was OK. I think it was the curiosity that overcame any animosity at the time. Most of the men present were in their forties, save the three Slovenians who were my age. They were people from outside big cities, hardened by war and its misfortunes, just like me. I am not sure how much education they had as I never asked. Their post-war time—the past eight years—was spent in camps and the MSO. Some were married to German women, had families and lived outside the compound. Few were of noticeably poor health. The MSO provided fair jobs and a livelihood. Our pay was about three hundred German Marks per month, room and board and medical and dental. Germany paid for everything. Our MSO group was partly exiled Yugoslavs, mostly Serbs. Our monthly pay was handed to us in cash.

I met the MSO commandeer the next day when Sgt. Nikolic took me to his office. He was chubby, medium-height and bearded with chimpanzee-like eyes; he had small fat hands with short fingers and his uniform was very tired. After entering and saluting, he asked many questions about me. When the questions of education and what languages I spoke came up, he was a bit surprised, I noticed. He gave me the usual short speech and we were dismissed. I have never seen him again (apparently, he had an outside business), we just briefly before my departure for Canada. Sgt. Nikolic was the one in charge of the unit. He spoke very good English and he reported to the English captain. I even forgot his name; I only remember his nickname—Brada (beard).

My first night was OK. Entering my room at bedtime, I saw there were only three men there. I greeted them, went to my bed and tried to sleep. A while later the other two roommates came in. One was in his late twenties (a handsome-looking man) and noisy. I think he'd had a few! Later, Butch and I became a bit more relaxed in our relationship till I found out how many different petty conflicts existed amongst a few of these men. He was very deceptive and cunning.

The next day after breakfast, there was a morning roll call at the vehicle park. Everyone was given his duty for the day by Sgt. Nikolic. I was the last one. He took me to an old stretcher Jeep and instructed me to clean it up. He then left. I attended to my Jeep. Older drivers came to look at what I was doing; some offered help and others remarks. In the afternoon, Sgt. Nikolic informed us that for the next two weeks there would be a German city police driving-school instructor lecturing us. There was a new regulation requiring us to have German driver's licences. Three weeks later, everyone passed and got a class 2 licence.

Later that day, Ostojic wanted to see me. He was a very nice man. He made every effort to explain to me the politics of the unit. We took a liking to each other, particularly because he also claimed that he was a Yugoslav who was born in Serbia. He was an educated man. I did not ask too much of his background. He helped me with an introduction to the good men's store, so I was able to buy stuff at a good discount. We met occasionally, and when he was in office he traveled a lot. We always sat with him during meals. He also pointed out who was who in the unit and mentioned to me that he would talk to Sgt. Nikolic about transferring to a room with the three Slovenians in it, because we had more in common. He felt that one or two individuals in my room may not be good, and it was not a safe situation for me because they felt strongly that I was a Communist—Tito's spy. A week later, the transfer was made and the three young Slovenes gave me a very friendly welcome. One I become a very good buddy with. His name was Josef Sipos. I lost contact with him after I emigrated to Canada. Later I heard that he got married to one of my girlfriends, Erika.

As we were half civilian, half military, my working days were Monday to Friday, 8–5. Weekends and holidays were free, to do anything I liked.

After five I could leave the compound and must return by seven in the morning. What a life for a young man. Socially, Butch took me to several nice places where one can meet all kinds of female company. It was an interesting period.

After my first paycheque, I went to explore the city. It was late fall and in that part of Germany that had "Shooting Fest" festivities everywhere, at night clubs and other civic dances. I was very busy. Socially, it was an interesting time. I tried to play field hockey for the local team. It was the end of the season and I think they did not want an occupier playing on their team, so when the spring came nothing happened.

Josef and I spent a lot of weekends together. He was really nice young man. When I went to meet Elke in Munster, I asked him to come along.

Elke and I kept in close contact, and just before Christmas she asked me if I could come to Münster while she and her mother visited her sister. Her mother wanted to meet me. We planned to meet the week before Christmas in the Kaiserhoff, the place where we first met. The weather was kind of cool with not much snow, none at all in Münster. Josef and I boarded a train in Osnabrück on the Saturday; I think It was 4 p.m. It had been a long time and I was excited to see Elke again. It was 7 p.m. when we arrived at Münster. By 7:30, we were in the Kaiserhoff. As we entered the restaurant, I asked the registration lady if Miss Baars was in. She politely smiled. "Are you Leon?" she asked. I said yes. "Please do come in, they are waiting for you." So, she took us to the table. We were a bit late. When Elke spotted me, she jumped up and ran to me, giving me a big hug. Then she took Josef and me to the table where her mom was sitting with her sister Ingrid and Hainke, her niece. I stopped at Mom first and introduced myself, and greeted her in the traditional European fashion by bowing and kissing her hand.

Right after that, she hugged me and kissed me on the cheek, saying, "You look exactly how Elke described you a few times, I must say. You and your friend both look very nice." I thanked her for the compliment. She was a very nice lady. She must have accepted me, I thought. Then I Greeted Ingrid and Hainke—she was seven, I believe; nice young miss. I then introduced Josef.

The table we sat at was decorated and set for dinner. I did not expect it to be ready in advance. Ingrid saw my confusion, so she picked up an upside-down envelope that was under a flower vase and gave it to me. I was really surprised. I opened the envelope and there was a beautiful birthday card: *Happy belated birthday, Leon, from all of us.* There were signatures from the whole family. I was honoured and thanked them all. I sat down, shaken. I told Elke that my birthday was over four weeks ago. "Yes, we know, but she wanted to surprise you. Today is our gift to you!" said her mom.

We had a pork roast with veggies, dessert and wine. Afterwards, the dinner music started. I had the first dance with Elke; some sensation. She held me tight and put her head on my shoulder. I noticed Mother was watching with a friendly smile on her face. She told me she was so happy that I could come. The next dance was Mom and I, so we talked about my job. I told her it was not my future, and many other things. She made a remark: "I see you and Elke look good together. There is a lot going on between you two, I see." I agreed. Suddenly she stopped and asked me, "Are you serious about going to Canada?"

"Yes," I said, "there is no future for me in Germany."

"But it will break Elke's heart."

"Let her come after me in a year, as soon as I get established. When I have a steady job, I will call for her."

"But she is so young."

"Well, by then she will be nineteen or a bit more. She will finish school and learn a little English."

"You sure know your plan," she said.

"Yes, I must think ahead because I might be called at any time." And that is where the conversation ended.

A few more dances and the evening ended. Mom insisted on paying for the dinner, then they took a taxi. We made a date for the next day early, because Josef and I had to return to Osnabrück. We met in the morning, had an early lunch and went for a long stroll into the park.

It was a memorable occasion. At 4 p.m., they all escorted us to the rail station. Mother invited me to their home at my first opportunity.

I promised I would go. There were emotional goodbyes and Josef and I left. "Some family," he said later. "You lucky man."

I re-established contact with my parents while I was in Münster. I obtained all my important documents; they were sent by my parents through some people travelling back and forth to Yugoslavia. It was very helpful in obtaining my new passport. I had all my documents translated by the University of Munster, faculty of Slavic languages.

Upon my return from visiting Elke, things became very busy. We had several exercises in pre-NATO manoeuvres. Then, in February '54, Josef and I were posted to transport the CO to various allied officer's clubs located in Western Europe. Socially, we were also participating in the carnival festivities; there were plenty of those. In one of them I met Erika; wow, my heart got split in half. Erika was older than Elke. Erika and I got really involved.

After my second visit to Elke, her father told me that there would be no future between the two of us. She will not marry a refugee and she will never go to Canada. Elke and her mom were crying. I thanked him, said goodbye and left. Boy, I was angry! Elke and I kept in contact till my departure for Canada, and after that till 1958. Then we lost contact. We met one more time in May '55; she was traveling through Osnabrück by train. It was very emotional, as I was also leaving in June for Canada. Forty-five years later, on Christmas Eve, the phone rang and a female voice ask me if I was Leon S. I asked who it was. "I am friend of Elke's, she was looking for you this past year and her daughter-in-law found you. She would like to talk to you." I asked her a few questions about Elke to make sure it was not a prank. It was a sure thing, so one hour later, Elke phoned. It was some conversation; it lasted for about two hours. She is a widow now. Elke came to Canada and we met on Vancouver Island, then we traveled a bit and came to my home in Kitimat where she revealed her whole life story.

The next year I visited her in Germany. There was a total absence of the old flame, but the good friendship was there. I returned home, and we kept in touch till June 2017. Elke passed away, may she rest in peace.

In March '54, I was called by the Canadian consulate in Karlsruhe, requesting my appearance for a medical. When I arrived, I was told that there was a gold mine opening in Thompson, Manitoba. Many people were needed there. After the medical, I was told to wait for further instructions. I returned to Osnabrück. A month later Manitoba was cancelled with regret, and they told me that if another opportunity arose I would be informed.

Erika was happy that I would stay for a while longer. She came from a well-off family; they had a large fish store in Osnabrück and Erika worked there—she always did have a bit of a fish scent. I must say that her family took a liking to me. One day, her father asked me about my future, so I explained to him that I wanted to go to Canada to make my life there. He wondered if I would be interested in working in his store. When he gave me a tour, there were a few not-so-friendly eye contacts. I related that to dating Erika. I said I would think about it. "You know," he continued, "Erika is just a year younger than you; you look like a good and healthy match and she is the only one we have. It would be nice to have some grandchildren." I just looked at him and smiled.

It was our beautiful summer. Erika said she would also like to get away from there. I told her that if I left soon, to give me at least a year until she would be able to join me. I needed a job and a place to stay. So, in the late fall, the second call came from the Canadian consulate. When I arrived, the official was very friendly and said, "After the medical, come back to my office." After the medical, I went back. He smiled and said, "Good report. Now, here is a map of Canada. Take a good look, and when you make a decision where you would like to go, put your finger on the location."

I stopped for a moment, looked at the map of the Canada and put my finger on Edmonton, Alberta. "Good," he said. "Edmonton it is, you will receive your instructions with all your papers early in the spring of 1955. One more medical will be done by your unit doctor. I can tell you that you will be sailing in early July with the *Castel Felice* from Bremerhaven." I remember when I saw it: it was a ten-thousand-ton Italian tin can. I could never figure out how we made it across the North Atlantic.

From that day on, a strange and curious anxiety set in. Erika and I talked for days about what would be. When her father heard the story, he kind of ... I felt he was not enthusiastic about Erika eventually leaving, but he would compromise if we came back. He wanted to be promised a wedding there before we left. I promised. And so, July came. I was discharged from the MSO and said goodbye to all in the unit. I left Osnabrück at noon; the ship was sailing at 8 p.m. that night. Erika went with me to Bremerhaven. She was crying all the way. She stood on the wharf while I went through pass control and then up the gangplank to board the ship. She was still standing there while the ship left the harbour. After I lost sight of her, I sat down crying, knowing that I had left Europe, Erika, Elke and my past. It was July 15, 1955.

A while later, a hand touched me and a voice addressed me in my native language, "Are you from Yugoslavia?" I said yes. "My name is Drago, I am from Lika in Croatia." He seemed to be a nice young man. We shook hands.

"I am Leon. I am pleased to meet you." He said that we should look for our cabin, and I said OK. And so began the second stage of my life into the unknown...

Geburtsort und -datum / Lieu et date de naissance: Ivancic, 9. 11. 1931
Beruf / Profession: Student
Wohnort / Résidence actuelle: Nürnberg
*Geburtsname u. Vorname(n) der Ehefrau / Nom (avant le mariage) et prénom(s) de l'épouse: /
*Name u. Vorname(n) des Ehemannes / Nom et prénom(s) du mari: Soos, Leon

Personenbeschreibung Signalement

Größe / Taille: 178 cm
Nase / Nez: gerade
Haarfarbe / Cheveux: d. braun
Hautfarbe / Teint: weiß
Farbe der Augen / Couleur des yeux: braun
Gesichtsform / Forme du Visage: länglich
Besondere Kennzeichen / Signes particuliers: keine

Kinder Enfants

Name / Nom — Vorname(n) / Prénom(s) — Geburtsort und -datum / Lieu et date de naissance — Geschlecht / Sexe

Nº 0071442

Nº 0071442

T/n "CASTEL FELICE„
SITMAR
No 280
Bremerhaven-Quebec
25. JUL. 1955

280

For use of Carrier

CANADIAN IMMIGRATION
IDENTIFICATION CARD
(To be shown to Examining Officer at port of arrival)

Name in full	Soos, Leon
STATUS	IMMIGRANT - "LANDED" IMMIGRANT - "REÇU"
Signature of Passenger	X
Port Stamp	CANADA IMMIGRATION JUL 25 1955 QUEBEC

FOLD HERE

DULY STAMPED BY AN IMMIGRATION OFFICER, THIS CARD IS EVIDENCE OF YOUR STATUS IN CANADA. IT IS REQUIRED FOR CUSTOMS CLEARANCE AND WILL ALSO PROVE USEFUL FOR OTHER PURPOSES.

RETAIN IT CAREFULLY

FRANÇAIS AU VERSO

.S. CASTEL FELICE

After the ship was out of Bremerhaven, Drago and I went to the quartermaster to find out where our cabin was. My instruction envelope from Canadian immigration included a ship fare ticket from Bremerhaven to Quebec City and a train ticket from Quebec City to Edmonton, Alberta. I noticed that my ship ticket had a stamp on it: "Category C." The quartermaster looked at it and instructed one of the attendants to take us to our sleeping quarters, so we went. The ship did not have any elevators that I remember. I think from the main deck it was about three or four stories down. When we finally got to level C, it clicked what the stamp "Category C" was for.

Level C was, from what I can remember, in the engine room area, next to or just above the drive shaft, very noisy. Our room was large with twenty to thirty sailor bunks in it, a very unfriendly area. I said to myself, *Aren't you glad that you worked on Tito's state projects?* (I guess Canada was too cheap to pay for a better cabin for a future taxpayer.) "Take your pick," the attendant said. Drago and I looked at each other. There were about ten others with us. "When you settle down, come up to the cafeteria for some food," the attendant said and left. I took the lower bunk and Drago the upper. I did not have a lot of stuff, I had sent most of it to my parents before I left Germany. I had two suits, working overalls, army boots, some underwear, shaving gear and some money, about a thousand German Marks, which at that time was probably just over $300 Canadian.

Then I sat down and said to Drago that I hoped our future would be better, and then for some reason I started to look through my passport and stopped in shock when I came to the page with the German stamp indicating my right to live on the territory of Germany. It was now stamped over with "cancelled." I was quite upset, as I did not pay attention to this in Bremerhaven. In my excitement, I asked Drago to check his passport, which was the same as mine. He handed me his passport and, sure thing, he did not have a cancellation on his stay permit.

Little did I know about Canadian law at that time: I have to wait five years for my Canadian citizenship and my Canadian passport; accordingly, in the first and fifth year I could not leave the territory of Canada, and I could be deported for any criminal offence. Then it dawned on me that there was no hope for me to go back to Germany and marry Erika. Suspicion came: Did Erika's father have his fingers in it?

The first night was horrible, due to the noise of the shaft and the engine. The voyage was supposed to last eleven days, and we arrived one day early.

The next day we passed the coast of Ireland and sailed into the open North Atlantic. It was beautiful weather and clear sailing for two days. I talked to the Italian quartermaster to see if we could get better accommodation; he said he would see what could be done. Before the night was over, I ran into him at the bar. Many people were sitting around (there were seven hundred passengers on the ship, mostly women, some single and immigrating to Canada, some joining their husbands who worked all over the country, some visiting their children). I had put two hundred Deutsche Marks into a napkin, and I sat next to him and greeted him. He was a friendly, handsome Italian. There were women around, so he would be softer, I thought. So, I asked him if I could buy him a drink. He accepted. We had a casual conversation in English. When he went for a dance, I discreetly put the napkin with the money under my beer glass and went to the washroom. When I returned, he was back at his chair. I sat to finish my beer. After a while, I got up to go for a stroll out on the deck. I said goodnight to the quartermaster, thanking him for the company and all he did, pushing my napkin to his side at the same time, and then I left. Much later, after talking to Drago on the deck, I went to bed.

The next morning at breakfast, Drago came with a German newspaper and said, "Look at this." There were four pages on the largest private development in the world of a hydro-electric station in Kemano B.C. and an aluminum smelter in Kitimat, B.C. We discussed whether or not we should go there after we finished our contracts, which were with the Northern Alberta Construction Co. and was supposed to pay good wages. Little did I know then how cleverly our contract was presented...

While we were sitting, an attendant approached us and gave us a key, saying, "Compliments of Quartermaster, please follow me. He took us to the B-deck two-bed cabin. All our stuff was there, too. Drago looked at me while giving a tip to the attendant and said, "This was not your doing, was it?" What can I say?

After breakfast, we went on the deck. It was so-so day. As I went by an attractive lady leaning over the railing, I said good morning in German. She turned around, smiled and said, "Good morning to you, too. I am watching the icebergs in the distance." And so, the conversation started after the introduction: she was Gerda B. from Hamburg Germany on the way to Vancouver B.C. to meet her son, Ralph B., who was working in Kitimat B.C. for the Aluminum Company of Canada—Alcan. We told her our story, and then it hit me.

"You know," I said, "we just finished reading a story in a German newspaper about Kitimat, and here you are. What an amazing coincidence." Then came a weather advisory on the intercom: "Atlantic storm approaching by midnight." Oh my god. I started to think about the unfortunate Atlantic; there were icebergs floating everywhere. Nature's beauty, yet so threatening.

Frau Gerda B. gave us her son's address in Kitimat and we parted for the night. I am sure most of us retired with a dosage of fear. At midnight, we hit the storm. The old Italian tin can was moaning and groaning under the stress of the waves of the furious ocean it was subjected to. We were—and I am sure everyone else was—woken up. It was a long, sleepless night; the ship was no more than a rubber ducky exposed to the mercy of Mother Nature's immense force. The ship was rocking in all possible directions, things were sliding on the floor. Finally, the morning light appeared. The intercom interrupted the situation, "This is your captain speaking, those that can make it to the cafeteria, only sandwiches and canned drinks will be available. If you need medical assistance, use your house phone..."

Drago and I decided to go up to the cafeteria. On the way up, the hallways stank from the people being sick and throwing up. There was not a soul to be seen, save the odd attendant keeping the ship as tidy as possible. It was rough going due to the ship's constant rolling; you had to hold onto the handrail. When we came up, only one officer, the chef, a bartender and two more sailors were in cafeteria. They greeted us and were apparently happy to see us. I looked outside: it was sure looking ugly. The sea was boiling, and the ship was rolling. There was no rain, just a strong wind and the occasional glimpse of an iceberg when the ship's rear rose out of the water. I turned to the officer and said, "This seem to be an old ship, do you have radar on?"

He said, "Fortunately, we do. It would be hard to navigate through the iceberg alley without it."

Then Drago said he was very hungry and asked what we could get to eat. Chef said that, seeing we were the only two guests, it was his treat. "Good," Drago said. "Could we have a loaf of bread, one Italian salami, some good cheese and two bottles of Cognac?"

Chef looked at us and said, "Are you serious?" We said yes, we were. He left and came back with our order. We thanked him.

"We will be back tomorrow for the same breakfast," Drago said, and Chef just smiled.

"Could we perhaps go up to the bridge and observe what is happening out there?" I asked the officer.

"I will ask the captain," he said, and went to the house phone. He returned shortly and happily announced that we, the only healthy passengers, were welcome to come up.

I must admit that, as young and strong as we were claiming to be, the bridge was an effort. Drago carried the bread, cheese and salami. I carried the Cognac, and by the time we entered the bridge Drago must have been very hungry, as he started to slice our breakfast right away. The Cognac was uncorked (bless the chef) so I had a drink out of the bottle and passed it to my friend. I offered the other bottle to the captain, but he declined.

The view was unbelievable. The ship looked like a galloping horse trying to jump over and under huge waves while icebergs glimmered in the distance. Actually, after one bottle of Cognac, nature's effects kind of started to retreat. By the time Drago and I started the second bottle, our bread, salami and cheese were gone. I think we'd had enough, I was ready to have a snooze. The young officer took us to our cabin and I crashed out.

The next morning, there was no change in the weather; it continued for the next four days and nights. Drago and I collected our daily food and Cognac. It was the eighth or ninth day of the voyage when the sea suddenly went calm, the icebergs stayed behind, the sun came up and many passengers came up on deck. These poor people looked like zombies. Frau Gerda came too, so we continued our conversation and had a nice social in the evening on a beautiful night on the sea. Early in the morning, we saw the land on the horizon—Newfoundland. What an exciting experience this had been. I will never forget: during the night the ship entered the St. Lawrence River ... I was in Canada! The next day at 11 a.m. the ship docked at Quebec City.

Canada

I will never forget the moment when I set foot on Canadian soil on the North American continent that day; the emotions were overwhelming. Unbelievable! As I stepped off the ship I fell on my knees and cried, just as I am now, writing about that moment it happened some sixty-two years ago. An immigration officer came to me and asked if I was OK. "I am not sure, Officer," I said. "I cannot explain..." He then helped me and directed me towards the customs and immigration building.

Writing this today, I think I have found the answer. I think by remembering that little boy many years ago as he sat on the floor in the old castle classroom looking at old maps of the world and wondering about distant people living there—a member of whom I became that day, July the 25th, 1955—and listening to the old American's stories and the words of a gypsy woman reading my palm at my Grandma Baker's place when I was seven, I knew what brought me here. Am I, was I, dreaming?

When Drago and I entered customs and immigration there were already long lines of seven hundred passengers going through the check. When my turn came, the immigration officer was friendly. "Welcome to Canada!" he said.

"Thank you," I answered.

"You speak English, I see."

"Yes, I learned in school and then I worked for two years for the British occupational forces in Germany."

He smiled and checked my passport and British discharge document, stamped them and returned them to me with the $35 cash, saying, "Compliments of the government of Canada. I said thank you. Then he continued to give us instructions on where to board the railroad coach. "Yours will have the sign: Montreal-Toronto-Vancouver."

Most of the people were boarding the coaches for Montreal and Toronto. There was only one with a Vancouver sign on it. Drago and I were the first ones to board it. After storing a few of my possessions, I went for a stroll and looked for Frau Gerda B. On the way to the next coach, I stepped into the washroom. At the sink washing my hands I saw a golden ring sitting on the ledge. I checked it out for a name: nothing. There was no one else in the coach, so I decided to keep it. I put it in my wallet and continued my search for Frau Gerda. She was not to be found, so I returned to my compartment. By 8 p.m., the train departed. A boring five days and four nights later Drago and I arrived in Edmonton, Alberta. It was 11 a.m.; two immigration officers were waiting for us. They welcomed us and took us to an inexpensive hotel on 101 Street just below the McDonald Hotel. They gave us instructions on our contract with the Northern Alberta Construction Co. We were to board the train the next night. They were to pick us up and take us to the train station.

The hotel's name was the Devon Hotel, an old frontier structure. We had no other choice; besides, it was cheap. When they left, we talked to the hotel owner. She was a Lithuanian lady, very nice and very helpful. She offered to store our stuff till we returned.

The Devon Hotel was a real old Wild West building. In the night silence, one could hear all the things that went on in the old three-story building. Oh yes, I was awake for most of the night. Drago was also tossing and turning, trying to absorb the continental transition and all that had transpired in the past twelve days as the reality slowly sank in. Then I remembered the ring I had found. I turned the bed lamp on and took a close look at it. I was surprised at what I discovered. The ring was broken. Is that the reason someone left it? I am not superstitious, but I asked myself what the reason could be to find an object like this after being in the new world just a few hours?

When I got married later in life, my wife had it repaired and a small Alaskan black diamond installed in it. I lost it when my wife and I separated; she passed away not long after. May she rest in peace!

I remember going for the medical in the Canadian embassy in Karlsruhe, Germany, when I was asked to put my finger on the huge map of Canada to choose the place that I would like to go, and my finger pointed to Edmonton, Alberta. And here I was; unbelievable!

Sure, the map was large, but after I boarded the train in Quebec City with short stops along the way to Edmonton, it took five days and four nights to get here. I said to myself, oh my god, that map in the Canadian embassy did not lie. The country is huge. It occupies half of the North American continent. But you can only get the true feel of its size by travelling on land.

I must have fallen asleep. I was woken up by Drago shaking me. It was time to get ready. We went to see the Lithuanian lady and made arrangements for our belongings, which we were to pick up and pay for on our return. She agreed and we thanked her, leaving a $10 deposit. She was happy with that.

The two immigration officers with the car were on time. Good mornings and how-are-yous were exchanged. I learned these Anglo-Saxon social formalities working for the English in Germany. Then they asked us if we'd had breakfast. We answered no, so they took us to the railroad-station restaurant. Surprise, they paid for it, just to get rid of us, knowing what was waiting for us. Then they verified our tickets with the ticket office and we boarded the train. The tickets read: "Post Copy B.C." We departed by 11 a.m. It was a real milk run.

By 8 a.m. the next morning, we came to the town of Grande Prairie. The conductor informed us that we had to be back by 1 p.m. We went wandering about. Drago went to a barber shop. Not too far from the railroad station was a lot with much activity; heavy-duty equipment was working on it. I stopped to watch. On the side was a parked pickup with an elderly man sitting in it; watching the operation, I assumed. A short while later the man in the pickup stepped out and said, "Good morning, young man. Are you looking for work?" He was very friendly. I greeted him, and we shook hands and introduced ourselves. I gave him a short story about myself. He complimented me on my English. I told him that I would love to, but that I must fulfill my commitment to the Canadian government. "Too bad," he said, "you look reliable and strong. Maybe you come back?" He gave me his card.

He then told me about the project and his family. He was married with no kids. Then I asked him how one gets a driver's licence in Canada. I showed him mine, which was rated for heavy trucks. "Boy," he said, "I sure could use you. As for the driver's licence, come with me. I will help you." He went across the street and asked me to come along. He led me toward a beautiful Cadillac convertible. "Get in," he said. "You drive and show me what can you do, and I will direct you to where we are going."

I could not believe my eyes and ears. I had seen Cadillacs in pictures and the movies, but never a live one. When Frank M. asked me to drive, I sat behind the steering wheel and for a moment a flashback came: *The little boy who drove his relative's car into a huge sawdust pile. Oh my god. I hope history does not repeat itself here with this beautiful car.* So, I didn't move. Frank asked me what I was thinking. "Let's go!"

I turned to him and said, "If I tell you the truth, I hope you will not change your mind. I hope you will laugh."

"Go on, tell me," he said. I told him the story and he sure had a good laugh. Then he said to me, "My boy, no one drives this car but me, you got this? If I made a mistake by putting you in the driver's seat of my car then my impression of you is a total failure. Let us not waste any more time. Let's go!"

After a brief instruction of the operational panel, I adjusted the seat and side mirrors—Frank was a bit bigger than me. I had never driven an automatic vehicle; it was the cat's meow for me. I started the beauty up. The car was amazingly quiet. It was a very large vehicle, yet it moved without much effort with all the power it had. I turned on the left signal light, looked out and moved out onto the street. Frank guided me for several blocks, then we came to a large building with the sign: "Government of Alberta." He told me to park there and wait. I parked at the front of the building and Frank went inside. A while later, he came out with a tall slim man who he introduced to me as Steven, a driver's licence inspector, saying: "Well, Leon, here is your opportunity to show us how good you are. Steven is my friend and I asked him a personal favour to give you a driver's test and he agreed to do so, so do not screw it up. No fender bending, etc." I politely thanked them both. Frank sat in the back and Steven in the front holding his writing board with the examination papers on it.

"Let us start," Steven said.

"I have not read the Alberta driver's manual," I said.

"It is OK, you are a new immigrant and I see that you have a class 2 licence. We need good people; I will allow you to show me what you know." So, I went through a full vehicle inspection: under the hood, lights, brakes, emergency systems, and off we went through the full test. He was making notes and asking questions, and then came parallel parking. A Cadillac Eldorado was, I think, over twenty feet long and close to seven feet wide. Most drivers have difficulty parking a baby carriage. Sorry, I had to put this in: the Cadillac was parked on the first try, 100%. Both Steven and Frank were impressed. After that, Steven said, "Let us go back, I am satisfied."

We went back to Steven's office, and a while later I got my first Canadian driver's licence! I thanked both men again and we left for the railroad station. It was close to noon and the train was leaving at 1 p.m. Frank and I said an emotional goodbye. He asked me to keep in touch in case I changed my mind, then we parted.

The train left Grande Prairie at 1 p.m. It was another milk run. It was after 4 p.m. when the conductor came and said, "In about half an hour the train will stop and that is where you will get off. There is nothing there but a wooden shed; wait there and someone is going to pick you up." Sure thing, the train stopped accordingly, and as the conductor said there was a wooden shed, all right. It was very, very hot as we stepped off the train. There were black flies like I had never seen before and they were pesty. So, Drago and I went into the shed. I can tell you, the next three hours in that shed was like solitary confinement in the Sahara.

Hours later, we heard the train coming. I said to Drago, "If it is a passenger train let us stop it and go back." He looked at me and asked if I was serious. "Most definitely," I said. Finally, around the bend came the train, but it was a freight train. It stopped, a man jumped off of it and called us by our names. He introduced himself as Mike, foreman for the "extra gang" of the Northern Alberta Construction Co., and welcomed us.

"What is an 'extra gang'?" I asked him.

"We repair and maintain the railroad."

I looked at Drago and said in Croatian, "Good night, they sure gave us a good construction job. It's a good thing Yugoslavia gave us good training on such jobs."

"Come to my office," Mike said, which was a rough, remodelled boxcar. There we filled out a labour form with an elderly bookkeeper who informed us of our wages: 91 cents per hour, of which we pay $2 per day for our room and board. We work ten to twelve hours per week, no overtime. After the registration, he took us to our accommodations. It was an old two-axle boxcar that had four bunks with straw-filled mattresses and two army blankets and a small wood stove in the middle. The other roommates were two young Italians. Here began the two-months long extra-gang saga.

At 6 p.m., the cook was ringing the chime for dinner. There was a long coach next to the kitchen car that served as a dining room. There were about eighty men in the gang; about one third were us young guys and the rest were old Russians and Ukrainian men. I never enquired how they got there. Were they POWs of WWII? Who knows?

Food was very good and there was plenty of it. All was fresh, particularly the veggies and fruit. The foreman introduced us to the crowd by our first names. Between the sleeping boxcars there were two washroom/toilet boxcars. It was quite a primitive set up. After dinner, Drago and I retreated to our bunks, and for a while we just sat and stared at each other. Then Drago said, "Perhaps after the second paycheck we should go back to Edmonton before winter comes. Or even all the way to Kitimat."

"We'll see," I said. "Perhaps I should contact the fellow in Grande Prairie."

"Maybe," he said.

The job was demanding, the tools were primitive, and everything was done manually.

5 a.m. was wake-up time, 5:30 a.m. was breakfast, and lunch was given in a paper bag. Lunch was half an hour. A shift sometimes went until 7 p.m. for a small group to finish up the job. Drago and I always declined. We let the old guys work as there was no overtime pay at all. By the end of September, I wrote to Frank. Ten days later, a letter came from his wife stating that Frank had had a fatal accident. In the middle of the month, Drago and I quit and went to Edmonton, back to the Devon Hotel. The Lithuanian lady found us a job the next day with a small concrete company. By the end of September, the chinook winds were getting colder, so we decided to go to Kitimat, B.C.

I think it was November 2nd or 3rd when we left Edmonton. On the 6th of November, we got to Terrace, B.C. in the afternoon. It was minus seven, with six feet of snow. We found accommodation next to the railroad station in a circa-1900 hotel. We were informed that the train for Kitimat was leaving the next day at 2 p.m. The night was cold and windy; I was falling asleep thinking that tomorrow would begin a new chapter of my life. I came as far west as possible. I remembered the map of Canada; the next province is on the Pacific Ocean.

It was the time when the Social Credit government was in power in British Columbia. The aggressive leadership of Premier W. Bennett moved the province at a fast pace, unions were grooving fast, as well, and so was the opposition to the government: the New Democrats led by Dave Barrett. In my opinion, the province, and particularly the Skeena riding—because of the strong forest industry and strong Alcan labour—was fertile ground that was easily infiltrated by many local, national and international Socialists of various degrees. MP Fulton, MLA Howard and others that followed.

The Kitimat population at the time was about 60% Portuguese, 30% Italian (many had only a grade-four education with no English), and the rest were other ethnic groups, mostly from Europe. Alcan built the town and provided the housing, hydro, water, sanitation, road and fire services. There were shopping centres, schools, recreation facilities (soccer fields, a golf course, hockey arenas and others). The municipal council was made of Alcan personnel. Kitimat was a real company town.

It was quite a night in the old Terrace frontier hotel—snow everywhere, just like back home in 1943, but not as cold. We got up early, and on the way to the railroad station there was a small coffee shop full of different immigrants all going to Kitimat. We stopped for breakfast. It was a while before it was our turn. Most of the people there were Italians and Portuguese, but there were a few Germans. By 2 p.m., there were probably over a hundred people at the station, all going to Kitimat to work, and to their new future. The train stopped at the Kitimat rail station at 3:30. It was full of people. Some came out of curiosity, some were leaving for a break. One German told us that we could store our luggage at the railroad station, which we did.

Outside the station there was a hotel, a large commercial building and a small strip mall. The area was called the Service Centre. There were two auto dealers, two fuel stations and several construction companies. We walked over to the taxi stand and got a cab to take us to the smelter site. Everywhere you looked were signs of enormous human ability and the effort to create. It was one of the largest private undertakings in the world—close to one billion dollars—that built that huge aluminum smelter on top of the Pacific Ocean's Douglas Channel. The hydro-electric project Kemano was some forty-five miles away; it supplied electric power for the plant and the city and had been built at an enormous pace. It was estimated that it served some fifty-seven-thousand people at that time.

The cab took us on a partially paved road along the Kitimat river towards the smelter site. That was the area where the aluminum factory was built. Line one and two were completed and producing the aluminum. There was also a hospital, bank and school, and most of the workers lived in a number of the bunk houses with a huge cafeteria and a Hudson's Bay store. Across the street from the Bay on the dry dock was a Delta King ship, which served as the original camp. Other personnel lived in numerous bungalows and many already lived in the town site, as the housing was completed. It was a real company town, where the company—Alcan—was the owner of everything. Some forty-five hundred people lived there. Halfway between Service Centre and the smelter site was Anderson Creek, a huge construction camp of the Saguenay Kitimat Company that was constructing the smelter. Forty-seven hundred workers lived there in bunkhouse huts and tents. There was a large recreational centre and gambling casino and cafeteria. On the other side of Anderson Creek was a bowling alley and a trailer court. Perhaps four hundred people lived there. The whole place was a real beehive. The whole undertaking started in the late forties, and by the time I arrived the infrastructure in the town site was in place. One high school and three elementary schools were operating, as well as a number of churches.

When we stopped at the Bay, we went inside and asked for directions to the address Ralph B. that Frau Gerda B. gave us on the ship. We walked up the hillside where all the large bunk houses were located, and there we found Ralph B., who had just come off a shift. He was surprised but very friendly when we told him who we were. He then said he would see what could be done for room and board, and that we should go back to the Bay and wait for him. A while later, he appeared and told us that we would have to sleep on the floor in his room for a few days, but there would be no problem with the food in cafeteria. He told us that he was off for the next two days, so he would have time to show us the union office and the Alcan personnel office. He gave us a couple of cafeteria passes from his buddies who were out of town. After dinner, he took us across the road to a Chinese restaurant. Next to it was a large building that served as a basketball court, meeting place, cinema, floor-hockey arena and dancing hall. There were a number of different huts housing offices of various companies. It was late, so we all went to bed.

The next morning, we first went to the union office. We heard that one hundred people were hired or quit every day. When we asked if any jobs were available, the union rep asked for $100 to sign up. "Up front?" I asked. Yes, was the answer. "Can I pay from my paycheque?" No, was the answer, he said to borrow the money. We said thanks and left. I was furious. This was blackmail, in my opinion. We went to the Alcan recruiting office. Ralph told us that they were advertising for English-speaking personnel. Most Portuguese and Italians had only grade 4. I was given a four-page application form. I filled it out and returned it to the clerk, who checked it out, looked at me and told me to come back in two days. We went to the Saguenay camp recreation complex. There we met a few Croatians, one of whom was from my high school, from a parallel class. It was a friendly and exciting meeting. He had already been here for two years, mainly picking and choosing jobs. He was also gambling. Very highly strung kid. As we were talking, he asked me if I had a job. I said, "No, why?"

"I got a slip today for a truck driver at the local lumberyard, if you are interested. Here, take it." So I did. I was lucky, as I had an Alberta driver's license. It was a commercial one and it was good for six months before I had to change it to a B.C. one. I went to the lumberyard after lunch and Drago went uptown. He found a job there and I did not see him for a while. When I went back to Alcan to check on the state of my application, I was told by a woman clerk that I was too educated for what they needed.

When I went to the Kitimat Builder's Supplies yard office, I introduced myself to the owner/manager, Don F., in English. He was pleasantly surprised by my good English. He checked my documents and the driver's licence and called the foreman, Dave S., to show me the yard and the truck I was supposed to work with. I got the job because one of the drivers, Bill C. from Saskatchewan, quit. Dave was average height, skinny, a heavy smoker, fishy-eyed and a closet-drinking individual who always had a mickey in his pocket. He was not a lover of immigrants, I noticed. It was a warning, as he was not impressed by what the boss had told him about me. He had also told him to take me at the end of a day to their crew's hut at Anderson Creek. Here I was paid $1.47 per hour and a bed in a four-bed hut. There was another kid, Len P., a nice, hard worker from Alberta. He was very helpful to me in explaining the materials, etc. In the crew were another two of the foreman's alcoholic friends, John M. and Norm B. John M. was a warehouse bull-shitter; he was never to be found. Norm B. was a specialist in creating overtime with the help of a foreman and a huge Portuguese, Joe R., who unloaded cement on the wharf.

There was a Royal Bank of Canada in the building. My first money was deposited there.

There is one hilarious episode about my crab fishing I will never forget. One day I stopped as usual for a bull session at Ralph's Chevron, when Ralph said, "I am going crab fishing, would you like to come along?" I said sure, and off we went. Honestly, I had never done any fishing in my life. And since my experience with the Atlantic storm I was reluctant about going on boats. I told this to Ralph, and he replied, "We are not going far, and I have a nice boat." I agreed, and off we went to the yacht club, boarded the Elratosa, the Germuth family cruiser, and took off down the Douglas Channel. When we reached Eagle Bay, Ralph cruised around for a while then he said, "There are a bunch of crab traps on the back of the boat, when I say throw them overboard, go back there and throw them." When the time came I did exactly what Ralph commanded (God forbid otherwise) and we continued to sail (funny expression for a motor boat, sail) down towards Jesse Falls and back to Eagle Bay. When we got there, Ralph was cruising around. Suddenly his face went red. "What the hell did you do with the crab traps?"

"Exactly what you told me," I answered.

"Did you tie floats?"

"What floats? You never said anything about floats." We did some trawling in hopes of recovering the traps, all for nought. I bought six new crab traps, but he never took me on the boat again. Years later when he passed away—may he rest in peace—his ashes were scattered in Eagle Bay. Sometimes I wonder if Ralph found his crab traps...

Winter came fast, with a lot of snow, so Portuguese workers came every morning after the night shift at Alcan to clean the snow from the piles of lumber and open an access to the building by 9 a.m. In those days, snow cleaning equipment was luxury.

Trucks had poor snow tires and chains were hard to get.

After our regular hours, Len and I were asked by the boss to unload boxcars at a railroad station that had all kinds of lumber, Gyproc and roofing materials. We took the contract on all lumber arriving for the next six months. The boss gave us two trucks and gas. We worked every night till 2 a.m., and weekends and holidays. It was quite an adventure transporting long lumber that hung over the cab on two short trucks. We sometimes had to hang counterweights on the front bumper in order to steer the trucks. It was fun! We made an average per night of $75 apiece on top of our regular wages. We changed gloves every day and heavy leather aprons weekly. In six months, I saved a lot of money. Len left the next summer. Teamsters were organizing. Bill C. returned and the foreman started playing politics. I joined the Teamsters for $160 and was offered a job at the Alcan construction site. I told my boss that the foreman was making it impossible for me to work, preferring the drunks in the crew and discriminating against me. He said he would look into it, so I asked him when. "Soon," was the answer. I thanked him and quit. He was surprised.

Before I go on to my next job, I would like to add a few words about the winter in my valley of snow...

Today is February 2018, a long way from July 1955 when I arrived in Canada. Looking at the subject while I am typing this, I take quick looks out of my window here and there and I smile at all the memories that instantly flood my mind, watching the snow that has piled up in the past week caused by the continuous persistence of the Pineapple Express (a severe storm from the Pacific Ocean) which was rushing to have a rendezvous with a gentleman by the name of Arctic Freeze, who has been busy spreading winter across the North American continent, and at no better location than our region. Oh boy, what a romance it must have been when they met, as they shed millions of tons of snowflakes for the past several days and nights. Then it suddenly stopped, like all hot lovers recharging, and we are told there is more to come. Oh, my valley of snow!

In my time here, the winter began by the end of October and left by the end of March, yet the snow in some areas was on the ground until the end of May. Snowfall ranged from between fourteen feet to thirty-six feet in this season. Snow equipment for residences was mostly shovels. Our geographical location blessed us with constant temperature changes, thus making the snow go from powder to medium-wet to wet to slush. It was hard work for many. Snow conditions most of the time required you to clean your driveway three to four times a day. It occasionally snowed four inches per hour, so accumulations were up to four feet in forty-eight hours.

The city was—for our times and still today—the best snow-equipped city in B.C. They ran the equipment around the clock, as access to the work site's hospital and the schools had priority. The population of the community was almost sixteen thousand people. I remember that the municipal staff would operate heavy-duty snow equipment while the regular crews needed rest, like the municipal manager Art C., the recreation director, Joe I., the municipal treasurer Frank G. and Fire Chief Audrey C. (I apologize if the names are misspelled.)

Most of the roofs had to be cleared of snow twice in the season. There were some structural damages—the Alcan River Lodge cafeteria, for example—and a few deaths. Snow had to be shoveled up, particularly from bungalows because of the height of the snow on the ground. Snowbanks in the Kildala-area streets where I lived at the time were between twelve and sixteen feet high; people tunnelled into their homes. It was most difficult for everyone. Homes had oil furnaces that were not very efficient, and oil delivery was difficult because the tanks were underground under the deep snow. It was a real test of human resilience by Mother Nature.

With the coming years, better and better equipment became available. One of my companies had some fifteen pieces of major equipment; among them were four large loaders, a grader and a snow wing with sander. We provided winter snow removal services for industry, government institutions and municipal, commercial and school properties. It was quite a task at the time to satisfy all my customers and make their sites ready for business. It was life in the valley of snow...

So, two days later I was at the truck pool office of Saguenay Kitimat, directed by a 213 business agent. Dispatcher Emil was a friendly guy; he took me out of the truck pool to see what I could do. I tried several different trucks, on their own and also with a trailer, then he switched me to Euclid and belly-dump trucks. I passed all the tests, but as I was junior in the pool I started with the flat deck as a relief driver. It was all good—I was assigned to the camp, had room and board and a good paying job.

Work was interesting, as there were different assignments every day. Emil the dispatcher was smart to accommodate drivers who did not want a daily routine. It was good practise operating different equipment daily. There was a lot of activity around the construction site.

Note: Once, later in the summer, I was alone on the job site. I suddenly had pains in my stomach, so I climbed down from the Euclid and went into the bushes on the roadside, thinking I needed to poop ... no go. The pain increased, and I crawled to the edge of the road. An hour later the foreman came and took me to the hospital. Appendix! It was leaking. If I had been an hour later, goodbye Leon, the doctor said. A priest came to give me my last rites and asked me for twenty bucks up front. Can you believe that?

When I went to my first union meeting, I saw guys with baseball bats standing there after the doors closed. I was not impressed. Even worse, someone got beaten once. I thought, is this Democracy? Is this Western freedom? I tried to avoid meetings, and after my last job in Prince Rupert—building the airport on Digby Island—I stopped paying my dues. No more union jobs for me. To note: Our shop steward later became a provincial executive and Pierre Trudeau picked him as a senator.

One day at the lumber yard, a trucker came from a local company, Kitimat Express. He introduced himself as Fred S. He was a nice guy. We started to talk, and he asked me if I played any sports. I said I did: field hockey, soccer and many others. I told him my story. He became very interested. Finally, he asked if I would be interested in playing floor hockey with him. I said OK, I would come and try, so I did, and the team liked what I could do. I became a member. There were five teams competing. It was exciting, and my kind of contact sport: no guards. All the games were played in the smelter site's recreation room. There was a lot of damage done to our bodies and to the hall. Heck, we were all young and full of it. I was in good shape due to the hard work I'd done for several months in the lumber yard. As I was on shift work, I could work some hours there when needed. I also drove a taxi. In general, there was lot of extra work available for those who wanted betterment in life and to do something with it.

As I lived in camp, there was no place I could take my girlfriend, so I bought my first car: a 1953 Chevy Bel Air ... nice bedroom!

The Kitimat Express won the league. Walter H. and myself were the top scorers. I was the only immigrant on the team. Most of the Europeans avoided the rough-and-tumble sports, especially the type of floor hockey we played where there were body-checks galore and plenty of fights, and the spectators went nuts. At the time, the ice arena was not built, so many of the ice-hockey players joined floor hockey.

At the time, I kept contact with Elke and Erika. Late in the year, Erika got married to my former buddy from Osnabrück, Germany. Elke got married soon after. I lost contact with them.

At Helen's Cafe, a Chinese restaurant just across from the Bay, I flirted big-time with a German lady from Berlin. The flirting went on for about three months, and we ended up living together for about a year and a half in mid-'58. Rumours started about a Saguenay closure, and by the end of '57 it closed and we got laid off. So died the big plant and the plan of a fifty-seven-thousand-person community. For a while I drove a cab, then went to work for Columbia Cellulose in Terrace, and two months later I got a union job in Prince Rupert. I was going to Kitimat every weekend to be with my girlfriend. Several weeks into the job at Prince

Rupert, my car broke down. It needed serious repair. I patched it up. I had some money, and being naive that my job would last to the end, I bought a brand new Pontiac Parisian from the GM dealer. It was a beauty; what an eye-catcher. There were only six built in Canada. I still owed $2K, and at the time that was a lot of money.

It was about this time I met my future partner, Artur Spanevello. Art was working at Alcan.

One day in camp, I debated the union shop steward on the issue of the sale of Canadian wheat to China. The debate got heated when I asked him if it was better for Canada to let the farmer's wheat rot in greeneries—some were not modern—and for rats to piss on it than to sell it for two cents less per bushel to China. He got really excited and called me DP (displaced person) Communist! Wow! Two days later I was fired. News travelled fast; by the time I got back to Kitimat my girlfriend was having a good time in Smithers. Nice. It was a short and sweet split.

I drove cab for a while, and then one day the phone rang. "Hi, Leon, Bill F. here. Still interested in working for Alcan?" I said sure, I would give it a try. A few days later I was hired and directed to do pot room service.

Just as I was about to leave Prince Rupert, I met someone from Toronto! So here is a photo of her, myself and my second car. There were only six in Canada, and I regret not keeping it. C'est la vie!

Artur and I kept in contact. We talked about doing some business. We recognized complimentary attributes in each other and a mutual trust. So, for a starter we purchased a taxi cab in '58 and, as we worked different shifts at Alcan, we drove it ourselves. This is how we started our partnership.

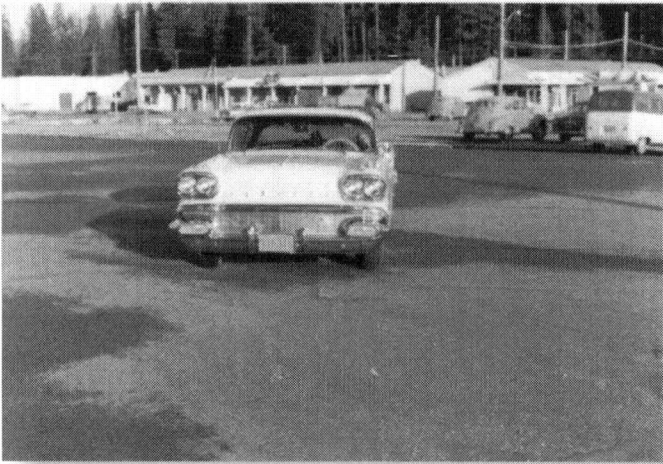

Art and I bought a brand-new 1958 Pontiac. I traded my beauty in and Art put up the cash. In between the Alcan shifts we drove the cab, and I rented a room in town close to Art's home.

At Alcan, my first week was a curiosity. It was quite a place. Smoky, noisy, dusty and gassy. Simply put: not for humans. In two weeks, I worked in every area of the plant, operated equipment, etc. I developed a good relationship with my foreman, Herb T. Nice guy. But his gang leader, a German named Frank R., was quite something else. He was after me all the time. He was skinny, white and ash-faced, with reddish hair and dead blue eyes and he smelled like a dead man. The "new" lines—three, four and five—had an area called the basement where you were able to get to the pots from underneath. It was quite a working area; I called it "the catacomb." It was dreadful.

On the tenth day, I surfaced from the catacomb in line three and I was just crossing the centre passage when there was Frank, coming towards me with a big aluminum wrench in his hands. "Come with me, you are going to pull the studs," he said.

"Like hell I will, I am quitting and going to the foreman's office for a pink slip," I said, and I went by him. Stud-pulling was one of the dirtiest, smokiest, gassiest, hottest jobs in pot lines. The summer heat between the pots averaged 172°F. It was very dangerous, as well. As I continued on my way, Frank tried to stop me physically. I got really mad at the bastard. At the same time, Herb T.—a really nice person—came between us.

"What the hell is going on, boys? Cut it out!" he said. I explained to him what occurred and told him that I would not take any orders from this German discriminator. Frank told him his side of the story. "OK," Herb said, "you come with me. You will not be going to pull the studs."

"Thank you," I said. "Get me away from this man before something happens to him."

Herb took me to his office, and when we got there, he said, "Sit down and smarten up. No more of this crap, or you will both be out of the gate."

"Yes, sir," I said. He then asked me if I would like to be a shift material distributor and a general relief operator. I said I would give it a try, because the previous driver had quit.

Work at Alcan was not hard for me. My job consisted of checking with each line-office foreman, where I picked up my written instructions. I was one of a few amongst the hundreds of workers who wore a face mask due to the poor air conditions, particularly in line one and two where the temperature in the centre passageway in summer was 142°F. I never took the mask off during the shift. Some brass got upset, but I pointed their official bulletin board out to them, saying, "Verbal orders do not go." The main gate on an afternoon shift read 90°F. One consumed a lot of water and salt tablets. We worked three shifts, six days a week, with two days off. Harsh. About every six weeks it worked out to have Saturday and Sunday off. Afternoon and graveyard shifts afforded three to four hours of sleep and a lot of chess and card games. It sure helped my private undertakings. Art worked as a stud-blast operator. Frank was always trying to interfere with something, but I avoided him as much as possible. It was an interesting community: while one group was working, the other one was sleeping.

With time I learned how divided the community was: big management and a big union that were forever at each other's throats. Because of the shift work you would see some of the people every six months. Socially, the community was totally divided. Each shift had a social club and activities. In the community, organizations and clubs was by invitation only, or if you were related to somebody or were a member. There were many of them.

Alcan had a major say in the city administration: permits, housing, land, sport, schools, hospital—total control. Later on, when the city centre was developed, the whole town was bustling. There were some fine stores around.

Our taxi under Totem Taxi dispatch was doing well, until first Art then I made strong observations of some unethical behaviour by two other members, who then took it very seriously. Being important officers in their organization, the Knights of Columbus, they must have complained to their chief, who was also local RCMP staff. Well, Lord behold, the wrath of the authorities was upon us. Art collected three traffic infraction tickets, and I two. Art would lose his licence if one more ticket was handed to him. But before I had a court date, the charge was: crossing double lane (winter) and making a U-turn. When I entered the court chambers, I was surprised to see staff instead of one of the officers who charged me. The magistrate was Mr. Hugh M. The magistrate asked staff to read the charge. He did, but went into an aggressive mode that was not acceptable to me. So, I stood up and said, "Your Honour, I apologize for the interruption, but I am a new Canadian citizen, not a criminal. I do not have to take Gestapo abuse that I fought against for five years. Please stop this."

Staff went pale (it must have been the first time he was contradicted in his service) and at the same time the magistrate said to him, "Cool it, Sergeant," and then he turned to me. "What do you have to say, Mr. Soos?"

"Your Honour, that day there was a lot of snow on the road and I could not see any lanes."

"But you should have remembered; you've driven here for a long time," interjected the staff, obviously very angry.

"Well, Mr. Soos?"

"Your honour, I am a professional driver and I obey the road signs when I see them. How can I see something under a foot of snow?"

"Thank you, Mr. Soos. Case dismissed!" And there was peace in Taxi Land after Art's charges were dismissed as well.

Another memorable event with the taxi came in 1961. Alcan shut down the smelter and Kemano due to tunnel maintenance, where rocks were falling and damaging turbines in the hydro complex. It lasted for nine weeks. Kitimat was almost deserted.

Art's family and I decided to drive away on a cruise with the taxi. It took us through Washington, Oregon, California and Nevada. When we came back five weeks later, we were tired and rested until the restart of the smelter and Kemano. It started up on time and it took a long time to get all the pots going.

Life continued. The town was vibrant with young people. The high school at the time had over twelve hundred students; there were some beauties in grades eleven and twelve. I remember the younger boys—eighteen, nineteen, twenty—brought their sweethearts into the camp late at night. Beds in rooms were separated only by sheets. Some of the older workers were drunk and snoring, others were understanding and accommodating to the young couples by being absent, and some stayed awake listening to the noises and commotion behind the partitions and masturbating. The girls were taken home early in the morning. Everyone wanted to get married. It was the standard/condition of the times. I was older: twenty-four. A few of those girls had crushes on me (and perhaps my car) but I never paid attention, so they called me stuck-up! I was too busy building my future and I did not want to get stuck with an eighteen-year-old wife.

I started to play lacrosse with my floor-hockey teammates. My team, under a different name—Nechako Cartage—again won the floor-hockey league. I also participated with the soccer team Blue Adriatic, made of Croatian boys. Kitimat at the time had eight teams of different ethnic groups. There were lot of heated ethnic games. After Saguenay shut down, many moved away after finding out that Alcan was not the kind of work they were looking for. So did the boys from Blue Adriatic. Only Portuguese, Italians and Greeks kept their teams. The rest of us joined a team called the Black Eagles—a few Germans and the rest of us. It was a great group of characters.

I think that in the short time of four years, for those of us who inter-related with the different people of the community, the world was kind of slowly eliminating ethnic nationalist zeal. Yes, the language was the most important. Sadly, those who could not handle it remained frozen in their past.

This is something that new immigrants and other self-serving groups, with our incompetent governments, are told: not to bother with learning Canada's primary language and laws but to infest it with their own. So they are, with the government's help, paid by all of us, and it is polit-ical correctness that creates powerful forces that are slowly making changes which will eventually destroy Canada as a beacon of freedom and liberty in the world. It is already drifting towards a dictatorship with its guaranteed false "freedom of speech" and "political correctness." Oh, my Canada...

I am not sure how it began, but I think Art and I responded to advertising: "Janitorial service for sale." "Let us check this out," I said. It was a small company operated by a husband and wife, John and Maria S. He was a custodian at the high school. We made arrangements to see their workplaces; they had several commercial and private contracts. We made an arrangement to meet Maria at her workplace.

Bear with me, I will come back to it, but there is an incident that almost slipped away from this story, yet it is so important as it could have changed my life and my partner's family forever. Here it goes: The Incident on Grouse street.

Art was working, I think; he and his wife Gisela had had their first baby Denise and there was also a newborn, Nicole. They bought the house on Grouse Street. By that time, Denise was three years old. I lived a few streets away. Later, I moved in with them. I had room and board there. It was practical for both of us, for our operation and financially. By the way, Art and Gisela were Austrians. It was also convenient for parking our taxi, as there was a large driveway. Denise could not pronounce Leon, so she called me "Gogo." She was/is some sweetie and I love her dearly.

In these days, the streets were full of small kids, so one had to be extremely careful while driving or backing out onto the street. I always checked carefully around and under the car. All the kids were little ones running around innocently and carefree in summer without clothing and playing in the dirt—which today is forbidden for some silly liberal-elite politically correct reason, yet at the same time we have nude beaches and gay and lesbian parades where the same nudity is allowed, and the little ones are exposed to it.

That particular day was a cold spring day, and as I stepped around our taxi there were no kids around, and Denise was nowhere to be seen. I sat in the car, started the engine and began very slowly to back out onto the street. Gisela was standing on the porch with Nicole in her arms. As I looked out through the passenger-door window, I saw a lady about four houses away frantically waving her arms. I stopped the car and shut the engine off immediately. As I stepped out of the vehicle, I heard the lady screaming, "Denise is under the car!"

I went to the driver's side and looked up; Gisela's mouth was frozen. Then I kneeled down and looked under the car; the left front wheel was about a foot away from running over Denise. She must have been playing next door; there was a green hedge between the driveways, so I could not see her, and when she heard the car start she must have run out behind the car and got pushed by the bumper, fell and ended up underneath the car. She was looking at me. "Are you OK, sweetie?" I asked.

In a soft, kind, confused voice, she said, "Yes, Gogo."

"Can you move your arms and legs?" She did, then I reached under and took hold of her snowsuit and slowly pulled her from under the car. One side of the snowsuit had tire marks—oh my god! I stood her up and she started to walk to her mother. She phoned the doctor's office and we took Denise there: no damage. Thank you, Lord. I said a silent prayer. It was a moment I will never forget.

I met Maria at the Kildala Grocery, where she had a maintenance contract. It was a medium-sized corner store, built and owned by a Swiss couple named Luis and Franca R. Maria showed me around. Luis happened to be there, so she introduced me to him. Then we went over to the city centre where Maria showed me the rest of her contracts. The next day, Art and I debated the matter and agreed it was a viable opportunity. We concluded that to do business in this country one has to be versatile, so we bought the janitorial company. Maria agreed to stay one year after. We hired a driver for our cab. I had a better background in cleanliness than Artur; my standards came from my mother. And so began the second venture in our lives in which we took a small company and made it a competitive, reputable and reliable one. Banks rewarded us because of our good standing and credibility.

A big celebration today: I proudly became a Canadian citizen!

This happened after returning from our multi-state cruise in the U.S., from which the most memorable places were Crater Lake, San Francisco, Yosemite National Park and the old scary road from there into Nevada, Old West cities, Tombstone, Carson City, Reno and the Columbia River crossing on a large raft.

Life in the community was slowly coming back to normal after the smelter was restarted. Art and I became workaholics. Some memorable things from that time:

In summertime, Saturdays were spent at the old Lakelse Lake Lodge, a very rustic and romantic place. Bring your own bottle, eat dinner and dance in the candlelight. Afternoon shifts were the best for parties. My working buddy, Walter P., used to leave a case of beer in Anderson Creek to cool until after the shift at 11:30 p.m. What a delight that was to drink after the unpleasant conditions in the plant, where after the shift you could never scrub the dirt clean from your body in the shower room. One time we came, and our beer was gone—someone was on to us. We had a good laugh. One particular Saturday night, after we went through our ceremony at Anderson Creek, we decided to go to Lakelse Lake Lodge to join the party. There was another buddy, Walter S., with us.

The distance to the lodge was about twenty-seven miles; the midnight dinner was just being served when we sat at the table, which had been reserved by Artur and his wife. My buddies produced a bottle of vodka and a bottle of cherry brandy. We had already drunk a bunch of beer, so by the time we finished the booze and food it was 2 a.m. The place was closing. I know I was loaded. The Walters left in their car; I was trying to get into mine, but no luck. Artur asked me to let him drive and finally I agreed, handing my keys over after some debate ... the usual. When I stepped out of the car upon arrival in Kitimat, I pirouetted and crashed onto the sidewalk, so I was told. They carried me into my room. Apparently, I refused to undress. I was out for two days. What a mess. When I finally got up, I took my clothing off and, together with my bedcover, put it into a garbage bin.

At work in the smelter, several serious issues occurred in the period of five years between 1959 and 1964, when Artur and I resigned due to the next engagement in our private undertakings. Two were serious safety hazards. We were all dressed in heavy woolen clothing—company safety regulations—and safety boots. I also had to have a hardhat, safety goggles and ear plugs. I always wore a safety mask that was capable of filtering some of the crap we were exposed to.

After my foreman engaged me as a shift driver, I also from time to time operated the small payloader that was capable of going in behind the pots and helping the poor pot-men collect spilled bath (spillage from the pots)—it was liquid but already cooled and hardened—and other crap. This small machine was very handy; however, it had a serious exhaust problem and I developed some serious headaches.

The foremen were responsible for identifying the moisture sensors and marking dangerous areas or situations; for example, the west passageways were used for laying down materials, mostly bath. In the rainy season there were dripping leaks in the roofs, so sometimes that bath got wet. As such, it was extremely explosive if it fell into an open pot. Bath was also re-used to close open pots by being put next to the pot to warm up before being carefully shoveled by the pot-men into the open cavern on the pot's crest itself. I usually got the list of pots to place cold bath next to from the shift foreman. So, after one rainy day, the list of pots was given to me by the line-two foreman. I picked up a bucket full of bath (there were no safety markings on the pile) and took it to the assigned pot. When I came to the location, I stopped the machine at a safe distance and slowly started to dump the bath on the floor next to the pot. One small piece fell on the pot's plate and rolled off into the pot. I could not get away fast enough, so I immediately covered my face with my bent left arm, and at the same instant there was an explosion like a hand grenade. Some hot bath—fortunately not the hot metal—caught and burned part of my open face on the left side. I was lucky.

Bath was moist or wet and not inspected and marked by the supervisory staff. I went to the pot-line office and reported it to the general foreman, who ignored the facts and nonchalantly told me, "You should have checked it out."

"You are wrong, I am going to my foreman to make an additional report." My foremen gave me a first-aid pass and said he would investigate. After treatment in the first-aid room, I was told by the attendant that it was fortunately a surface burn, and that I should go home and see my doctor, of which he will inform my foreman. My doctor kept me home to let the burn crust up and prevent infection. I stayed home for four days.

When I returned back to my shift, the supervisors were checking the machine log. As Alcan emphasized safety, each piece of equipment had a log book where operators of each shift were responsible for checking the equipment accordingly and entering the findings into the vehicle log book. If they found that you had screwed something up, you were disciplined. As I mentioned before, they failed to act on my reports, so one day I had had enough and I stopped at the foreman's office. There was the acting foreman on duty, Mr. Hickmore. I called him out to show how badly a machine spewed smoke and asked him for a first-aid pass. As I had severe headaches, he gave me the pass for the first aid. The attendant was Eric M.

I had left the machine twice before in the heavy-duty shop and the mechanic on duty told me that they had a replacement engine sitting there in the crate for six months, but that the shop general foreman did not authorize replacing it because in his opinion, the machine is good enough as it is. Nice, I thought...

When I went to the first aid, the attendant checked me out and told me my eyes were all glassy, and that I look gassed. He put me on oxygen for half an hour and entered a report of what had happened into the book. After that, he phoned the foreman's office and sent me home. The next day when I came on the shift, I was told that I was suspended for three days without pay for leaving the plant without permission. That did it, so I went to the union office and filed a grievance.

After I returned, I refused to operate that machine unless it was repaired, and my foreman told me to be careful or I could get fired. "Go for it," I said. The next day I went to see the superintendent, who acted surprised at my grievance. I told him that the company did not act in good faith, and left a new engine sitting for six months in the garage. He was trying to talk me out of the grievance. "First," I said, "you and the company owe me an apology for wrongly accusing me of leaving the plant without authorization. Pay back my wages in overtime. Discipline the acting foreman and demote him for lying [at the time I did not disclose to Alcan that I still had the pass in my pocket] and finally, repair the machine. I will not operate it unless you do so. You and the WBC [Worker's Compensation Board] wrote the safety rules. I follow them. Your payloader is unsafe to operate, period! Check the machine's log-book entries with my signature. Then I will consider stopping the arbitration." It was not accepted by the superintendent so I went to the second stage, but the union chickens withdrew, so I was left alone to defend myself.

Meantime, all the records from the incident were removed from the company's records: the page from the first-aid report vanished, the first-aid attendant was gone and the copy of the foreman's pass was not to be found. This looks like a conspiracy, I thought. The group of incompetent supervisors had to protect themselves, probably thinking that there was no way that they would lose arbitration. So, they played hardball to the end and lost.

(Several decades later my suspicion was confirmed: In the safety instructions for supervisors the story was recorded; sadly, it was fake, the absence of truth again. Shame on those who made that entry! Most importantly, after I stopped working in the Alcan plant their property department was the most supportive in Artur's and my undertakings in the community. It sure makes a difference who is running the show.)

Then came the date of the third stage; the chair was a UBC arbitrator. I sat on one side alone and on the other side was a large group of Alcan supervisors and middle management with their main witness, Mr.

Hickmore. He was asked to testify first. He stated that he never gave me the pass for first aid and said there was no record of a Mr. Soos being there. He also stated that the attendant in question did not work there anymore.

The arbitrator took a few moments, looking at the Alcan witness. Then he said, "You, sir, you are a liar. Shame on you and all those that contributed against Mr. Soos. I am ruling in favour of Mr. Soos. Case dismissed." There was dead silence in the room.

I got up, approached the arbitrator and thanked him by saying, "Sir, I do have the pass in my pocket."

"I know," he said simply. "Good luck, Mr. Soos."

After the arbitration, I became a hot potato for the company supervisors and middle management. In regard to public relations, the loss at arbitration must have been embarrassing for Alcan. I was transferred to the conveyor system that supplies the pot lines with different materials. I stayed there till July 1964.

My God CHILD NICOLE & HER SISTER DENISE MY SWEETIES

The Arbitration case at Alcan, the traffic charge and many other instances—observing as a child, a student and an adult—proved to me one simple thing in dealing with human kind: Humanity, in my opinion, consists only of two kinds of people: the good and the not-so-good, regardless of the blood relations in families, ethnic origin or legal documents that one may have. Perhaps, if you try hard, you can find a few fair ones in the not-so-good group.

By the end of the WWII, the cold-war cloud had started to build and was hanging over the whole globe, creating the Korean War in 1958, the Cuban Crisis, President Kennedy's assassination in 1963 and then the Vietnam War. I was lucky to live in Canada, regardless of the daily incomprehensible political acts of our prime ministers and some provincial premiers and all the members of parliament, who conveniently forgot that their service and obligation lies with Canada and its citizens first, not just to their respective political parties through which they attempted to promote socialist and even some communist ideas, of which they had very little knowledge and even less experience with, or even less of an idea about what kind of consequences their Socialist-utopia exercise may create. Some of them had no real value, yet they were popular with the voters they needed because they were freebies—someone else paid for it!

These make-believe political illusions were guaranteed by a mixture of private enterprise and capitalism that was still functioning, and was needed to provide the financing for these political illusions. Sure, there was some economic abundance created periodically, so that the credit rating by Wall Street or the IMF was approved, so that the economic pains were not felt or were simply forgotten. By the time, they took care of their own futures. They then stepped aside for the next group to do the same thing under a different name; again, only for themselves, not the nation. A new political illusion began all over, new items were announced to the populous, such as political correctness, which is supported by hate laws, civil-rights laws, and more laws to protect you. In fact, it does not allow freedom of speech. It is a form of dictatorship that is slowly disabling and arresting the nation, yet the fake drum beats: Democracy ... Democracy ... Democracy...

Through all this, another opportunity knocked on my and Artur's destiny doors...

One day, when I was cleaning the windows at the Kildala Grocery, Luis the owner came out and complimented me on how good the service was that we were providing. I thanked him, and we began a casual conversation; amongst other things he asked me what our future plans were. I told him that Artur and I will look into any opportunity coming our way, provided it is a good deal and we can afford it. He looked at me and said, "You guys are serious ones."

"Yes, and careful. Sure, there is always risk, which makes it a challenge," I said.

"OK," Luis continued, "what would you say if I offer you the store with the house?"

I looked at him seriously. "You serious?" I asked.

"Yes, I am."

"Thank you for the offer, let me pass it on to my partner, Artur." I was sure excited inside. "Thank you, I'll be back to you in two or three days." We said goodbye and parted.

Artur and I complemented each other. Whatever one was short of, the other had. We respected and recognized each other's qualities. It was all good and benefited us both. We also had arguments that were healthy and beneficial without being begrudging.

It was all for our good in the end. Sometimes he took too long in weighting the odds. He was not a high-risk taker. Yet he took the risk on his own—I was with him but without consent. A strange statement, but it was so, as I was never comfortable with the operations. The other concern was that he did not have proper communication in writing with the contract supervisor. These lapses cost us some money. In the end, what we had the most in our relationship was an abundance of trust!

Later, when I mentioned what Luis offered, I was glad to see that Artur's interest perked up. We sat down and discussed the matter, and we were in agreement to see the owner to tell us what he had in mind and also what we were looking at. We met with Luis; he was positive and receptive about us seeing the books and at the same time he gave us a price with the terms.

It actually looked not too bad, so we checked to see how much cash we could put together for a down payment, which would include the sale of the taxi and Artur's house. We went to the bank, laid out our plans and accordingly asked for the bank's assistance. The bank agreed. Artur then went to Luis to hash out the details, which were then submitted to a lawyer. I think it was July of 1964 when we took over. The store at that time had the burden of a considerable amount of people's grocery charges that we took over. Art was the first to resign from Alcan, and I did the same a month later. The taxi was sold. Art concentrated on the store, I looked after the building maintenance company (I also pursued new contracts) and the repair of the house that was part of the purchase with the store and the collection of outstanding charges. It took me almost two years to collect the money, which in some cases did not create many friends for me.

The Alcan property department was most receptive to Art and me; they were happy with our service on their properties, which consisted of some two hundred and ten homes and thirty three-hundred-unit apartment blocks. Another year later, I added landscaping services, but my partner was not too enthusiastic. Little did he know about the little boy watching the professional gardener on his father's farm. All these experiences came to fruition and turned into a good, profitable business. Not too long after, we bought the lot adjacent to the store to prevent the competition from moving in on us.

After the house was good enough to move into, Art and his family moved upstairs. They needed to more room for the family. I had a very cozy one-bedroom apartment downstairs. In time, I made a lot of effort to expand our building maintenance, one of the largest in the community. I also added to it a pest-control service that I earned a ticket for in San Francisco, as British Columbia did not have a Ministry of Environment. To that, I added caretaking, snow cleaning, carpet cleaning and installation services. We purchased a small Ford tractor which I froze my ass and jewels on. In another year, we added a large 966C loader. I still had good contact with the Portuguese people from working in Alcan. One, who also became a close friend, was Manuel C., a fantastic individual with whom I made hundreds of gallons of wine and moonshine for years, which we drank mostly in the winter and every day after work on the construction site. His dear wife—may they both rest in peace—always served fresh Portuguese sausage and bread.

Through Manuel and others, I was never short for hired help. I guaranteed immigration to Canada to several Portuguese families by my charitable heart and of my own free will (Artur was not so charitable), I always remembered Frank in Grande Prairie making the effort for me to obtain a driver's licence after being in Canada just one week. I had collected some forty-five individuals who worked for us with Manuel's help. With Christmas time coming, there were gifts for about thirty families—many with little children (some of them later babysat my girls)—loaded into the van at noon on Christmas Eve. From house to house I went, eating and drinking, giving and receiving the gifts. By 6 p.m., I returned for our Christmas dinner prepared by Gisela, Art's wife, stoned out of my mind. This continued for some twenty years. How I lived, survived, who knows? One thing is for sure, I believe the Lord and my guardian angel were always with me!

After Art and I got involved with the Kildala Grocery, life for us really shifted into high gear. Art took on the managing of the store and I took care of all the building maintenance operations. Business was flourishing. An average day was between twelve and sixteen hours, 24/7. In summer, I grabbed a game of soccer, practise Wednesdays, game Sundays. Late on a summer day I would take a trip to the lake with my buddy, Otto S., or I would take a pretty teacher or a nurse with me and have a lover's picnic on my private beach close to Swan Bay. Wow, what times they were. Young, with trains of energy, and love was always in the air.

On Saturdays, there was always a party or a dance. Besides that, the community was very cliquey. Due to my interactions and being now in the business ranks, the social gate was opened, just not quite 100%. Most of the time, the parties were in my place—there were many because everything was free, I am sure. Most of the people who came were good, but some were not so good. Sometimes up to forty jammed into my small place. Basically, it was wall-to-wall people. Boy, did the place used to stink of cigarettes—awful! Everyone was smoking. I was an expert barman. Imagine that in those days wine was very seldom served, with the exception of sit-down dinners. Some beer but mostly hard liquor. I used to make some cool drinks for the ladies; they were in high gear in no time. Men were primitive drinkers. Rum & Coke or Pepsi, beer and rye. They were poor eaters, particularly the regular Brits and Canucks, so some of them got loaded quickly. Their wives or girlfriends would take them home and then come back to party and dance up a storm until the early hours in the morning. I was always a good host and accommodating. My buddy was a good assistant. By eight, I had to attend to my crews. And so it went, day in and day out.

Winters were harsh and long. Lot of snow; the battle with it was continuous and never-ending. The first traces came in late October and lasted until the end of March or mid-April. But the summers were just as beautiful and hot. In the store we had our manager, Lady Tilly B. She was very efficient. Art and I could afford some time off by covering for each other. Tilly and her husband Ruby were Swiss. There were lots of family dinners and fondues together. They had a son named Rolland, and as mentioned earlier my partner and his wife had two girls, Denise and Nicole. They were real sweethearts. I probably spent more time with them than their father. I love them dearly. I am also Nicole's godfather.

Kildala Grocery (1964) Ltd.—new name—had a bowling team of nice people in the winter. I was captain. We bowled for two years together. As time went by, I lost a track of some of them. Three passed away. One, Joan H., not too long ago—cancer took her after a long battle. She was also a good golfer.

By the end of '65, I came up with the idea of building a laundromat next to the grocery store. Financially, we were sound. I had collected 85% of the outstanding charges; our bankers loved it. I shared my idea with my partner by saying that it would be a complement to the store. Our area had a large population of Alcan workers with plenty of dirty laundry, which the housewives were not enthused about washing in their machines. I tell you, that woolly stuff surely collected dirt in the Alcan smelter. So, I let him think about it. Art, as usual, took his time, so I reminded him that that was the time, because it was wintertime and we had to find a contractor and talk to the banker and a laundromat equipment supplier. While Art was having his debate, I quietly found a reliable contractor, an electrician and a roofer. Finally, it was a go.

Things went reasonably easy with the administration. We obtained all the necessary permits. Then we had a deliberation on what kind of laundromat equipment to buy. Maytag was the leader in the industry, so we choose their equipment. We also found a supplier in Vancouver: Neifer Installations. The manager/owner was Ernie, very knowledgeable in the industry. He came up to Kitimat and gave us all the info for the cost and plans, and indicated the size of building we needed for the facility. After receiving firm prices for everything that was required, it was decided we would start up in the late spring of '66. Then, just before we started, my mom became very ill.

I had a very difficult time making the decision to go or not to go. I kept in regular contact with my family and friends in Yugoslavia. It was also a considerable risk for me to go there due to the fact that I left the country for political reasons, and I was probably facing jail or being put into the army for the eighteen months that I did not serve. Here there were considerable commitments with Art. We had a long discussion on the subject. In the end, he was totally supportive of my risk and assured me that he was capable of looking after our mutual interests. In support of that, we purchased insurance for protection if one of us was not there anymore because of unforeseen circumstances.

I made traveling arrangements and left in the beginning of autumn. I had two stops, one in Vancouver and one in Nürnberg. It was important for me to see my team friends, Mladen and Japa. I had a fine reception there. Both were doing very well and married. I was happy to see that Japa had a considerable fur business outside Munich. He perished in a car crash years later on Christmas Eve.

In Vancouver, I had to stop for a Yugoslav visa at the Yugoslav consulate. It was quite an experience. When I entered the building, I could see right away that it was not just any regular construction. I had the feeling of being in a bomb shelter. I noticed that the only door that had a door handle was the entry into the waiting room. We were allowed to enter at 9:30 a.m. There were a few of us. When I entered the waiting room, I noticed another door on the left, and in the middle was a kind of odd, small kiosk-size window. I had to reach up to in order to hand my passport to the individual when I was called through the intercom. The ceiling was very high. Against the opposite wall were a few chairs, and high above were narrow windows.

A man came out from the side door. The room behind was smoky and there were more than a dozen people sitting around a long table. Security and probably spies. Tito's counter-intelligence was very active in keeping tabs on various Yugoslav emigrant groups and individuals (some were assassinated) around the world that were politically undesirable and dangerous to the system. He handed us short visa application forms and then quickly vanished into the back room.

Suddenly, there was a loud bang that I thought was related to electric or magnetic security locking systems. You knew right away that there was no way out. Then the person appeared behind the kiosk window. I was third in line. When I was called upon, he was holding my passport in his hand saying, "You are from Kitimat?" I said yes. "You do not have an entry for your place of birth?"

"In Canadian passport it is an option," I said. "I was born in Kloštar Ivanić, Croatia."

"Thank you," he said. "By the way, would you do me a favour [here it comes, I thought], when you come back or you are here in Vancouver, would you send me or bring me a Kitimat telephone book?" There is no harm in it, I thought. It was a bit of blackmail or play, who knows? I said no problem. Then he stamped the visa into my passport signet and gave it to me. Telephone books are publicly available, so I did not see anything in it. Perhaps he was testing me?

Mladen became a representative in Bavaria for Hoover vacuum products. He married the only child of a famous Nürnberg Lebkuchen family. The last time I spoke with him was in 2005. I think then we lost contact. I think I should try to reconnect. I will. It was quite a moment after thirteen years. In the end, all was good.

While parting with my friends and boarding the plane in Munich for Zagreb, I was suddenly overcome with a mixture of strange emotions: anxiety and fear. Once in the air there was no way out. I was the last one at the departure gate; I almost turned back but I think being the adventurer and the risk taker helped. Perhaps it was the cat's curiosity, but in the end an overwhelming desire put me on the plane.

It was a beautiful sunny day when the plane crossed the Yugoslav-Slovenian border. My excitement grew, particularly when it started to drop altitude upon entering Croatia. So many beautiful familiar sites appeared. While I was looking intently out of the plane's window, tears started to run down my face; the stewardess came and asked me, "Are you all right, sir"?

I turned my head and said in my native language, "Thank you, I am just happy. It has been a long time."

The landing in Zagreb was smooth. After passport control, I exited into customs area to pick up my luggage. In the distance, through the glass, I spotted my brother. His face was pale and worried. My sister-in-law Nada was smiling and waving. At customs, an agent was directing the flyers; I recognized him. He was also a field hockey player on another team. I called him by his name, one of the few I remembered. "Hey, Vlado, how are you?"

He looked at me for a moment. "Is that you, Soos?" Yes, the original.

"Strange things are happening every day, but to see you … wow," he said. Than we shook hands and went into a big hug. Other agents watched and smiled.

I was watching the carousel for my suitcase, and when it arrived, I picked it up to take it to one of the officers. Vlado said to the officers, "It is OK, he is one of ours." They waved; I thanked them all and went for the exit. My brother, who is a highly strung person, was pacing like a fart in the pants, totally stressed out. My sister-in-law ran to me and gave me a big hug, saying, "Welcome. I hope my husband does not have a heart attack." I thought, here we are, caution, Leon. So, I just said hi to him, holding my suitcase. He was so desperate to leave. The poor guy, he was one of those humans who was forever thinking he was constantly being spied on. Which is quite possible when living under a dictatorship.

And so, first we went to their place. It was pretty stressful. He was very nervous, constantly cautioning me not to talk about politics or say anything derogatory about the government. When I had enough of that, I simply told him to shut up because his car may have been bugged. Boy, that did it. He just went mum. Then we went to Mom and Dad's. We phoned them before we left, more excitement there.

It was about an hour's drive, fifty-eight kilometres from the city. When we arrived at the gate, Father came out, he was pale-faced and evidently excited. He opened the gate and we drove into the back yard and stopped at the porch. I stepped out. Father closed the gate and Mom stood there on the porch with her hands together in front of her, cold blue eyes watching me, like general troops after a battle looking for the missing and wounded. I am sure she had the same emotions I had: Is it a dream or reality to see her son again? When I came up to her and tried to give her a hug she put the palms of both her hands out as a stop sign and spoke in a calm, cold voice, "I will never forgive you that you left me." Then she got hold of me and I of her, and for quite some time both of us were crying. Huh, what a moment. The others scattered and left us alone.

At the same time, my father was running around in the circles not knowing what to do with himself. My sister-in-law went to the kitchen to tell Mom that she would prepare something to eat. My brother went to wash his car, smoking nervously. Then my father appeared with a bottle of homemade cherry brandy, poured two tumblers and handed one to me, saying, "Welcome home." After we finished, he said, "It is important that you and I see your godfather. I just phoned him and told him that you have arrived, and he is expecting you in an hour." It was a short, silent dinner, like we were in a dog house, sniffing each other. I am sure Mom was worried about what was next between Dad and me. My brother was silent. Most of the conversation was with my sister-in-law. So, I said to myself, keep cool and everything will be all right. Remember, you are just visiting.

My godfather by profession was a doctor, a pharmacist. By that point, he had become the secretary of the local Communist Party and a mayor of the community. I guess when he heard from my father that I was coming to Yugoslavia, he got a bit worried, knowing my circumstances.

It was after 6 p.m. His office was located in the old municipal building. I knocked on the door and entered, saying, "Good evening, Godfather."

He looked up smiling, saying, "Good to see you." He put a finger to his lips. "How was your trip? I said it was very good, thank you. I was immediately on guard. There must be a camera with a recorder somewhere, I thought. "I am glad that you dropped by."

"Nothing like paying respect to the nicest person in my life," I answered. He was evidently pleased with my answer, so he continued by pushing a sheet of paper at me, saying, "Just in case you need something and you cannot reach your parents, let me know what your agenda will be." I was writing and detailing my intentions at the same time. It was their way. You were not interrogated, you were called several times before an official who would hand you a sheet of paper every time and say, "Write!" That could go on for days, and if you started to make lots of mistakes the real, cruel interrogation would start.

Remembering the instances of the interrogations from the past, I totally understood his intent in helping me.

I started to write with the help of the small address book that I always had with me. I think it took over an hour to write down my Yugoslav itinerary. When I was done, he got up smiling and hugged me, saying, "I am so happy to see you. Tomorrow you come and see my new family." I thanked him for the invitation and went home. It was quite dark already. Walking back on the old familiar elevated promenade with the main road on one side and a doctor's home on the other, and a school, a pharmacy and an old church that was severely damaged in WWII, along with the Franciscan monastery. On the other side of the promenade was a line of very old, huge, wild chestnut trees with rest benches beneath them.

As I walked, old childhood memories were floating before my eyes like a movie. I stopped at the old school and I could hear children's voices; I wondered where everybody was now, thirty years later. Then I stopped at the old church where we went to Mass and I had been an altar boy sometimes. In winter we used to sled from that point.

The church was damaged in 1943 during the hard-fought battle between the Partisans and the Fascists, who were fortified in the church tower. They placed a number of machine guns in the openings of the church-bell gallery and the large forestry service building that was next door to my grandparent's home, separated by a one-metre-thick and two-metre-high brick wall. Part of it is still standing today, as it was damaged by the constant machine-gun fire while Partisans were hiding behind it. After an all-night battle, the Partisans withdrew. During the battle they tried to blow up the church tower by placing a large amount of explosive under it. The church was severely damaged, but the tower stood up and my godfather lost his beautiful Mercedes Cabriolet; it was in his garage, which was in his backyard close to the church.

When I arrived back home, everyone was tense, pacing. I think they were in fear of something. Surely not for me, except for my mother. Their normalcy was interrupted, I thought. It was the weekend, so their regular routine was to prepare a big lunch, as my brother and his wife were going back to city. I was riffling through my old writing desk and found a lot of my old stuff. Mom must have saved it for me. My sister-in-law was the only one making conversation with me. Mom was always busy with something. I felt that it was likely very emotional for her. My brother and father were like two excited monkeys in a cage. Something was amiss. The family warmth, the dance of the soul, the melody in the heart ... who knows why there was no spark in the eye, a welcoming atmosphere? It was a feeling of being a guest who everyone was trying to please but not knowing how to begin. I was a stranger in the home of my birth.

Sunday lunch was proof. My mom and my sister-in-law sure cooked up a storm. The table was nicely set, then the surprise came. I was placed at the head of the table ... wow! Before we began the meal—my father had already started to eat—I stood up and said a short prayer in English: "Oh Lord, bless this food, my family and friends that we are privileged to share." Then I said it again in Croatian, and before I sat down I thanked them all. My father was vividly confused and upset, as was my brother. My poor mom, not liking any conflict, just froze. Seeing all this confusion, I calmly apologized by saying, "Living away in foreign countries, one learns many different customs." Not much was spoken after that, except between my mother and sister-in-law, debating the food. My father ate, never looking up. He must have been very uncomfortable, feeling that my eyes were on him. My brother avoided eye contact as well.

After lunch, my father had a nap and my brother went to the garden to do some work. My mom asked me and the sister-in-law (she liked her very much) to sit with her on the veranda. I was pleasantly surprised; it was a hint that Mom wanted to talk. She told me later that there was too much hearsay about me, and she wanted to hear my story from me. I noticed that the absence of my brother and father made both ladies relaxed. Once I started to tell stories, they both asked additional questions ... I really had lot to tell.

My mom ... I have never heard her being so talkative. You know, she said, "When you stepped out of the car, you were a reality that wiped out all the stories I was told about you. Now I am proud of my son; you look prosperous, healthy, big and strong."

"Thank you, Mama. You know, my journey has just begun. I am also happy that my presence here has stopped half of a mother's grief for her son."

"Never," she said. All three of us were slowly melting. We were all Scorpios, so no wonder things were running smoothly. In the process, my sister-in-law and I finished a bottle of wine. I think she took a liking to me. Mom just had cherry brandy.

Then Dad and my brother showed up and joined us. I just kept on talking about my thirteen years of absence. I think it was a good way to prevent and keep away tensions. It was very late; Mom and Dad departed and so did my brother. My sister-in-law declined, by saying, "I will stay and talk to Leon a bit more." Through a half bottle of plum brandy, I was told what had transpired in my absence. In the end, I asked her, "How did you get married to my brother?"

"Our mothers gave us an ultimatum, by saying, 'Enough dating, get serious!' So we married." There were no children, sadly, as she had only one kidney. It was 2 a.m. when we parted for the night.

At seven the next morning I was up doing my gym. There was a soft knock on the door, and when I opened it, there was my dad holding a small tray with two tumblers filled with cherry brandy. He looked shaken and humble, and my guard went up immediately. "Good morning, son, may I come in?" he said.

"Sure, please," I said.

As he came in, he handed me one tumbler, took the other, held it up and said, "To us! There is not much worth in talking about the past, let us talk about tomorrows. I need your help, please."

I looked at him for a while. "What about your other son?" I asked. "OK, tell me what is on your mind." So, he started...

"This place was really run down when we moved here. We all put a lot of effort in to make it look good and comfortable, but there are legal issues that make this home and its properties vulnerable due to the poorly constructed wills of your mother and her mother before her. I tried to talk with your brother about this important matter, but he just goes ape and refuses to discuss it. Your mother reacts the same way."

I thought for a while. "OK," I said, "I am staying here for a month, let me think what I can come up with. Give me, please, all the documents to see what is what, and who is on it." Later that evening, my brother and his wife departed. I struck up a casual conversation with my parents and I asked when my uncle, my mom's brother, was coming.

In the coming days, the house was like Grand Central Station; different members of society came to see my father to try to engage him in creating a vineyard for them, of which my dad was an expert. Among many who came was the county judge. A super individual. He and I had an instant and strong connection. My good school buddy was the main prosecutor for the city of Zagreb. Oh my god, here are my problem-solvers. The judge asked to see me before parting. I was surprised, and I thanked him. My father had made a beautiful vineyard for him, of which he was very proud and thankful. I smelled it right away. My dad pried the door open.

At night-time I was looking at the document of the properties and the names on it. It sure was complicated. It will take lot of horse-trading between my mom, her brother and me. My uncle had an ex-wife and a daughter, and my mom just my brother and me. I took them for a ride one day, and casually attempted to make conversation on the subject. There was quite a bit of resistance. My uncle had more of an understanding, and that was enough to start the project. In about two weeks I made a plan that I presented to my school buddy in the city.

I realized that I had all the aces in my hand, and I would start with a scare tactic. It was simple but clever (I think both the judge and my buddy asked me if I would be interested in working with them; I declined, not being a lawyer).

"You all should agree with my proposal. Remember, I am not a Yugoslav citizen anymore. Slowly, changing times were coming. And the government, when they get broke, may nationalize the properties of foreigners. So, I will be the first to give my interest in the house, with property, to my brother, but in return my mother must give her part in the land and vineyard to her brother, who will in turn give his interest in the house with the property to my mom, giving him the right to live there to the end. I will pay the costs. You do it or you may lose it."

I went to my buddy, who prepared all the transfers and amendments to the land registry and signed them. I took it all home. On the way, I stopped at the judge's office and asked his secretary for an appointment. He was busy, but she went in after I told her who I was. He called me into his office briefly and was glad to see me. We sat down, and I showed him the documents. He glanced through them, looked at me, smiled and said, "Good work. Everybody come on Monday." I thanked him and left. When I got home, I showed the documents to my mom, uncle and dad, telling them that the judge approved them and was waiting for them for certification. Amazingly, all agreed.

Later they all thanked me, except my brother; he was ranting for a while because he was not consulted. "Really!" I said.

A few days later, my father came into my room with tears in his eyes. "Thank you, my son," he said, and left. No cherry brandy this time.

I went in search of my old team and school buddies and spent a few days on the Adriatic coast with my brother and sister-in-law. Surprisingly, nothing to note. My old buddy Kruno from the university loaned me one of his cars, a French Simca. I spent some time with my old teammate Boris and many others. It was a very touchy-feely time. I had to be very careful.

Every day, my dad came with cherry brandy. We took long walks into the vineyards so he could show me his work for others, and I think to show me off. He also took me to the family vineyard; he was thinking of putting a fence up and I talked him out of it, as the ownerships of the family had been sorted out and there was no more need for him to worry about it, aside from the regular maintenance. He agreed. Evidently, there was an attempt to melt the ice between the two of us. I played ball because of Mom, and because I was soon to go away.

It was customary at certain times to be at the front of the house as people passed and greeted my dad, as he was very popular with many. When women passed, he knew them all, young and old—it was his nature. And he told me who was who.

Dad was a clever old fox, and knew I was single. He had seen in me a very masculine sample with an eye for ladies. There was an attractive lady present for afternoon coffee. She was a professor of English. She went by many times when we were standing in front of the house, and one time she briefly stopped and greeted my dad, and then he introduced me to her. There was an instant chemistry and my dad noticed it. It was like high school. Boy, my mom was steaming. She disliked other women around her men—her brother and her sons—with a passion, particularly those who were not of her choice, save for my sister-in-law. So began a real Balkan dance...

There was a few days left before my return to Canada. I spent two days with my buddy Kruno, and when I returned in the late afternoon, Mom seemed to be all excited and refused to talk to me, except to tell me to follow her. She led me to the dining room. The door was closed, and when I opened it there were about ten old friends of my parents, all old men, and my dad sitting at the head of the table ... evidently, they all had had a bit to drink. As I entered, all of them got up and one gave me a toast. I was confused; what has this to do with me? It appeared to me that my father had invited his friends, not mine, on my behalf. I was furious. I thanked them all and went around and shook their hands, excused myself and left. Late at night, I heard my father lamenting angrily.

Morning came, no cherry brandy. Mom said Father had to go and help someone. Bull, I thought, he did not want to face me. I asked her what he was angry about. "You know, we as a family should have celebrated together with maybe a few of my friends, if it was done for me. I know it was his selfish deed and he put you through a lot of work, which is not nice, and I am upset about it. Let you and I talk, we are alone now." Mostly she talked, nothing more, with more questions about the future, like, will I ever come back? I explained my involvements and responsibilities to her. "I would love you to come and visit or stay if you would find it acceptable."

She was very firm, and said, "If dad would not be afraid of flying I would. Otherwise I will wait till they both die (my uncle and my dad), then God-willing I will be there." I laughed and thought, what a tease! "Please do not worry about last night." I heard Dad coming.

She confided in me that she'd had bad breast cancer and lost both boobs. Uncle suffered from lung cancer; both were kept alive by injections of Interferon that was developed by my brother, who was a doctor and scientist working at the institute of immunology in the city of Zagreb.

I smiled and greeted Dad. I could see he was uncomfortable. "Sorry about last night, but I was bushed. I sure missed cherry brandy this morning, maybe you are able to offer it now, please. I have something to tell you both." He looked at me, surprised, and left. A short while after, he returned with cherry brandy and three tumblers; the ice was melting. My mom never drank but this time she did. "Good health to all of us," she said, "and bottoms up." Dad and I looked at each other and obeyed the command.

"I have a plan that you have two years' time to think about. I am in the process of buying a beautiful property. House, vineyard, orchard and garden. When I complete the transaction, I will send you photos."

"I will come over only in a horse and carriage," said Dad.

"It is OK," I said, "we will put you to sleep for a few days."

"Never!" he said.

"Two years, Dad!"

My last weekend came quickly, and everyone was present. After lunch, only my uncle, my sister-in-law and I kept talking, while Dad and Uncle went for nap. I sat on the porch. Mom and Nada were cleaning the kitchen and making some preparations for Sunday brunch. I sat on the porch alone; suddenly, my brother appeared from the garden. I could see something was on his mind. He walked straight up to me. "Could you loan me fifteen hundred dollars?" he said in his usual unsure manner.

"What for?" I asked.

"I need to buy a better car."

"You have a 1500 Volkswagen."

"It is old and needs repairs."

"OK," I said. I did not question him anymore. To me the car looked OK. I got up and went to my room, got him the money and gave the rest to my mom. She was surprised. I said, "Mom, this is for room and board." She just gave me a big hug.

I will pay you back," my brother said.

Both Dad and Uncle appeared. I asked my uncle if he felt like going for walk. We went for about two and a half hours, covering all the years that went had gone by. "You are sure a different man from your brother," he said.

"Thanks to you and your wise guidance that I will never forget." He was pleased. As we were sitting on a bench under the old chestnut tree in front of the old church, I asked him how his daughter Lea was. His mom and my mom managed to divorce him. What a family! I handed him an envelope with cash by saying, "This is your vacation in return for the many you gave me. Thank you for helping in the family trade." We both cried for a while.

Late in the afternoon came the usual farewell from Mom, Dad and Uncle, as I was leaving the next day for Canada. I stayed the night with my brother and Nada. The next morning, I left Zagreb and changed planes in Amsterdam to Canadian Pacific. When I stepped into the plane, my tensions left me; I hugged the stewardess and said, "Thank you, Lord, for bringing me safe home to Canada!"

Happy 50th Anniversary

Kitimat, My Home, My Town

Many years ago, when I came with many others here
Into this valley, big trees,
Eagles high and deep snow.

There were no moose, no deer,
Save for the small Haisla village
On the Douglas Channel shore, here.

We came from all the corners of this land
And the globe
To build this town, our home.

We worked hard, in sweat, rain, mud and snow
In heat and cold,
Through the rainbow watching
Our town grow.

The wood and the oil were the only heat,
Living in the Delta King, tents and shacks,
Sleeping on the hard bunks of railroad cars and camps
In darkness, sometimes with batteries and oil lamps,
Yet life went on in a beat.

Many days were spent with desire and pride
Watching miracles of the valley rise in stride.

Today, looking back at a lifetime spent
With tears in my eyes,

I glance at the channel, beautiful valley,

Mountains around, people and the town,

Remembering friends and others that went.

My heart beats with excitement, full of joy,

My children were born here.

The work is done for now, the sun has set,

The new generation is taking over.

It is time for me to rest.

I am proud to call it my home here,

I love Kitimat the best.

By Leon Dumstrey-Soos, 49-year resident

On the way to Vancouver, I had over nine hours to contemplate the many fundamental changes for the better of my inner self over the past thirteen years living in Canada, particularly my beautiful British Columbia. I realised that there is nothing in the world that would make me want to live back there where I came from. Besides that, Yugoslavia has changed and prospered since Tito opened the borders to prevent the steadily growing unemployment of Yugoslavs who wanted to work in the Western European countries.

There were other reasons that I was troubled. After WWII, Tito divided Yugoslavia into six republics and two autonomous regions, Kosovo and Vojvodina (where Vojvodina after the civil war became part of Serbia as well as Backa and Baranja) at the expense of other republics: Slovenia and Croatia.

After the civil war, "wisdom monopolists of the UN and EU" took a part of central Dalmatia as an access to the Adriatic Sea, Bosnia and Herzegovina and the Republika Srpska. I understand that in the past if they traveled on land, Croatians needed a visa to cross the narrow corridor. So, the bridge was apparently built over: no visas.

At the peak, there were some two million people working in different countries that funneled all their earnings back into Yugoslavia, building homes and depositing millions of international funds that made banks and the country prosper. Tito knew what he was doing. This economic boon lasted for some twenty years.

When I landed in Terrace, there was no one waiting for me. Then I heard people talking about a slide at Williams Creek, where a section of the highway—some fifty yards—disappeared into Lakelse Lake. Transportation was provided to Williams Creek, and then we had to walk across the portion of the missing highway to the other side. There was Artur waiting for me. "Boy, am I glad to see you," were his first words. For the rest of the trip he briefed me in detail on our operation. I realized it was high time to go back to work full steam ... and so it was.

The number-one problem was the completion of the laundromat. The roofer was over-extended—it was a scam of the times that became a habit of many in the future: get as many jobs as you possibly can, start most of them, finish none on time as originally promised. Artur and I had never done any roofing. Here we did not have a choice. As the contractor brought all the materials, we literally forced the owner to get his son to operate a tar burner. And so we began roofing our laundromat. The young man gave us basic instructions. Art was hoisting pails with hot tar and I was mopping it, and together we were unrolling roof paper. It went on all day, and in the end we did it—the best roof in the business. I think it was the only flat roof in Kitimat that never leaked.

In the spring (I believe May '67), the interior was ready for new equipment—wash machines and dryers. With the equipment in place, some sheet-metal work had to be done for the dryers, and month later we were in business. We named it L & A Laundromat.

More business, more work for us. The parking lot was also prepared and paved. On opening night, the stand-up ashtrays were stolen. Later, some chairs started to disappear, which I later recovered. Vandalism was up, as well as the equipment abuse, and that required more supervision ... ah, the human race! Yet nevertheless, all cylinders were firing well.

Another winter came early with nothing but snow; it created a lot of extra business and a lot of work for many of my Portuguese friends. Certainly, it was difficult getting around. My truck's tires were always chained up to be able to get around, particularly in the early mornings, picking up the crews for work. Another Christmas Eve came with the punishing-my-body round. My guardian angel must have been with me, as I always managed to come home safely with no tickets. Ah, so many wonderful moments...

There are a few moments that I have missed ('50s & '60s), so I will bring them in line ... unforgettable, adventurous and daring. It was a miracle that I stayed alive...

There were unforgettable trips to the Okanagan, A & W drive-in Papa Burgers, drive-in theatres, backseat romances, night clubs, beach parties and girls ... oh my, oh my! To get there in those days was an adventure. The highway between Terrace and Prince George was all gravel except the parts that were paved through each community. The speed limit was 60 mph. In summer, the dust cloud behind you stretched a long way, with rocks flying. Anyone trying to pass you was suicidal. Damage to reckless driver's cars was substantial. Paint from the hood, rocker panels and fenders were chipped away. Broken windshields and hood dents were the daily norm.

In my opinion, I traveled three of the most dangerous sections of Highway 16. Terrace to Prince Rupert was all gravel and very narrow—two cars could pass with caution and it was very dangerous on dry dusty days. A car and a big truck had almost no room to pass by each other; you would be wise to really slow down or pull tight to the side and let the truck pass and proceed when the dust settled, as your visibility was almost zero. If you traveled from Prince Rupert, your attention to driving was even more demanding. Gravel could be just as slippery as snow and ice. If you were totally foolish and speeding or somewhat impaired, your chances of ending up in the Skeena River were 100%, and there were many that did. In late '57/'58, I drove this section twice a week while working at the Digby Island Airport near Prince Rupert. Once I had a blow-out on the front-right tire driving my Chevy; fortunately, it happened on a slight uphill curve and it was early in the morning.

My vehicles in these days were a '53 Chevy Bel Air, a '58 Pontiac Parisienne and a Karmann Ghia Volkswagen.

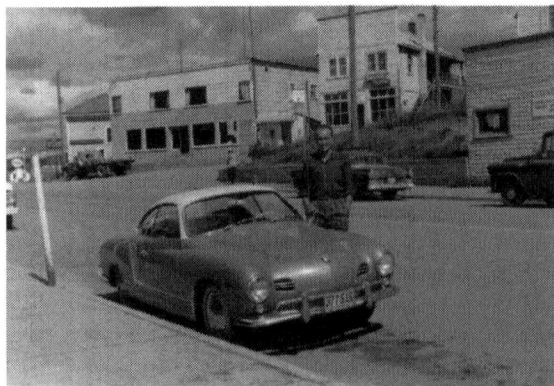

The section between Terrace and Kitwanga along the Skeena River was quite a piece of highway to drive on; there are stories where people disappeared and were never found. I am glad I was not one of them.

Perhaps most dangerous and adventurous was the original Hell's Gate, where the descent from the Fraser River Crossing into the deep canyon, practically over a goat trail (if I remember correctly, it was one-way traffic), was an extreme experience for every driver.

In '63, we traded the Karmann Ghia for a Ford Mercury station wagon, and in '68 we purchased a 327 SS Camaro. It was a steal. In '74 when I got married, I sold it (what a mistake) because my wife had a fancy Mustang automatic and the Camaro was standard, which she did not like to drive. The Camaro is still here in Kitimat at an estate sale.

Winters had a lot of festivities, of which the most popular were October Fest (live imported bands playing) and the Mask's Ball presented by the German-Canadian club. Tilly B., our store manager (what a cutie), and I won first and second place.

Other classy dances were the hospital and the annual RCMP dances. Lots of fun. Many pretty women were in town at the time, particularly single teachers and nurses. Judy, Lonny and particularly Pat B. the Australian—what a woman! Yet she really p— me off when one day after a romantic picnic on the lake (wow!). We returned to her apartment and the phone rang, and guess what? She asked me to leave the room. This was after we had been dating for a while and having s— like rabbits. I just left and went home. Shortly after the phone call, there was Pat trying to explain in vain. I was aware that I was competing with the local doctor. I had met Pat one evening in a Kitimat hotel where my buddy Otto S. got married. She was on the phone in the hallway, and as I went by, handsome and dressed to kill, I said hi. She took a long look of appreciation, so I stopped and asked her, "How about a date?" She said OK, and so began a short, fiery affair.

Winter sports like skiing and floor hockey, and broom ball in particular, took a heavy nightly toll on me. One SOB stuck a stick between my legs and I fell; the consequence was a total separation of my right shoulder. I was out for six weeks.

Recovery was frustratingly slow and a burden on my partner. It was very difficult to get around, as my right arm was tightly strapped against my body and I could only move my fingers. Driving was difficult. One of my boys did the driving while I checked the job sites and organized the crews.

As I started to write this, the phone rang. The call was from a Croatian neighbour/friend of my brother's, saying, "Your brother passed away this afternoon." Thank you, and may he rest in peace. It never stops! The funeral was the next day, so it was impossible for me to attend on such a short notice. I also had my treatment coming up. I said a prayer and lit a candle.

This was a period when my partner ended up with hepatitis. He barely survived. It happened twice. The second time he was in Vancouver for nine weeks. Somehow, we overcame.

In the summer of '68, I visited my parents again. I got a game together with my old team mates. I looked around for old girlfriends to see if anyone was ambitious enough to get married. Luckily, I was out of luck.

Again, I started a revolution at home. First, I went through the same process with the airport customs officers yelling that I was one of theirs, and there was to be no control for me. My brother and his wife picked me up in a brand-new BMW. When we came to Mom and Dad's, there was also a small Fiat parked there that belonged to his wife. I never said a word, but I asked my brother why he chose a BMW. He said it was for prestige as he is a doctor. I told him I had given him money for something practical and not for prestige, but he ignored my remark. I said, "By the way, now that you have two cars would you rent one to me?" He said he had to talk to his wife. OK. A few days later they both came over, and without further ado, his wife said, "We do not give cars to no one!" I thanked them. I was not surprised, but I was surely p— of. So, I phoned my buddy Kruno to ask if it was OK to stay for couple of nights at his place. I needed to cool off. Mom and Dad knew nothing of what had transpired.

When I got to my friend's place the next day, he took me to the airport and I went to Wien, Austria. My partner's sister's boyfriend had an auto rental. I picked the nicest deluxe Volkswagen and drove straight back. When I arrived and rang the bell, my dad came out to open the gate. He did not recognize me right away. He was excited seeing the Austrian plates; he opened the gate and I went in, turning my head the other way. Surprise, surprise, my brother was there again, washing his car. As I stepped out, my father recognized me. My brother just kept staring at the car, then said, "I did not know that they make such a beautiful model." My father asked where the car came from and I told him the story. Then, for some reason, they got offended by it.

My mom was unhappy. The next day I said I was going to visit my cousin Melika. I think that was wrong, for my father and brother started saying very negative comments. I never found out the real truth about why there was such a dislike for my cousin. I went anyway. I had renewed my contact with Melika on my first visit there in '66. What a joy it was to see her and her two children, Maja and Mario. We had a lot of fun together.

This time, Mario and Maja were not home. Melika and I were sure happy to see each other. It may have been totally wrong, but I had the idea for her to come with me to see my parents. She did like my mom, and she finally agreed to come. Boy, was it ever a situation full of tension, yet somehow civil. One thing was for sure, peace and forgiveness were not achieved. I took Melika back to her home and departed the next day.

Upon my return, I asked Mom and Dad if they would like to go for a ride and cover some old trails. Dad was immediately enthusiastic, Mom declined. The reason was that neither of them could sit in the back of a car, due to motion sickness. We spent all day driving, and went to our old place and met some people who worked for my dad. We stopped a few times at nice taverns and had something to eat, rested a bit and continued. We stopped at the village where my mom's relatives live. Dad was not very comfortable meeting many nice people, he being a blue-blood. After having a schnapps or two, Dad relaxed, and it was all good. With many good hugs we left. We came home late; Mom was worried. She told me that Dad had a heart problem. Dad was tired and went to bed. I gave a full report to Mom on what had happened that day.

The next day Dad came with cherry brandy, and said, "Thank you for the trip, I could never do this with your brother. He never has time, he is always in a hurry." In a few days, I left back for Canada. My mom kissed me goodbye and then said, "I will never forgive you for leaving me!"

The next several years of my life kicked into high gear. First, there was an insurance man by the name of Chuk C. who sold my partner and I protection insurance then succeeded in getting me into golf (the big story of my life) and finally succeeded in getting me to join the Kiwanis Club of Kitimat.

The next thing was that my partner and I decided to go into a different venture: land developing.

One day he came to me and said, "You are getting on in years and should get married."

Partnership in the Chimo Cabin on Hudson's Bay mountain in Smithers with Ralph and Elske G. was offered to me by Mr. Stew M., former Kitimat works manager at the City Centre Mall.

Golfing turned into my new passion. Kildala Grocery bought a debenture and so I became a member of the Kitimat golf club, which later changed its name to Hirsh Creek Golf and Winter Club. I took golf seriously, so I used to go and practise before I went to work. My first game and most deadly experience was in Terrace, when a bunch of us went there to play. My second shot ended by an alder tree. Not having any experience, I asked my companions what to do. I followed their instruction by leaning against the tree. There was the stub of a cut branch about two feet long at shoulder height and, being inexperienced, I swung hard and my upswing ended with the club hitting the stub and breaking the club head. It missed my head, but not by much, and the club head flew about thirty feet away. I was lucky I didn't commit suicide. It turned out that I became good at the game, and won quite a few trophies.

I began to play in all the tournaments between Prince Rupert and Penticton. My favourite was the Simon Fraser pro-am in Prince George. So it went for some thirty-eight years. The last one I played in PG was the year the tiger killed my daughter, Tania. It was May the 10th, 2007.

Ever since, I played the game as often as possible, in Kitimat as well as in Terrace. In Kitimat I play with Ed. M., his son Tim and Paul V. In Terrace I played with Gus G., Mike B. and Fred L. Both Mike and Fred declined after some ten years, due to various reasons, so Gus and I occasionally played with Jim R. and some others.

The Kiwanis Club that Chuk got me into was interesting at the start. I became the director of international relations. My duties were to seek out good students in the world or organizations in need. I speak four languages and communicate in two more. I am loyal and dedicated when I commit. In the first instance, I established contact with an orphanage in Bogotá, Colombia managed by Catholic nuns. How did that happen? Well, on my last trip to Yugoslavia I went to New York then to Azores, Portugal, Spain, France, Switzerland and finally Yugoslavia. In New York, I ended up on the Empire State building. There was a young lady and a nun—evidently South American—so I said hello, and they returned my greeting and we started to talk. It turned out that the nun was the sister of a young lady—Maria Teresa Huertas—who was living in New York. Her sister nun was on the mission to seek help for their orphanage in Bogotá (the country was in a civil war.) What a coincidence, I thought. So, we exchanged addresses and parted.

In Yugoslavia, I also visited my godfather and asked him about poor students in need. I found two that would qualify for a Kiwanis grant.

On my return to Canada, I brought in these two instances as worthwhile projects in my report at the following Kiwanis meeting. My proposals were accepted, so I got to work. The students were the easy part, Bogotá took some organizing. With the help of the club members, we built a large 8 x 8 x 8 crate, and it took a while to fill it up with all kinds of clothing and other goodies. The crate was shipped cost-free thanks to Bill H., the manager of the Northern Dock in Kitimat. Another Kiwanian in Vancouver who was in import/export made sure that the crate continued to Columbia. I also informed Maria Teresa what was transpiring by phone. She was crying as she thanked me. Month by month went by, with no news on the crate. I did not have a report for each meeting. After a few months, a member, Max P., raised a critical concern, accusing me of wrongdoing ... that did it. I stayed calm. Two weeks later a letter came confirming the crate's arrival. It had been ransacked on the way to Bogotá several times. I brought the letter to the next Kiwanis meeting and asked President Art O. to read it. At the same time, I pointed out that an apology was in order from Max P. (he was also an alderman, a big-shot three-hundred-pound cheesecake). He ignored the situation. No one offered an apology. I got up and said I was resigning, with a letter to follow. I left, never to come back.

Years later, there were two attempts by Tim G. to reinstate me, and when I asked for the written apology no one ever came back. Shame on them all!

Land developing became our new vocation after we paid off the store, house and laundromat. Both of us believed in versatility. So this became our fourth venture, financially larger than the previous ones. We began negotiations with Alcan for a parcel of land that today consists of Konigus, Driftwood and Dees street. This sure piqued the curiosity and envy of local "well-wishing individuals." When we got out to inspect the property with the city engineer, Clark B.—an ignorant SOB—we pointed out to him that a city road was crossing our property. "So what?" he said, and that is how our battles started with city hall.

One of our grievances came before council, which was: the engineering was slow in processing subdivision plans and their staff was harassing us. Alderman Max P. said, "This is a crock of shit; you have no idea what you are talking about." Nice guy, nice alderman, nice citizen. Somehow, we always managed to succeed. As time went on and we applied for another subdivision, it took longer and longer to get these incompetent public parasites to approve one—almost three years. Scandalous.

The most ridiculous part of the whole issue was that the individual developer has to have their own engineer to provide all the drawings according to the building code, yet it took two or three years for a city engineer to approve another engineer's drawings. I remember stopping in the engineering office many times to check how things were progressing. Tim G. was a clever one. He covered the desk with stacks of files. "See how busy I am? Come back in ten days," he would say. What a specimen.

Before I continue ... Alcan, in building the community in the Kildala area, have by design created the Kildala drainage channel that runs from the city centre under Columbia Street and Kuldo Boulevard Bridge, along the dyke south to the Kitimat River. I worked for a short period on the project, and from what I heard it was necessary for the channel to be maintained on a regular basis, about every five years. The channel was designed to pick up Columbia and Kuldo storm-sewer water. When

Alcan handed the community administration to the civil one whose department heads were perhaps not so experienced, some things like Kildala Channel and the one along the east side of the Kitimat River dyke were ether ignored or simply forgotten. So, when some thirty or forty years later the shit hit the fan (the department of fisheries became omnipotent) and fish showed up in Kildala Channel, it became law or myth, I am not sure which, that the channels could not be touched anymore, and later this became even more complicated due to land claims.

Yet had the administration applied regularly to the DFO for permits, they might have been successful. The DFO was giving permits that allowed activity in these waters. The same thing happened with Radley Park; it has eroded where a huge gravel bank east of it had developed with trees growing on it. You cannot touch it, cannot restore it—what bull!

At one time I served on the planning advisory group and also served as Chair for a year. The planner, Mr. Brian M.—may he rest in peace—was a wonderful person. We always debated to achieve positive results; however, his assistant who is today a director of planning—oh, boy—was a totally different person. I will stop here, as my time is more valuable than this. Screws were tightening up more and more and battles with the administration continued. Duncan and Baxter Street went reasonably peacefully.

It is worth noting the double standard applied to a former city engineer who resigned and started the Smith subdivision, which was approved in no time. I wonder who approved it so fast. And so it went...

Our last development was the Alexander subdivision. The city planner passed away and the subdivision plans were still not approved. Yet the work went on full blast. The weather was atrocious. We had a contract with the new petrochemical company, Ocelot, to build thirty homes for them. The city's engineering technician was spying on us and making reports to the WCB, harassing us, etc., until one day I had had enough, so I started to spy on him. I took some photos of him running around in sneakers with no hard hat and jumping over trenches, scaring the guys working in them and distracting operators, so I wrote a memo and gave him a copy, and the other I send to the WCB. From then on, he had to come properly dressed and first report to me, as this is protocol for a construction site, for safety reasons, and he had to tell me what his purpose for being there was. This was also a private, not public, property. That stopped it for a while, until...

The city's crew was installing the main water shut-off. They had to dig a trench across Alexander Street to make the water connection. When the trench was dug, the crew entered it *without shoring* to install the pipe and the water valve. The city engineer was waiting along with my partner, our engineer and myself. I was taking notes and photos of the event. When they were done, my partner and our engineer looked at each other, knowing that they had installed a water valve some two feet into our property. I finished writing about it, and after signing it gave it to my partner and my engineer for their signatures and handed it over to the city engineer, who became furious after he read it. "I am not moving it; you redesign the subdivision," he said and stomped away, throwing the memo on the ground. I picked it up and handed it to the city crew foreman, a really nice man.

"Sorry," he said. "I will fix it right away while the trench is open." I said thank you, and took the memo out of his hands and ripped it up. Everybody was happy. Three days later, the city engineer was gone and the new one—a real piece of work—arrived.

The next episode was with the carpenter's union objecting to our different contractors not being unionized. So, we took them out on the public road and had a short discussion, and I asked for a copy of the contract, which they gave us. It was about eight or twelve pages of small print, so we asked them politely if they would leave it with us so we could carefully read it. We all agreed, and told them we would give them an answer in about a week's time. They came back as agreed and I handed them the contract, saying, "It is a good contract; sadly, there is not one paragraph about what the union will do for us. Unless you come up with something, we will not sign." They left, never to return.

We presold all the lots to people giving us their down payments, and then the crunch came, and people asked for the money back, and my silly partner conceded.

The last thing came from the city after the subdivision was completed, and the city took over their responsibility. A long letter came from the new engineer who was an expert in writing letters (less so at doing his job), that we should remove and clean the street of the silt being washed from the lots on the hillside. I asked my partner to let me go alone. I took all my correspondence with the city with me; one of them was a demand to shape the subdivision in a certain way, which had caused the silting on the street when it rained heavily. Well, two of them came out, the city manager and the city engineer, Tim G. So I asked what all this was about, and handed them the letter of their demands, which were the real cause of the silting. It was now their road that I am paying taxes for, so provide service, I told them. Try me some more and it will not be pleasant. They continued pushing, and I told them that we were taxpayers now and have no intention of maintaining a public street. We parted, and I send a letter confirming our conversation.

We were hard at work on Alexander Subdivision. As we were completing the Kildala subdivisions, more work and opportunities were lining up. One day when we were preparing for Duncan and Baxter subdivisions, Art and I were chewing other new ideas. "You know," he started suddenly, "don't you think it is time for you to build a family? You are getting close to forty." I looked at him, surprised.

"I guess I have never thought about it," I said. "I really have not looked and met someone that could come to a serious relationship. Besides, our commitments and work kept me away from the thoughts of marriage and a serious proposition. There are not many options here, but I will give it some thought, because I feel it would have to be someone committed and supportive to our efforts. Let me think…"

One option was the City Centre Mall, offered to us favourably by Alcan. We kind of chickened out, so we bought a large crusher that we had no direct control over, as it was entrusted to others, thinking it was a better money-maker. How wrong we were.

Option two was the hot springs. We had all our ducks in a row. Suddenly, there was severe opposition to the concept from various powerful groups, and the project was scrapped.

Two new subdivisions, Duncan and Baxter Street, were almost completed.

Later, Ernie N., our laundromat equipment man, appeared in Kitimat to see how our laundromat was doing and to show me some repair tricks. At the time, I was the fixer of all and pretty good at it, thanks to Ernie. Art and Ernie did not develop the warmest of relationships. Golf became a common dominator for Ernie and me, and with time we became good friends. Later, when I got married, he was my best man.

I knew enough about Ernie, who was a hustler always trying to peddle something. "What does he have up his sleeve this time?" I would say. I was right; later that day we were having dinner together at a hotel, his treat, and it just confirmed my suspicions.

He began, "You know, boys, I am not sure if you may be interested, but I have a proposition for you. I have just finished installing a brand-new laundromat and dry-cleaning store on Robson Street in the West End of Vancouver. Good location, lots of traffic…"

Surprisingly, Art was the first to answer. "Leon and I will talk about it and we will let you know."

So we did. "We should look at it," he said, "and you know what, this may be your opportunity to meet someone…" I thought this was not the only reason; I had observed that he and his wife struggled.

It was the early '70s, so Art went to Vancouver. After that we bought the place, found a convenient apartment next door and operated the place on a one-month rotation. Ernie was happy; he took me golfing when I had the time. When I was in Vancouver, social life was hectic. At that time, I had back surgery done by Dr. Kuntz. The problem with my back was chronic. Dr. Kuntz did a super job on me. I have never had a problem since. It took a while to recover. And then one night I met Babette, my future wife, in one of the ritzy places of Vancouver where I always had a table after 11 p.m., thanks to the barmen who were kids from Greek parents in Kitimat. She came with two other friends and they sat at the next table, and when I saw her I said to myself, "Here is my wife." Boy, she was beautiful. I went and asked her for a dance and after that it was all good.

The seventies era was an economic boom, you might say, yet interest rates were quite high. The federal liberals were driving the country into the red. The gold reserve for our dollar was gone. The African dictator Amin had expelled East Indian nationals, and many ended up in Canada. They did not need to do much in order to obtain federal loans. I was told that a simple letter confirming their status was sufficient; the rate to them was 7% and we were paying over 23% on commercial loans. Many ended up in Vancouver. One day, a group of them appeared in our store on Robson Street and wanted to buy it. I happened to be in attendance at the time. I did not accept their offer. They were not impressed and left.

Babette and I were dating frequently, and we had a good time. After six months she decided to introduce me to her parents. It was an interesting meeting. Her dad and I took a liking to each other, and her mom scanned me by asking what my intentions with her daughter were. I answered that I planned to marry her daughter by the end of the year, if she accepts. They all looked at each other and smiled. Two months later, our store on Robson Street burned down. We pulled back to Kitimat. I said goodbye to Babette and asked her to phone me by the end of November if she was ready to get married. We parted and kept telephone contact. Art and I were swamped with work. One day the phone rang, and Babette told me that she would like to see Kitimat. It was a beautiful late February day when she came. I could see that this city girl had some slight discomfort. She asked about homes, so I took her around. I introduced her to Art and his wife. Two days later, she left. I did not hear from her for two months. Then she phoned me and said, "I will marry you!" So, I asked her to come and help find a house. She did, and we settled for a home on Tweedsmuir Avenue. The wedding was to be in Vancouver on December 18, '73.

I prepared the home and kept very busy. Then I went to Vancouver to get married. I was forty-two, Babette was twenty-nine. The wedding was held at her parents' home on Sunset Drive in North Vancouver.

That was a funny day. Ernie was my best man. He also had both the rings for the wedding. But first we went golfing, and we were late and in a hurry to be in North Van on time—there were no cell phones at the time—and as we were crossing the Lion's Gate Bridge he remembered the rings. We crossed the bridge and made U-turn back to downtown to pick up the rings. In the meantime, Sunset Drive was a boiling pot. I was told later that the general feeling was that Leon had chickened out!

Finally, Ernie and I arrived, and a thousand apologies later everyone calmed down and the ceremony began. Assembled was a small group: the priest, Babette's mom and dad, Ernie my best man, Joan—Babette's best girl—and myself. The ceremony was short, and we exchanged vows. Congrats went all around. My father-in-law came to me, gave me a hug and said: "Thank you. Now she is your problem." It took me a long time to understand what he meant. Babette and her mom considered themselves big-city girls, that is why I brought her to Kitimat to see if she would like to live in a small town. Seeing what she and her parents had in Vancouver, I knew I could do better.

It all felt like I was in a trance and not sure what was happening, as the whole thing to me was very emotional, and the new route of my life began—it sure did.

A dinner was arranged by my father-in-law at the Hyatt Regency in downtown Vancouver. Later, my wife and I ended up in the Vancouver Hotel's On the Roof nightclub where we met. The bar boys prepared my favourite table with Champagne, and the band came over to play "My First Dance With You." It was some night.

It is perhaps worth noting in a very simple way, and for the first time: Before I was paid out and moved out of the house, they invaded my premises due to their discord. Moved my furniture, etc. Never asked me about it. Sad.

For the next two days we went shopping for some furniture, and then we drove off to Kitimat in her Mustang. Two days later, we arrived and the homemaking started. I could see right away that it was not my wife's cup of tea. So, I said to my wife, "Just look after you and me and the kids when they come, and I will take care of the rest." We still had a tenant in the basement. It was to help with our mortgage, I explained. It was skeptically received, and that made me remember her father's words. It's life, I said to myself!

"I LOVE THAT MAN OF MINE!"

HAPPY FATHER'S DAY

My business relationship and friendship with Art is some sixty-one years old as I write this. December 18, 1973—my marriage to Babette—completed the walls of my castle, in which my total devotion, energies, commitment, integrity, loyalty, responsibility and trust would from then on include my family to secure and protect—so I thought—against the storms of life. All of that was immensely rewarding to me, and just as immensely destructive, personally. Was it because of mistakes or wrong choices, or just not paying the utmost attention to all of my things equally and responsibly? I introduced my wife to my community contacts at a reception in the North Star Inn. I think it was all good.

The 1973/'74 winter was the one with the most snowfall. The workload was endless. It was all good, life was rewarding in every way. One night in the early spring of '74, my dear wife gave me a big hug and whispered in my ear, "I am pregnant." I never thought this possible.

"Congratulations, the hard work paid off," I said. As the spring progressed, she grew very big. Her close friends Joan and Jim came from Vancouver. Then her parents came for the first time. I also noticed that my wife had more to drink than a pregnant woman should. We talked about it, but somehow our communication failed.

We had a visit from my friend Kruno and my brother. Kruno was an expert investigator for insurance companies. He was in a symposium in Chicago, so I helped him to visit me.

My brother was a scientist, one of three who developed Interferon. He was in a symposium in San Francisco. It is worth pointing out how things changed with the functionality of our federal government. We had a customs and immigration office in Kitimat and Prince Rupert. In both cases, I just picked up the phone or walked to the office to speak to a customs and immigration officer who had a name and a number, and who expertly advised you on what you can or must do to provide access to Canada for the people you were trying to sponsor.

Today, if you phone the offices of the federal government, you are put to the test of electronics, and if the magic happens—maybe—you are told to wait and someone will be with you shortly, usually a while, and the answer finally comes: "We are too busy, call back later." Have you noticed that no letter from the federal government is ever signed with a name attached to it? Or when you are called, sometimes the person that is calling cannot pronounce your name because of their lack of English.

Today is January 4, 2018. A devastating day in my life. It is two years since Vesna was murdered and it was the reason that I woke up early and started to think about the continuous writing of my story. It is so hard to write as the tears pour.

My life began to be more and more a part of this small community in the valley of snow, and at the same time, more and more people of this community entered my life. Some helped to mold it, some I helped to come to Canada, some became lifetime friends, and now that I am going through the list of names in my mind, I find that there are not many left. Many moved away, while others of my age are slowly and quietly disappearing into the sunset of life.

Respectfully, I would like them to be remembered and also to be a part of this book, particularly because their lives were a big part of this valley of snow, this community, and my life as well.

Here it goes: Don Forward; Norm Hartnel; R. & E. Germuth; R. & T. Bachman; A. & G. Spanevello; Wayne Ashley; Ed Schrier; Wilf & Paul Owen; N. McRitchie; A. Charneski; S. MacKenzie; E. Sykes; R. Baumeister; the M. Cabral family; T. & M. Mendes; A. & C. Mendes; the Francisco Silveira Family; the Papa Viera family (Dora, Maria & Maria S.); the Barcelos Family; M. Silva; Members of the building committee, Christ the King church (Max, Arnie, Lui, Bernie, Frank, Marie, Father Ken & Jewels, Bishop O'Grady); Ken Minifie & Arnie Kokesh, my sponsors to the Masonic Lodge Kitimat 169; Al Worden at Finning Tractor; John Morgan Engineering; Wesley Owen; Ed Marin; Tim Martin; Paul Voykin; my Kemano crew (Bill, Paul & Ian); W. & S. Eynon; Al Brownlee; K. & C. Vidalin; C. Sted; B. & K. Campbell; P. Germuth; W. Hickman; E. Henriksen; Members of KHAG; my friend, mentor, wine maker and councillor, R. Wozney; my friend, golf partner and confidant, Gus Gerdei from Terrace; K. & P. Blassing; Dr. S. Kay and Dr Miller in P.G. who saved me; and Dr. E. Feldhoff, who recovered my smile. And particularly Mr. Eric Sykes, Alcan plant manager, for his love of our community.

1974 was moving fast; Babette was growing more and more every day. There were so many beautiful exciting moments, especially at night-time. Babette used to wake me up to feel her tummy, where inside our child was bouncing. This was another level of feelings for my wife and the little life's miracle inside of her.

I was in work up to my... I was finishing the Duncan subdivision and moving on to Baxter Street late in the year.

And then the big day came in our family on August 24. I took Babette to the hospital and she began her eight-hour labour. What a fighter she was, yet she emerged as a queen. Then the delivery room: a cold, unfriendly, sterile place, charged with anxiety and the difficulty of labour beyond the comprehension of any man who hasn't experienced it, the encouraging voices of the doctor and the nurses—"Push! Push!"—that sounded in my ears like war drums, the moaning of my wife with perspiration pouring from her forehead, her whole body trembling as I sat at her foot rest, cold and shivering, excited and confused, with the doctor standing between her knees, his arms outstretched with open, expecting hands—all that was like an eternity, and then here she comes, said the doctor. And there it was, a miracle of life, a little head protruding out of her mother's womb, and then the chorus really intensified: "Push, push, push..." I just stood there mesmerized, watching the baby entering this world in an unfriendly O.R. room of a hospital and the face of my wife that suddenly relaxed as the baby exited.

"It is a girl," the doctor said, and the baby started to mutter. My wife and I looked at each other, smiling. The nurse wrapped the muttering baby girl up and placed her on a warm plate; I bent over and softly spoke to her: "What is wrong, sweetie?" At the same time, I put my left hand small finger into her right hand and she went silent—I am still crying typing this—emotions overcame me, thinking how I lost her later in life, it hurts so badly. I cannot say more. She was thirty-three and mauled by a tiger, gone. What a sight in the morgue.

We named her Tania and later, when she was upset sleeping in the crib next to me, I would always just give her my left-hand little finger and she would grab for it and fall silent. Or when something went wrong, she would snuggle up to me and take my left-hand small finger, and she would become calm.

Both my wife and baby Tania were heavy sleepers. At night when Tania was hungry, I had a lot of fun waking Mom up and handing her the baby and then keeping them both awake. It was quite a performance. It was a wonderful experience, never to be forgotten.

Today, I will interrupt my story for the moment with the state of my bone cancer. On December 19, 2017, I received my sixth injection (the first one was administered some eighteen months ago) of Zoladex. I call it synthetic female hormones, which are getting rid of my manhood (the male hormone), which slows down or stops the prostate gland activity that creates bone cancer. I am slowly turning into a girly-boy!

In November 2015, I received my first treatment, which was a simple shot in the dark, according to my doctors; the only thing that may stop my demise, The original diagnosis gave me eight months to a year to live. With the hormone treatment, I inherited all the symptoms of menopause; it was and is a constant ordeal. On January 4, 2016, my younger daughter was murdered; she was thirty-eight.

On January 4, 2018, I had a Skype conference with my specialist, Dr. Stacey Miller. It was 11:40 a.m. "Good morning, my miracle, how are you?"

"Well, shitty, thank you," I answered. She started to laugh.

"What do you mean?" she asked.

"Doctor, this is my short definition of a one-page small-print version of your diagnosis." We had a good laugh. What a nice lady she is.

You know, to write all this takes a hell of a kick out of me.

The other day I asked my good friend Gus to remind me of my Skype interview with my cancer specialist in Prince George. Gus looked at me and said, "Are you planning to forget?" We had a good laugh.

Life was going at a fast pace on Tweedsmuir Avenue. Tania was growing, and Babette was a busy mom. She decided that we should have a pet. There was a German fellow in Terrace who had a Kennel. German Shepherds. When we arrived, there was a litter of thirteen pups. Babette went for the largest male, but it was already spoken for. I suggested to her to just stand there and pick up the one that came to her. And sure thing, the smallest little girl came to her and tried to jump up her leg. My wife picked the pup up and we took her home and named her Maisha. Now she had two babies to feed. It was fascinating to watch: breastfeeding Tania with Maisha at her feet sucking on a bottle. She sure fed that poor-looking pup. After two months, she had her potty-trained and the pup really started to develop. Maisha became a lovely family dog. She spent most of every day traveling with me in the truck from job site to job site.

I was busy, and whenever I could I went to the golf course. Golf became one of my passions. I gave up other sports. I did not have much time for skiing. Babette did not pursue any sports that I could see. I started to participate in various golf tournaments in the Pacific Northwest, from Prince Rupert to Penticton. I was lucky that my partner covered for me. I became a good competitor and collected some trophies in my time. My favourite tournament was the Simon Fraser Open pro-am in Prince George, where I had to play with the Canadian and American pros. Sadly, as much as my Babette supported me, she participated with me only twice.

There was a lot of entertainment at home and in the community. I think my wife started to drink a bit too much. I was not happy. We communicated poorly on the subject, which later took a very costly toll on our family. Visitors were frequent and many: Ernie and his wife Phil, Joan and Jim, my brother and, naturally, Mom and Dad.

Work and golf created a serious a problem with my elbows. I ended up in the UBC hospital and had lacerations on both elbows inside and out. I was off of heavy work for about a month and never had problems again. It was quite a relief.

Duncan and Baxter Street subdivisions were completed, with Art and I contemplating one more. Tania was two and a half when Babette surprised me. "I'd like to have one more baby," she said one night. She conceived in July '77 and our second daughter was born in March '78. It was a struggle to agree on the name. So, finally, knowing that for my wife it had to be something exotic, I proposed a name from old Slavic Mythology: Vesna, for the goddess of spring. It was accepted.

Oh boy, more work, one more subdivision—Alexander, we decided. And then Ralph and Elske accepted our offer to buy out their partner's half of the cabin on Hudson's Bay Mountain in Smithers. They took us out to show us the workings of the cabin. It was lot of fun, work and friendship. Skiing was always superb.

With Babette's cousin George and his wife Sharon, and their children, Norman and Ron, as well as Cousin Ursula and her husband Ron—with whom we did some business—and their kids Edy and Allan—who lived in Terrace—we exchanged many visits. Ursula and Ron still live in Terrace. George and Sharon moved to Qualicum Beach on Vancouver Island.

With the birth of Vesna on March 7, 1978, things were changing in the community. Another industry had been announced: Ocelot, a petrochemical plant being built by Partec-Lavalin. I participated in their previous presentation, and there I met their general manager and president. I introduced myself and offered them the services of our companies. The general manager also pointed out to me that they have a small office on the third floor of the Century House. One day, we the contractors that provided service for the Alcan property department were meeting as usual with the supervisor to receive instructions for the respectful services of our company, Palace Office Cleaners, to provide caretaking, janitorial, complete carpet service, snow clearing, and landscaping for over two decades for thirty apartment blocks (three hundred units) and two hundred houses, including the Alcan guest house. As I stepped out, there came from the adjoining office Ocelot's general manager, Mr. Al. B., with another gentleman by the name of Bill E., who was at the time supervising construction of the petrochemical plant.

Al, Bill and I in time became close in our work and private lives for many years, where I was successful in providing work with competitive prices and in advising many times on cost-saving factors, even when the company struggled. This relationship became a cause for envy and resentment to some of Bill's staff, who conspired and accused us of corruption. The matter was heard in the court and dismissed. Some of the accusers went into the sunset of their lives, while others suffered from the burdens of life that they had imposed upon themselves. I continued to work for the company after a short absence until the plant closed—sad for the community. My Willy, as I call Bill, is retired now. We often share our memories.

By the time Vesna was born in '78, life had shifted into high gear. Work on the new Alexander subdivision started in '77, with grubbing and clearing and continued into the spring of '78. The weather was horrible; the two-level excavation for the main sanitary line was some experience. Surveying was progressing. Mud was everywhere. We purchased a D-3 Cat with multiple attachments, as it was the only piece of equipment able to go through that mess, yet work progressed as the weather improved. On the other side, we had a commitment to Ocelot to build thirty homes. The district was slow in cooperating, and conflicts, harassment and disputes between engineers occurred daily for over three years. I had the feeling that the district was trying to sabotage our project. Finally, the project was approved and completed, and the houses built.

My partner had an acquaintance who needed money, who had a nice lot on Oersted Street and suggested to me that I should build him a house, which I did, thanks to the good work of Lyn H., Paddy S., Paul O., Hans S. and Lani S., and my friend Manuel Cabral, who was a great support. I worked every night from five till midnight, decorating and moving furniture as the rooms were completed. The house was completed by the end of October and the family moved in. It was a beautiful three-level, four-bedroom house, 1280 square feet per floor, three baths, a huge garage, office and laundry. Full-length balcony on the back. Thanks to Mr. Ron Baumaister, who put the design together from the photo Babette and I chose.

Manuel, his wife Magdalena and kids Leo, Angie, Leonilda and Johnny were a big part of our lives. The girls were trusted babysitters for my children. Manuel and I made wine for some twenty years, some hundred and eighty gallons of it. It was customary that after work the crew went to his wine cellar, where his generous wife always served fresh bread and Portuguese sausage with a gallon of wine. With everybody happy, we went home. Sadly, Manuel lost his wife to leukemia. He loved his wife dearly; the loss of his wife had a serious effect on him that finally created a sad and tragic end. May they rest in peace.

I was pleased and wild about the house. The framer was absent, I was busy, and his crew made a cardinal mistake by pocketing the joists of the first floor, thus creating a seven-foot ceiling in the basement.

I landscaped the place beautifully, and after I finished the basement, the girls and their friend had a nice place to play. And it was good for adult party time. The first winter clearing the snow, I pushed some on the neighbor's curb and he came barreling into my driveway without introducing himself—what a neighbor, I thought—being all business and saying, "Hey mister, you cannot do that." So, I stepped out and introduced myself and he did the same—Adam C.—we had a good conversation, and all was good. Adam was a superintendent of the Alcan power line. With time, we established a good relationship and I did lot of work in the Kemano and Kildala area.

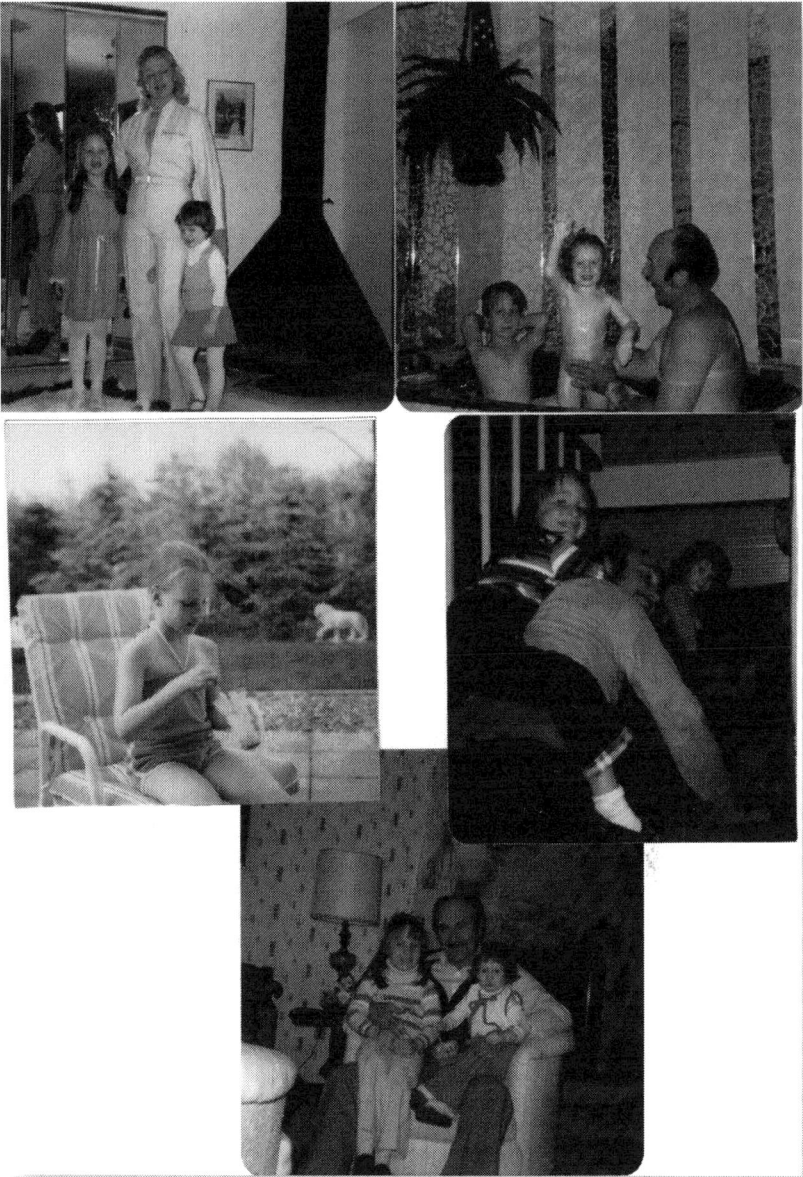

Tania came home from school one day and left this in my den on the desk. She was in grade 4. I love it.

By the end of the October '78, the house was completed. My wife inspected it and accepted it—lucky me—so the family moved in, and thus began the most happy, memorable, interesting, exciting, turbulent and tragic period of my life.

We dream, plan, build, enjoy, do some foolish things, save for the future, watch our children grow, suffer from political blunders ... we take it all in stride and hope, along with the fast-moving clock of life, yet little do we know what destiny has in store for each one of us...

The children were growing. In winter, we spent our most memorable times on Hudson's Bay Mountain. We went a week at a time as it was quite an adventure to get there. My dear wife was always worried about us going hungry. She was great at preparing food. I had a one-ton super-cab pickup that we loaded with five gallons of drinking water, two one-hundred-pound bottles of propane, a skidoo, one week of food supplies, clothing, sleeping bags, skis, boots, a set of chains, one large dog, dog food, two kids and two adults. We usually left mid-week, thinking there would not be much traffic. The roads up to the hill from Smithers were kept clear. It was a sixteen-kilometre ride. I chained up every time, as the truck was not a 4 x 4. It was quite a ride up to the upper parking lot. From there it was a real effort to get to the cabin with all that stuff.

Later, we changed our arrival to Sunday mid-afternoon as all the trails were packed.

The cabin was on the top of a steep hill, a one-hundred-and-fifty yard ten-percent slope. The first effort was to make a trail for the skidoo, clear the path to the cabin and clear the entry—as it was always blown in with snow drifts—get inside the cabin, light the fire in the beautiful wood stove and turn on the lights. It was a great understanding and cooperation between our families that the last visitor always prepared the stove to be lit. Naturally, the cabin was always left clean.

Making a trail with the skidoo was some effort. Sometimes, the snow was deep and fluffy and it was hard to pack. While doing this, I frequently had to check the fire in the stove and add wood. (We had quite a wood storage underneath the cabin.)

In the meantime, the family stayed in the pickup in the parking lot—which was some distance from the cabin—keeping warm. Maisha followed me, all the time having fun in the snow. Once the trail was ready, I hooked up the skidoo, picked them all up and brought them to the bottom of the hill, and then took them one by one up to the cabin. (Tania began coming up with us at five years of age, and Vesna at four.) Then I would go back to pick up all the supplies. First the cooler with the food for the kids and the dog food. My wife was busy feeding the kids and the dog. The cabin would be getting warmer. It took me three to four hours to do the move. The last thing was to clear a path to the outhouse. My women used the porta-potty. Then I'd had enough.

It was so much fun skiing with my girls. Certainly, Tania was almost four years older. She was a real carnivore. She had just started to walk, and the first time we went grocery shopping with her at SuperValu she was so cute, pressing her face against the delicatessen's glass case looking at all the meats. Hilde K., the lady in charge, smiled at her and asked her if she would like some, so she sliced her two slices of ham and gave it to her, and she said thank you, took one in each hand, raising them proudly, and started to chomp them. From then on, every time we went shopping Tania would rush in and claim her prize from Hilde.

The girls were totally different kids. Tania was intelligent and a fast learner, smart, yet of a short attention span. She was an adventurer and a show-off. Vesna, on the other side, was quiet, sensitive, very observant, spiritual and very caring. This announced itself as she got older; something happened there but I am not sure what it was. Perhaps when she left Kitimat in '88, the experiences she went through—no care from her mother or grandmother, and then a tragedy in the family of her best friend—prompted her to take up the child-care profession, and from then on I noticed she would always be involved in rescuing someone, which in the end cost her her life. She was definitely an angel.

On the hill, Tania was a daredevil, but Vesna was a schussboomer. I had great trouble showing her how to turn and stop. Left and right turns simply did not register, until one day when I was on the green chair with Vesna and a lady with her daughter. We talked about how kids progress on the hill, and I shared my problem with Vesna. "Oh," she said, "I had the same thing with my daughter, so a lady told me to change 'left' and 'right' for 'toast' and 'jam.'" When we got to the top, I said to Vesna, "We have different names for turns; let's go and I will call them toast and jam, and you follow."

And, sure thing, it was like magic: toast to the right, jam to the left and down to the bottom of the hill. She was waiting for me with a smile and sparkling eyes, saying, "It was fun and so easy, Dad." From then on it was the cat's meow.

Things were changing rapidly: Arnie and Ken M. sponsored my candidacy to the Kitimat Masonic Lodge, I was accepted, and I became a Freemason, then a Royal Archmason, then a Knights Templar and finally a Shriner and a Shrine Clown named Gogo. Today, I am very thankful to Arnie, Ken and my good friend, brother, co-worker and golfing buddy Ed Martin. Later, my close brother and friend, Richard W.

Masonry equipped me and changed me forever with a new character, strength, philosophy, identity and dedication. Its teachings of tolerance, faith and charity helped me survive the most difficult challenges in my life. With my dedication to the craft, I served in all the chairs in the lodge and the chapter (Royal Arch). It was a lot of memory work and travelling. I did a lot of charity work and support for many through What Cancer Cannot Do, of which I became terminally ill and survived. I also served as a Shrine Hospital representative for our Pacific Northwest region, helping those that our regular healthcare doesn't.

89

Alexander was finished. The paving of roads and cementing of side-walks were just completed. Thirty houses for Ocelot were in the finishing stages. My wife ended up with a serious liver infection. She ended up in Vancouver for nine weeks and survived by a miracle. I certainly had a situation. Thanks to the Lord, she returned, and shortly after agreed to enter the Victoria Life Enrichment Society. She was there for two months. I joined her in her second month. At the end of the program, we ended up as strangers. Slowly, the fear was creeping in: my family was starting to fall apart ... oh my god, do not let it happen. She complained about having nothing to do, so I suggested she take a course in real estate; we had so much land to sell. Babette was a very smart lady and she completed the course.

In '84 my father died, and I could not get an air ticket out of Kitimat for three days. I phoned my mother about the situation. She said, "We will wait for you, you have to come." Finally, I got it. I also did not have a visa, so I phoned the Yugoslav Consulate in Vancouver, and he remembered me.

"Do not worry," he said, "just go and the visa will wait at Zagreb Airport for you." It sure did. When I arrived, my passport was checked and the officer looked at me and said, "No visa, how come?" So, I explained to him that I was late for my father's funeral, and people were waiting for me. The consul said that my visa was waiting for me here and sure thing, he checked it out and found my visa, stamped my passport, and mumbled that this had never happened before. Boys at the carousel picked up my luggage; the pass control told them to let me go. My brother and sister-in-law were nervously waiting, and in a hurry we left the airport. When we arrived, there was a huge mass of people waiting outside and inside the yard. Later, I was told there was over four hundred people there. They were quickly going by, and I saw many old familiar faces that I had not seen for decades. I smiled, waved and greeted them as I rushed into the house to change. My friend Kruno helped me, then I went to see my father before the casket was closed. And then off we went to bury him in the family grave. A few days later, I returned home to Canada. Parting, I asked my mother to visit me, which she accepted.

The next year in May, she arrived with my sisters-in-law's niece Nina, who spoke English. Mom was in transition shock as well as suffering from jetlag. I did not spend too much time with them during the day, but my wife did. I showed my mom everything that I did, and she inspected it all. In a few days, she recovered. Sadly, she could not communicate with the kids; Nina helped a lot. I am not sure what she thought about my wife. About two weeks later, she said, "Now that I have seen everything, I am satisfied and understand why you have no desire to return. You have done a lot for your family." Two weeks later she left, and I have never seen her again.

Two new contracts ended up in my lap. The first was landscaping for the new Ocelot office building. I completed it on time and it was late in the year, four days before Bill the official came to me and said, "What about some flowers?" I told him the season was over, but I would try my best. I got some from a nursery, but most I dug out from my front and back yard. The result was a surprise for everyone. I guess the customer has to be satisfied.

The Christ the King Church building program was in high gear. We acquired the land and the grubbing and clearing began. Money was coming in. People of the parish were extremely generous, which enabled us to change the plans for completion from seven years to three. Arnie and I traveled to Unity, Saskatchewan, and visited a brand-new church designed by Ted Rusik. His design was chosen, and we completed the task. With the Lord's blessings, our building committee overcame all the road blocks, and the house of the Lord was completed and dedicated. I am humbly proud of this achievement for my community. Arnie and I became operative Masons through this effort. Thank you, Lord.

THE MEANING OF THE SYMBOLIC ROOF DESIGN OF CHRIST THE KING CHURCH

IN KITIMAT, BC

Roof slope represents the road of our life; In the beginning it is easy, we are care free children, then, our life changes and becomes harder and harder with pressing responsibilities and for many of us it becomes very difficult and for some of us extremely difficult. The road becomes very steep and climbing up the last length demands extraordinary effort and then comes the moment we lose our strength and we stretch our our arms to heaven, praying and asking Our Father In Heaven for help to complete the journey. This is represented by the two beams above the steeple pointed towards heaven.

Designed by Ted Rusick, Architect

Submitted by Leon Dumstrey-Soos
Past V.P. of Christ the King Church Building Commitee

1760 Nalabila Boulevard, Kitimat BC

Lightning-speed events were happening...

A new company was created—Kildala Road Construction Co. Ltd.—through the initiative of my partner. He thought it was good idea, and I gave my unwilling consent. Meeting my third partner confirmed my instincts. The company was involved in extensive construction of the forestry roads, where extensive repair of equipment was the result of poorly trained operators due to the third partner's alter-ego motives and poor supervision in the field. I was not happy, as every year our financial statements proved the fact. The company was eventually terminated, shortly after the new B.C. NDP government brought in the New Forestry Act. I was relieved.

My partner and I were going through some very difficult family times. He divorced and remarried; I was trying to salvage my situation, which was slowly deteriorating. I think we both were distracted enough to make some cardinal errors in our judgements. His children were away and dealing with the hardships of life. The younger one—my god, the child really struggled. It was sad and hard on me watching our world crumbling.

The company also constructed the logging bridge across the Skeena River for the Columbia Cellulose Company.

We also won the contract for the Shames Mountain road, and after the completion of the first half, the former minister of forestry for the Socred government, also a local individual, arbitrarily awarded the second half to a Terrace contractor. Nice guy.

Another memorable contract under my supervision was the preload for an ammonia tank and its completion, and the gate at the river-water intake for the Methanex (previously Ocelot) pump house. With my simple proposals and go-ahead, a lot of money was saved by the company. Everybody was happy! Most of our contracts with Methanex and Alcan were under my management.

Another project, the Alcan power line tower retaining wall, was a fiasco, as construction procedure was not followed by-the-book. I was beside myself upon hearing the news.

And then, big things happened: In October '87, there was nasty weather; eight or nine inches of rain fell in twenty-one hours. The river was fourteen feet above normal. I forget the date, but it was about 3 a.m. when the Ocelot supervisor, Mississippi Al, called me. "Emergency, Leon, the ammonia line is fully pressurized and it swam up by the flood, being poorly buried by the contractor. I lost my loader trying to stabilize the line; could you come and help as soon as possible?" It took me some time to get the loader and two excavators to the ammonia line that ran along the EuroCan pulp-and-paper haul road. When I arrived with the loader, he already had a cable hooked up. What a scary sight it was. Everything was under water, the ammonia line was floating on rough water, the line was buried and all washed away. There was a great concern that it might break up. It was an eight-inch pressurized ammonia line, which would be a good buoy to us, for sure, but also for many at the Alcan facility and the community.

I am not sure if the community was ever informed of the deadly danger that existed that dreadful night.

As soon as I pulled the Methanex loader out of water, the first excavator arrived on the low bed. It was unloaded and marched carefully into the deep water, then the operator swung the boom to pick me up with some rubber mats, which were to be laid over the pipe, so when the bucket was placed to hold the pipe it would not get damaged. The second excavator arrived and was placed into position in the same manner. Thanks to God, the line was secured, and no one got hurt. After, the operators stayed in the idling machines, and we all monitored and waited for the water to recede—it had stopped raining—to make sure that the line stayed as originally placed. We were there until the late afternoon. The water receded enough for the operators to retire; the machines were left in place, just in case. The next morning, I was asked to go to the manager's office and it was decided that we would cover it with some rock-mixed material, 2 metres wide and 1.5 metres high. It took me two days to organize and negotiate with Alcan for the rocky material from their quarry to cover the 2.5 kilometres of exposed pipe. It was a difficult process, due to the high tides at the time. Water was rising in Williams and Anderson Creek, and it did not help with the power line being so close to the ammonia line. The excavator had to be extremely careful. I was there full-time for the duration of the project.

This was the period when a new person entered my life, a young lawyer who took over a local law firm, Richard W. It became a long business relationship and later a close personal relationship. Rick became my mentor, advisor, confidant and friend. He shared the most difficult times of my life and supported me professionally and as a friend. He was very active in the community; he served on the school board, became mayor and engaged in a war with Alcan over power sales. Rick joined the Masonic Lodge and also became a Shriner; thus, our relationship became even closer. His dear wife Chris and I had many hot debates over education in this province. Today, Chris, their son Andy—who had a 100% match in a lung transplant—and I have shared similar experiences in life miracles, for we have slammed the door in the black lady's face. We are all doing—my favoured expression—shitty-well, thank you.

Rick is now retired, so we enjoy our time. He went through some testing times due to Chris and Andy's health issues. However, we corrected the situation by exercising our wine-making skills. We were quite successful in the past few years. It is our Christmastime special Port made by the recipe my father left me a long time ago...

At home, things were changing fast upon my return from my father's funeral, and my wife surprised me: "I booked a Christmas trip to Hawaii for the whole family, and also, I found a house in Penticton and made a small down payment, subject to your approval. You should go to Penticton and see it." That was an earful. I made a choice and a decision, but you complete it. My second surprise were the rumours that had started in the community over my wife having an affair with the local jeweller. It was a shocker to me, oh boy, right down to the core. We were exchanging visits and outings with these people, as with many others. Sure, things had not been the best between us. So, one day, when I had booked a golf tournament, I canceled it and returned home late in the evening. A babysitter was with the kids. My wife was not home. I took my dog Maisha and drove to the Alcan yacht club, but there was no Mercedes parked there. Then I drove to the MK marina, and there was the Mercedes, parked behind a boat on a trailer. That was enough for me. I went home and played with my girls for a while, then went to my den, and after a long meditation decided to do nothing, just let it go and see what would happen. I knew that things were going to fall apart anyway, as our personal relationship was limping heavily, even though we maintained family decorum. I realized my wife had pre-planned everything, so I went with the flow. The damage was done; who needs total destruction? We both could not see a foolish exit as a solution, there would be too many injuries to the kids and a huge material loss to us both; besides, I had to protect my business with Art.

There was also a surprising visit from Lady Y., my wife's niece, and her husband Steve and daughter Nicky. They came with the camper and stayed for a few days. It was wonderful to meet them.

Babette worked for the local real estate company, Johnston & Barkley Realty, so she got a tip on the house from one of the agents in Penticton who had renovated the home. A few days later, I left with my pickup loaded with tools and my old helper, Papa Viera. I spent a week doing the cosmetics. It was a beautiful place. Upon my return, there was another surprise: my wife had a buyer for our house with a trade-in that I could move into, and enough money to mostly pay for the one in Penticton.

Then one day, sitting in the living room, I heard the sound of a large diesel truck in the driveway. It was my wife with the Mercedes; oh my god, I said! Things were really piling up. When she stepped out, I looked at the temperature gauge; it had a red light on. I asked her how far she had driven, as there was no coolant in the car. The water pump had gone kaput; let us pray that the engine is not gone. She answered that she had driven just from the city centre. Well, it will be parked until I can get it in my shop to take the engine out and inspect it. I hope there is no damage to the engine block, because then we can kiss it goodbye. She was concerned about what she would have to drive. I went to see what was available locally the same afternoon. I found a diesel VW. I brought it to the house and my wife went bananas. I calmly said she could trade it in on a Cadillac if she had the money. Miraculously, she accepted the reality.

Late in the summer, the moving truck arrived. Before I left, I asked my wife to leave some furniture for the other house. She did, and the next day I moved it with my boys. They left, and I was broken-hearted, knowing it would never be the same. I was devastated.

In the meantime, progress on the Christ the King Church was immense. My situation demanded an extreme effort to keep my balance, and I was so involved with my work and golf, and particularly my utmost dedication to the church building, where we succeeded in completing and dedicating this magnificent edifice in three years, not seven, as originally planned. And there was Masonry, where teaching, lectures, memory work and friendships kept me above it all, and I am a very thankful, lucky man.

My dream home and my family were gone; I was desperate. I missed my children; they were without my protection and I was deeply worried. I felt like a caged animal: helpless, trapped...

The first night in the other house was sleepless. I debated with myself how stupid, irresponsible and selfish people can be, destroying the lives of their children and their own in pursuit of their own selfish who-knows-what?

When one leaves a family castle, it is never the same. I sure wanted my own home, as WWII took my family castle away, and afterwards nothing was the same. And now the same tragedy repeated itself. I hurt so badly writing this, tears are pouring out of my eyes—unbelievable! Such a loss!

So, my work and my commitments were the best medicine, and I kept plugging away. I went to Penticton. There was a Shriner ceremonial, and two of my friends, Bill and Rick from Kitimat, joined the Shriners. At the same time, I tried to visit my family. I was not invited by my wife, but I visited my in-laws. When we all met, it felt cold in the room—my mother-in-law was not happy with our situation and I felt like a stranger. My older daughter was working; she had left her school, and the younger one did not look happy as she was emotionally involved with her friend's family tragedy. The jeweller left, and another boyfriend stepped in. It must have been some show for the kids. It was clear to me there was to be no reconciliation with my wife. The love I had for her turned into total pity.

The Lodge and Shrine, particularly the clown unit that I engaged with, were my sanctuaries. Ed M. was my all-around mentor and instructor. Our clown unit at the time numbered eight, I believe. Locally, in Terrace, Prince Rupert and Smithers, we were engaged with most of the public organizations and industries. Many little faces were painted, and many balloons given. I was the one that participated in many Shrine ceremonials, provincially and across the country. I obtained a hurdy-gurdy—a handmade street organ—that I purchased in Germany. It was an attention-getter in various parades.

Ed is a marvelous, loyal, trusted friend and a brother, a high-energy individual and a handyman. When he retired and his buddy Bill left the community, Ed joined me and participated in one of my companies by looking after the crew, thus enabling me to golf more and be away when I needed to. Through him I met Steven and Stephanie J. Stephanie I had met before through my wife. Stef was a secretary at the real estate company where my wife had an office. Stef ended up as a Kitimat queen; my wife was her sponsor. Steven joined freemasonry. Years later, Steven progressed to be a Worshipful Master. I was proud and privileged to be his Installing Master. Steven and his family become very close with me; today I consider him my son.

Steven and Stephanie were with me in my tragedies—in the death of my older daughter Tania, my terminal bone cancer diagnosis and the murder of my younger daughter, Vesna. I have no words to thank you, my son.

In the early nineties, the NDP came into power. In no time, the forest industry collapsed, as well as the economy in general. We got stuck with a few properties in the Alexander subdivision due to their poor judgement, but now it is water under the bridge. I decided to build a new house. It was an activity project on the subdivision. In '92, I finished the bungalow and moved in. Later that summer I went to visit my children, of which I had not heard from for two years, and to hopefully reconcile with my wife.

Oh boy, I am not sure where to begin now as so much was happening all at once. Here at home, my family, the economy... In the province, the old socialist NDP came back to govern, and the outside world went nuts with war in the Middle East, and then it hit my home: civil war in my home country of Yugoslavia.

In '88, the family moved away; there was a different home for me, my car was apart in the shop, the family was struggling in Penticton—it was all an immense burden and pain. Then suddenly, an investigation into Methanex regarding apparent corruption was instigated by some nice envious local individuals that was dismissed by the judge at preliminary hearing. My younger daughter came back to live with me; the older one I lost track of, and the hope of my wife and I getting back together was lost forever. All this took a toll on me. I did not surrender, but it took some time to stabilize. I had to, Vesna was in school and now I was Mr. Mom, as she called me. A big chore.

In the community, we the ethnic groups organized into the Croatian-Slovenian Society, making an all-out effort to help children's hospitals in Zagreb, Croatia the best we could. A shipment of various hospital items was flown by the German airline Lufthansa from Vancouver to Zagreb for free! An unbelievably charitable act by the German airline. We all thanked them. I would like to point out that the provincial NDP government declined assistance upon our request, yet they made a nice contribution to disaster in India.

CROATIAN-SLOVENIAN SOCIETY
33 Banyay Avenue
Kitimat, B. C., Canada V8C 2P5

Pres. Mr. L. Dumstrey-Soos
Sec. Mr. W. Sarkotic

Telephone (604) 632-6755
Facsimile (604) 632-2410

August 24, 1994

Premier Harcourt
and Government of B.C.

Fax #387-0087

Dear Sir;

RE: Secret negotiating of Native Land Claims

Many years ago we immigrated to Canada for what this country offered and for what was required of us to become Canadian citizens.

Today, Federal and Provincial Governments, yours in particular, are taking great pains in cultivating multicultural and aboriginal ambitions without regard to the wishes of the majority. You are supporting small interest groups and others who in fact, are making sure that the Canadian identity (ours included), is destroyed at our expense forever.

In our opinion your secret negotiations about Native Land Claims is the final attack by those who do not wish Canada to retain its distinctly Canadian identity. These secret negotiations are also an attack on our livelihood.

You, as the government of B.C., have no mandate to take this identity and livelihood away from us.

We are tired of paying for political blunders in the past by the Department of Indian Affairs on the issue. Now you are starting the giveaway madness over again at the Provincial level. We do not want to pay for any more. Enough is enough!

In fact, we demand to be compensated for decades spent developing this country and this province in particular, as we with our efforts did contribute to the betterment of all life including the Native life. In our opinion, you are endangering our Canadian identity, our homes, and our livelihood by your secret negotiations. You have no mandate to break an alegiance to Canada and force upon us multicultural and aboriginal anarchy.

Pacific Northwest

CROATIAN-SLOVENIAN SOCIETY

33 Banyay Avenue
Kitimat, B. C., Canada V8C 2P5

Pres. Mr. L. Dumstrey-Soos
Sec. Mr. W. Sarkotic

Telephone (604) 632-6755
Facsimile (604) 632-2410

2

Each group, including ours, should preserve our heritage values on our own, provided we fulfill our obligation to Canada first. This obligation is to commit ourselves to be Canadians first and one nation — Canadian. Those that suggest that the public at large has no qualified information base or intelligence to participate on the land claims issue, should examine their own intelligence. Did we not all come here and commit ourselves to be Canadians? We resent your beureaucratic affrontery in secretly giving our children's heritage.

Your Government makes repeated public statements regarding "Fairness". Where is the fairness in these land claim issues? We are not fools and, in the fullness of time, we will roll back unfair legislation enacted by your Government. As a consequence, we will pay a price and the Natives will pay a price. There will be no winners. This is not even sensible.

Yours truly,

Leon Dumstrey-Soos — President

Pacific Northwest
CROATIAN-SLOVENIAN SOCIETY
33 Banyny Avenue
Kitimat, B. C., Canada V8C 2P5

Pres. Mr. L. Dumstrey-Soos
Sec. Mr. W. Sarkotic

Telephone (604) 632-6755
Facsimile (604) 632-2410

March 20, 1995

Premier M. Harcourt
Parliament Buildings
Victoria, B.C.
FAX #: (604) 387-0087

Dear Sir;

RE: Nisga'a Land Claims

Price Waterhouse recently compiled a claim for compensation by the
Nisga'a in the amount of four billion dollars in cash and 24,000 square
kilometres in land to make up for deemed exploitation of their land by
the non-native community.

We believe the corollary of this is - what value can be placed on the
benefits received by the Nisga'a in the same time frame. Some on the
benefits to be itemized should be health care, welfare, education,
housing, utilities, highways, railways, airports, food supply, life
enhancement, law, defence, stable finance, government, cash, etc.

Before any realistic land claim can be negotiated, you - the
Government, who claim to represent all people equally and fairly, have
a responsibility to show-case this value.

Where, to date, has this value been illustrated on behalf on the non-
native community in B.C. and Canada? How are the interests of non-
natives protected and how are their rights guarantied? What other
claims are being made behind closed doors without our particular
evaluation? Why are we - the non-native community kept in the dark?
These are not the Middle Ages when the Princes and Dukes made all the
decisions and the peasants had to live with them.

Yours truly,

Leon Dumstrey-Soos - President

Copies to:
Prime Minister of Canada FAX #: (613) 941-6900
Minister of Aboriginal Affairs B.C. FAX #: (604) 356-1124
B.C. Report FAX #: (604) 682-0963
Vancouver Sun FAX #: (604) 732-2323
Northern Sentinel
Prince George Citizen FAX #: (604) 562-7453
Penticton Herald FAX #: (604) 492-2403
Kamloops Daily News-FAX #: (604) 374-3884
Mike Scott MP. FAX #: (604) 635-4109, (613) 993-9007
Reform Canada FAX #: (604) 269-4077

During the time of war, I lost contact with my family. I had no information. My mother passed away and my brother assisted in the war effort.

In the '90s, our riding, Skeena, elected Mr. Mike S. as our MP, who
disclosed secret treaty negotiations with the Nisga'a. It was none of the

B.C. government's business to initiate the process. Yet they did it by creating huge economic uncertainty for the future of all British Columbians, and at the people's huge expense and discontent. (See enclosed letters to that effect.)

The NDP continued with failure surprises: Bingo-gate, the closure of Kemano II, the building of two ferries that had to be scrapped, financing the Prince Rupert pulp mill into failure that resulted in the total collapse of the forest industry here in the PNW. Some ten thousand jobs were lost and IWA—one of the strongest unions in B.C.—was decimated and never recovered. They even had the gall to import wood chips from Alaska at the expense of our woodworkers.

Quo Vadis, British Columbia / Canada after sixty-two years here, I ask myself often. What will the future of my children and their children be? And mine...

One day after work, Vesna came home and said, "Dad, I heard Tania is back in B.C., in Kamloops, from Norman Wells in Alberta. She is in Kamloops, has a baby and lives with a guy." So, I made contact and went to visit my daughter and granddaughter. My wife and grandmother came at the same time. Wow, I thought, lucky me, a small family reunion to celebrate our new member, granddaughter Adrianne. I visited Tania one more time after that and took them some essentials. What a sad, heartbreaking moment for a father to see his child living in poverty unnecessarily. I cried all the way home to Kitimat. What will be next?

Politics in the country and the world were changing rapidly. Politicians, in order to avoid their responsibilities towards the economy, jobs and the wellbeing of their nations, were panicking people—practical politics—with the doom and gloom of the global climate, tar sands, etc. So, the important topics of the day became not bread-and-butter issues, but rather pot, same-sex marriage, abortions and welfare. Every idiot in politics really deserves a Gulag holiday in the Gobi, the Sahara or Siberia. Above all, what they have created is a multiethnic society that lacks communication skills in absence of good English, thus successfully dividing the country, which is what they wanted in the first place. It's an old Roman trick: *"Divide et Impera."*

An Immigrant's View of the Nisga'a Agreement In Principle

As an immigrant some 42 years ago, I was invited by the Canadian Government, after meeting certain conditions, to become a Canadian citizen (which I am). I had to take an Oath to Canada to receive my citizenship. This, I believe, has become a contract between Canada and me.

Today, Federal and Provincial Governments, by misguided cultural and aboriginal policies, are actually cancelling my contract with Canada.

Nothing in B.C. or Canadian law or in the Constitution requires that natives be given land or money. Neither does the law or Constitution give natives the right to set up Governments, courts, police forces, and so on. The law does not require that natives be given rights to fish except for their own consumption.

Why then do we have this Nisga'a Agreement with its gift of land, money, native government and fish? Simply put, it is a political gift rather than a legal matter and is offered because politicians and bureaucrats have a guilt complex brought about because their policies and money have failed to bring most natives into a twentieth century lifestyle.

Looking at what these politicians and bureaucrats have done with the Nisga'a Agreement, we can conclude these politicians have learned nothing from their past mistakes.

page 1

If all 185 ethnic immigrant groups can live under the same law and in the same neighbourhoods, why would we want to create separate laws and separate neighbourhoods for some 100 different native groups? This will only lead to massive friction, violence, hatred, and failure.

Will we have 100 native ministries of external affairs? Will there be 100 official languages of their ambassadors? Will there be work permits both ways? Will there be 100 toll booths? For those who think this is humorous, may I suggest reality will be much worse.

For the last 100 years, the Federal Department of Indian Affairs and the Federal Department of Fisheries and Oceans have overruled British Columbia in matters relating to Natives, fish, etc. How is it that, now, the Province is required to put up all the land and half of the money? This is a Federal problem and we in B.C. are not responsible for the costs, whatever they might be.

By now it is evident to everyone that all British Columbians must be given an opportunity to vote on all the fundamentals of native agreements. Voters must decide how much land, money, self-government, fish, etc., are to be gifted to Natives. Any Agreement without this will ultimately break down. Bad laws are inevitably broken.

I am concerned for my family, particularly in the future. I am sure many Native families are also concerned. None of us need or want the divisions and hostility generated by imposed Agreements.

page 2

My efforts and contributions of 42 years in building my country, my province, and my community are diminished when politicians impose bad decisions on native and non-native alike. I did not commit injustices on Natives. My family should not be expected to feel guilty as a consequence. My contract with Canada has survived for 42 years and I will not permit it to be diminished by guilt-ridden politicians.

Leon Dumstrey-Soos, President

Pacific North West

Croatian-Slovenian Society

Kitimat, B. C.

LEON DUMSTREY-SOOS
33 BANYAY ST.
KITIMAT, BC, V8C 2P5

February 8, 1999

OPEN LETTER TO:
Hon. G. Clark, Premier
Parliament Buildings
Victoria, BC, V8V 1X4

Dear Mr. Premier,

RE: Nisga'a Proceedings In House - January 14, 1999.

I watched the above on January 14, 1999 and was astonished when it was pointed out to you and others that changes had been made in the Nisga'a Agreement after it had been initialed by all concerned and after it had been given to the public. The revised document was given to House members without the courtesy of advising them of the change. They, of course, were upset.

You and your then Minister of Indian Affairs shrugged off the House reaction and laughed about it. In discussion, you suggested that the document is too complex, not for lay people to understand, and is something for scholars to deal with.

Well Mr. Premier, you and your fellow N.D.P. scholars may consider yourselves superior to the rest of us in you arrogant and insincere way, but I believe that the rest of us British Columbians are ahead of your Government collectively in both scholarship and intelligence.

Watching your management of BC and listening to your Goebbels-style propaganda, one can only assume that your Government has been cursed by an arrogant and deeply-rooted imbecility of pathological proportion.

Your obsession with power and your casual casting-off of anyone with concerns about the Nisga'a Agreement reflect a lack of understanding of a Democracy. People are allowed to vote on contentious issues in a Democracy. Perhaps you were not aware of that.

The Nisga'a Agreement is flawed, particularly in the primacy of its self-government. As well, it infringes on neighbouring aboriginal claims. Any treaty must have the unconditional support of the non-native population or Balkan bloodshed will result down the road.

The "template" you are creating will be a disaster. It will be multicultural discrimination fathering hostility and revenge. What you are creating did not work in India/Pakistan or Yugoslavia. Why would it work here?

We all want a fair and just settlement and we are prepared to pay for it. Let us do it right.

Yours truly,

Leon Dumstrey-Soos

33 Banyay Street
Kitimat, B.C.
V8C 2P5

January 7, 1998

To the editor:

SKEENA CELLULOSE - "CHIPS AHOY"

Dear Sir:

Of all the things that happened with the Prince Rupert pulp mill and its satellite operations, in the last seven months, the BCTV news report on January 2, 1998 tops them all!

Skeena Cellulose' Prince Rupert pulp mill is importing wood chips from Alaska. A contract was signed December 1, 1997 at a price half that which Skeena would pay in B.C.

Thus, while the creditor group of logging contractors that have historically supplied the logs for chips are laid off and are owed millions by Skeena, the Government controlled mill is buying chips from Alaska.

Even if, as claimed by Mr. Giesbrecht and his associates, the quantity is small and the quality not as good as the best B.C. chips, the fact the price was half the normal price indicates something is drastically wrong with B.C. wood costs and this problem will not go away if Skeena continues or does not continue to operate.

If Skeena Cellulose continues to operate to protect the mill workers jobs in Prince Rupert, common sense suggests Skeena management buy low-cost chips from Alaska to assist in making the plant viable.

This will protect jobs in Dan Miller's riding and will destroy jobs in Mr. Giesbrecht and Mr. Goodacre's riding. It will effectively export jobs to Alaska.

The highly advertised job-creation plan for the forest industry claimed by Clark, Miller, Goodacre, and Giesbrecht is a farce. Regulations, stumpage fees, and other charges imposed on the forest industry by Clark, Goodacre, Giesbrecht, and their government is bringing the industry to a stall. Jobs will be lost in large numbers. Income tax from forestry companies and unemployed foresters will plummet and the provincial government revenues will not cover provincial expenditures.

The provincial government is killing the geese that lay the golden eggs.

Mr. Giesbrecht defends all of this while some of his constituents face bankruptcy, others joblessness now, and others joblessness later.

Chips Ahoy Mr. Giesbrecht & Mr. Goodacre. May you soon be jobless too.

Yours-truly

Leon Dumstrey-Soos

I think I have enclosed enough pages of politics in the hope that the readers pay attention now, and in the future, and do something about politicians who act without principles and character.

My life continues temporarily without any unusual surprises. Vesna was making good strides towards graduating and told me that she would like to enter college, having an interest in early-childhood education. As a parent, I was very excited, which is natural when you see a child's progress. Vesna was quiet and serious accomplishing her tasks on time.

I must admit that I was a bit lonely, but on the other side, between work, golf and the Mr. Mom job there was not much time for any heart activity. My girls encouraged me to find someone, yet I could not put them aside, as they were still not set on the right path of life. I also knew I could not live their lives for them, which was quite a struggle within myself. So, I had to go with the flow in assisting and protecting as situations would allow or require.

I found my relaxing time in Masonry and golf. I participated in many tournaments. I was able to do so while my partner was still here, and when he left Kitimat, Ed M., my friend and brother, looked after my interests when I was away.

I kept a regular connection with Tania, be that by phone or letter. I must admit I did not care very much for her choice of man. On my first visit there she was all excited about their lives, so who am I to say anything? I parted with pain in my heart seeing my child living in poverty and in a beat-up place, and my granddaughter under-nourished. Oh my god, how could that have happened?

I also kept in constant contact with my mother-in-law who—it must have been a year after we all met in Kamloops—invited Vesna and me to Penticton for Christmas. When we arrived, I could see that my mother-in-law suffered from what was going on with the family; it was falling apart. She was not well. When my wife appeared for a short visit, she had changed so much that Vesna asked, "Mommy, what is wrong?" She kind of shrugged it off, yet I could see that she was very ill. Life on the dark side is not so easy, and if you do nothing about it you will slowly slide away. She was just a shadow of her past self. Such a beautiful woman she was, so able, so smart...

On Christmas Eve, we were sitting in my mother-in-law's living room when the doorbell rang. Vesna got up to answer the door, and all I heard was Vesna saying, "Oh my god, what happened, Tania?" Then Tania walked into the room, she was badly bruised and beaten up, she was blue and green and holding baby Adrianne, who was skinny and pale. I went cold.

She came forward and kneeled on the floor before me, saying: "Dad, please help me."

"You know what you need to do?" I said.

"Yes, Dad, I know, and I will do it."

"OK, you will come to Kitimat and put your life in order. I will make arrangements to bring up your things, your flight and your accommodation. I will see you there." A short while later, I gave her some money; she said thank you, Dad, and departed. I did not question her about her injuries, the only thing she offered was that "her live-in beat her up." Grandma and Vesna went to see her out.

Sometime later I found out what really happened. She had slept with her live-in Steve M.'s friend, Mike M. One day we were having a conversation, and suddenly I said, "Tania, you have knee disease; learn to keep them together. It will destroy you if you are not careful."

Mike came to Kitimat; he worked for me for three days than he left. He was one person who considered work a social burden."

Tania kept her word. She graduated and her knee disease continued. She moved in with a young local boy. Later they bought a house together, planning to get married. That never materialized. They split up and Tania ended up with the house. I offered her a job, saying, "Tan, you are such an intelligent, able and talented young woman, why are you destroying your life?" Two months later there was a new live-in. I just shook my head. She was very good at the job she was doing in the Methanex warehouse; sadly, it lasted only a short while. In that period, I was not visiting very much, as I did not want to interfere.

One weekend the phone rang: "Hi Dad, I left Kitimat with Mike, would you look after the dogs? They are locked in the house." I could not believe my ears. No goodbye, Dad, nothing. I asked if she was coming back, and what she was doing with the house and mortgage, etc. "Can you rent it for me?" Oh boy, that was all I needed.

"Ok," I said. "What about the dogs?"

"We will come and pick them up."

"Why did you not take them right away? They are destroying the house. Show up or I will give them to the SPCA," I said, and I hung up.

Eventually, they picked the poor beasts up; the house needed some repairs and was rented. I had three years of peace.

Dear Dad,

I wrote you to stop all this unnecessary hurt. Life is too precious to be doing this. I want us to put aside all things that were said. You know I love you very much. And most of all I'm am sorry for judging you whatever your intentions were. Steven if I made the decision we did (to move here) because if things go wrong, we have no one to blame but ourselves. It is better this way, seeing as we aren't all that secure yet, there are more opportunities for us here. But don't worry, we have a very nice home (as Verna hopefully has told you) lots of garden work for me. Plenty of room for us (dog & cats included). And number one, we are very central. It's in the best part of Surrey (doctor & lawyer area) Not downtown Vancouver no CITY feeling but still in the city. And Kathleen is just a hop, skip & jump away. As well as my girlfriend Shelley Russell.

We also see Ed & Diane so Adrienne can interact with her cousins, her age.

Yes Adrienne is doing very well Dad. She is so cute. Her two front bottom teeth came in, she can sit up by herself and she is always smiling.

I am very happy Dad. Steven is very good to me. He is the guy I always dreamed of meeting but never thought I would. And even though it wasn't a "normal" way for a relationship to happen I thank my lucky stars it did. Because in this world today what could have happened. He could have had kids, he could have been the guy that would beat or he might have left me to be a single mom at 18. But no he has done so much for me and keeps on doing it. And he loves his little girl so much. I never imagined he'd be the way he is with her.

So, dad, please don't pass judgement on him, if you do, because you two met under the wrong circumstances and in the wrong way. And we'd both like you to be apart of our lives. You are pretty well Adrienne's only Grandpa. Steven's stepfather hasn't really shown interest and thus upset Steven because he has tried to make things stronger between him and his dad. But when he came up from B.C. to visit his father in Vancouver he didn't even do so much as call us.

But enough of that, I'm sorry we didn't see each other while you were down here but you have to understand I love seeing you all on your own but there is too much tension for me when we are all together.

Dear Dad,

Your response to my letter meant a lot to me and I'm glad it is behind us. One thing that still disturbs me is mom. Yes I know just as everyone else says "Get on with your own life" But I'd like her to be more a part of it to and I feel that her "problem" is keeping her away.

Dad from a friend point of view not ex-husband or ex-lover or whatever but friend. You've been through it with her before and I need advise on how to help her Like I told Vesna its very hard because some times I never want to see her again & other times I "miss my mommy" Well like they say Alchoholics don't just affect th selves they affect those around them too. I'm pissed off because there's no way I want to be at her bedside praying that one worst won't come about but then I know I will be anyways. And worst of all it gets between Steven's & my relationship. She'll be rude & cold and plainly unmotherly especially when drunk. And I complain about it to him & he'll get mad because I never confront her with it and that's hard to because don't

get me wrong, there's a part of me that wants to & then there's a part of me that doesn't think it'll do any good. I don't know what's up but I do know that she's hurting everyone around her & she needs help badly. Anyhow I should take a nap I'm still not at my best.

Adrienne & I send our love.
love
Tania
xxxx

I am not sure if I will ever understand my family members and many others who do not really comprehend what life is. Many think it is a privilege, others consider it a parental mishap. I think it is a gift of a miraculous creation, a precious gift that needs a lot of our respectful attention. It is our short moment of existence in eternity, like the strike of a match that flashes briefly in a dark night and then is gone forever from this dimension where we humans live. Remembering my wife and my daughters, I cry wondering what went wrong with their gift.

It is hard for any parent who cares to navigate through the sea of changes, moods and sometime ignorance, particularly of young women called daughters. Sometimes I would just sit down and look up, saying, "Lord please protect them, give them some sense, please!" Both of them were so far away and in opposite directions.

They both picked young men who were spoiled brats and who had no clue about anything that pertains to real life, to whom working for a living was not a necessity. The multiethnic one was a mommy's baby, very restless, not dependable and spoiled beyond imagination. Heavy smoker and drinker, cigarette butts and empty beer cans were everywhere; I think he also took dope. And my younger daughter went for him. Later I got the picture—her nature was to help anyone who was in trouble at her own risk. She tried to be a caretaker. The poor girl, I felt sorry for her to no avail, no matter what I said. She was so liked amongst her bosses, her coworkers, the children who she worked with and their parents. The conditions they lived in inside their trailer were deplorable; my heart bled. His parents and I got them a new unit. From there on, hoping that all was well, I did not talk to my daughter for a quite a while. I phoned one day, no answer, so I stopped at her working location, where I was told that she resigned. I did not know what to say so I went to their trailer. It was empty and looked abandoned. I just shook my head and left and went to his parents' place and was told the kids had left for the Yukon. We talked about what to do with the trailer, and we decided to rent it—another head ache. I left, I was in the dumps.

The other one, I don't want to waste too many words on him. A few months after they left, I got a happy letter from my older daughter that they were fine; he had bought a house on a nice property. Thank you, Lord, at least peace on one side.

The next spring, the father of the boy in the Yukon phoned me and asked me if I would like to go visit. I accepted. It was still winter there. My daughter did not look happy or healthy, yet she was stubborn as ever, and to me that was the sign of bad relationship. They lived in a rental home. All I can say is that people must hate themselves to choose to live like that. The next day I got up; it was a beautiful day—forty below. His parents decided we should look for another place. Knowing that my daughter does not follow my advice, I agreed. I put up some money for a down payment on her behalf. Another trailer was bought and a few days later we left for Kitimat. There again it was quiet for a while, surprise. Thank you, Lord. And life went on...

It's hard to believe it has been fourteen years since my wife and I parted in peace and respect. Through that period, my daughters have encouraged me to seek the companionship of someone else. True, I made a few attempts, but nothing lasting. This proved to me that something special, a complete relationship, is not easily encountered, considering that you just know when the right person appears, and that it is a real miracle.

I remember the night in Vancouver years ago, when the lady who later became my wife appeared. I knew instantly: This is someone just for you. You become transformed, mesmerized, swept away by emotions of immense force that can also be destructive. I am the kind of person who plays for keeps when I commit. To fall in love is one thing, to stay there is another. That is perhaps the reason I sat back in my emotional cellar. I am sure I was still in love with my wife.

Here comes an August weekend, and off I went to Prince George's Simon Fraser pro-am golf tournament. It was four days of golfing, fun and friendship, so after the closing round my foursome agreed to go for beer at the Legion. We parted at the clubhouse; they went to shower and change. I did not feel doing anything, so I went straight to the Legion, grubby and unshaven, and sat down, had a beer, listened to the live band and waited for my buddies. Only one showed up, and he left not long after. The place was fairly full, with people still coming. The majority were of different ages and, just like me, victims of highway-of-life crashes.

I sat there, not seeing anyone appealing to me and contemplating going to my hotel, when suddenly she appeared: white slacks and a beautiful emerald-coloured sleeveless top. Oh! And the shape she had, particularly her butt—wow! Confidently, she crossed the floor and sat down two tables away next to another lady. Later I discovered they were colleagues. I thought to myself, wow, better not fail, ask her for a dance. Yet my appearance was my enemy...

Here I was, a grown man sitting like a scared little rabbit, and this lady looked so perfect, immaculate. I tell you, *amor* hit the bullseye again—five arrows straight in my heart. I got up as if in a trance, walked to her table and asked politely for a dance. She looked at me briefly and declined. I thanked her and walked back to my table. Ten minutes later, I walked back, saying, "I would really like to dance with you. Just once, please?" I was determined not to take no for an answer. This time she looked up with her beautiful dark-brown eyes and looked me over. "Please excuse my appearance," I added.

Suddenly she got up and said, "OK, just this one time." I took her hand and lead her to the dance area. It was like a jolt of high current, a high sensor exchanging vibes, and then we started to dance, just like one body, totally in a trance, lost in sensations of two gold-seekers hitting a strike. We introduced ourselves; her name was Janice. There was no conversation, just a silent overwhelming one—unbelievable. Perhaps we danced for a good hour, then came a pause and I asked if I might join them at their table. Her friend was leaving shortly after, and asked her to come along.

I said, "Please stay and give us a chance to tell each other about ourselves. I will take you home."

Janice looked at me and said, "Good idea, before we both make a mistake." And so began a mesmerising relationship, where two souls totally surrendered to each other. It lasted seven years, and afterward remained as a solid friendship.

In the morning, I took Janice home, and on the way we picked her car up at the friend's house. We had a small breakfast, I gave her my address and phone number and we parted.

The way home was some seven-and-a-half-hours' drive from Prince George. Leaving my P.G. lady's house, I was filled with a joy and happiness that I had not known for a long time. 630 km went by like I was in a trance. When I arrived at my home in Kitimat it was early afternoon. I went straight to my den and started to write, I had never done this before in my life. I was writing a poem to my newly found object of admiration. In the period of seven years of our relationship, I wrote many. Here is the first one:

The Day I Met Jana, My Lady from P.G.

Remembering life's many moments,
Pains, losses and gains,
Some that made me lonely and sad
And others that made me happy and glad.

Some that I forgot, some that I forever
Lost, and some I never got.
Some that seldom enter our heart and soul
Yet do stay with us deep and strong,
Forever, long.

Remembering back years five...
It was a beautiful summer day in '98
I was ready for adventure and
much alive, yet lonely.
I could hardly wait.

After three days of golf
I was grubby, sweaty, tired
And slightly bent
After a few beers with friends
Miserable, off I went...

Cruising around like a featherless,
Lame pigeon,
I have never been there before,
Of all the places
I ended up in the Legion.

I sat in the corner of this shabby
Semi-lit place
My mind wandering in the space

Band started to play
in gentle beat, music that brought
me back as I watched
bodies on the dance floor sway

Sitting for a while with an empty mind
I looked up, like a sonic boom,
She entered the semi-lit room.
Strange static filled the air
And my mind started to grind.

Beautiful silhouette in the tight

White slacks and blouse

With deliberate stride and sway,

sat down a few tables away.

As my excitement grew

I spilled my brew.

I lost track of the time.

Staring at the lady,

My body felt like lead

I wanted to dance

Emotions were so powerful,

A grown-up man felt like

A shy little boy, without a chance.

Finally, I stood up, like in a trance.

Barely able, I walked over

To her table, it seemed like an eternity.

I asked her for a dance.

She lifted her eyes with a
Critical look, declining...
She looked so desirable, so neat,
I almost lost the ground under my feet.

I knew I was not an impressive sight,
In a flash I thought of exit or a flight.
My emotions were the mixture
Of a strange brew, yet this was
A chance of a lifetime, I knew.

I returned, determined, and asked
her again,
There was a flash in her eyes,
Pretty smile occupied her face,
suddenly she got up
and we started to dance.

The moment we touched
Our beat was perfect,
Chemistry's fully charged
Our bodies welded, I knew
It was the beginning of an
Awesome romance.

As we danced away, our bodies
Close in a sway,
Perfectly harmonic,
my heart and soul celebrating with

Joy, what a tonic.

My senses were ringing with a
million alarms,
Clearly, I knew that I have someone
Precious and special in my arms.

Evening was winding down
Its tone,
I offered the lady to take her home
To my place.
She looked at me, a total stranger,
Into my eyes with a straight face.
Feeling the trust, she accepted
With Grace.

The way she accepted it,
So excitingly serious, simply and blunt,
I felt respectful, honored and shy,
Knowing deep down that this is not
A one-night stand.

At the hotel, we entered my room
Without a word or sound
Taking our clothing off
Moving around.

As we lay down beside each other
With trembling bodies and
Hearts in a panic,
Gently kissing and touching,

Contended and happy, like carefree

Children, where nothing else matters

Except for a blessed day, where we

Were lucky to find each other.

Yes, my life was relatively peaceful...

Vesna came home one day all excited, face all pink. "Dad, Dad, look what I got!" she said, showing me the rose in her left hand. Oh boy, here we go, I thought—romance is born. It was the first time in a long time my Ves looked happy; back off, I said to myself, and see what happens.

"Wow, tell me why you are so happy." She met a boy who approached her with a rose in his hand and asked her for a date. They went for a long walk; evidently it was instant romance. I asked if I could meet him. OK, she said.

Upon my return from Prince George I had to attend to our activities in Kitimat. Ed M. was a support, for which I will be forever thankful. As a Mason I can state: Ed is a true brother and a friend, always there, always supporting.

Right now, he is away in Yuma, Arizona, enjoying sunny days. However, I know he is missing my good port wine. I promise I will save some for him. Actually, I have been a good boy; Paul probably thought that I've been sick or something, as I have not invited him for a glass of wine since Christmas. Ah well, when Ed returns we will get together and I will be forgiven, I hope.

My P.G. lady and I had a few phone conversations. Three days after I returned—it was early in afternoon—my doorbell rang. I looked quickly out of the window, and I could see only the white roof of a car on my driveway, so I went to open the door. The world disappeared; I was totally mesmerized, speechless. There she was, just like I met her a few nights ago. Without a word, we wrapped our arms around each other. We must have looked like an octopus not willing to release his prey. It was a very tight hug, believe me.

Her beautiful dark-brown eyes looked at me—happy, smiling, full of desire. Oh boy, what days, weeks, months and years those turned to be. The next two days there was no exit from our... I am glad I had some food in the house. A beautiful week went by under sunny skies—golfing, lovemaking, loving each other.

Distance did not matter for the time being. Also, I think that I made a huge mistake in the beginning by telling Jan that I would not get married. We travelled quite a bit: Mexico twice, Alaska, the Yukon, a few Shrine ceremonials. We travelled a few times to visit Tania, to whom Janice was very generous. Janice retired shortly after she had back surgery around that time, and I babysat her and her cat Sam, a very special kind of cat. It took me quite some time to get friendly with him. When Janice went to Eastern Canada to visit some friends, I looked after the house and Sam. Janice gave me a new nickname: Pedro, the Mexican handyman. Sam, on the other hand, got used to me and it was an interesting relationship.

In the same period, I wrote some thirty or forty poems for my sweet P.G. lady. After we split, I never wrote one again. They are all in Janice's possession.

Then the tragedy struck: Janice's son of thirty-six died while in custody in North Vancouver, B.C. Janice was devastated. I stayed with her and comforted her for quite some time. We scattered his ashes on the flower-covered slope of Tabor Mountain. Janice changed. We had a few differences and I sensed that she was cooling off while starting to flirt with and date others. I was hurt, really hurt, and so we parted, yet kept in touch. Strange, she never ever invited me to her home again when I was coming to or going through P.G. I never asked why. I think we stayed very good friends, which is good.

Janice was always there and supportive when my tragedies struck, she still is. Thank you, my JW. JW is my nickname for Janice, and it is related to the wiggle of her butt. She always wiggled it whenever we met or parted. Some butt it was, I can tell you.

It is February 23, 2018. I woke up early and started to think about how to continue to write my story as I approach the most difficult stage of my life. A life that was very generous to me, where I was very successful in my work, regardless of a few ups and downs. Yet on the other side, I lost all my family one by one in such tragic, incomprehensible, different events. The latest victim was my brother. May they all rest in peace!

I think I will add a few lines that relate to me. My split with my P.G. lady was a quite a blow, it made me realize how deeply I was in love with her. I sure was. So, my thing was to compensate that out-of-balance state with golf and work. About a month or so later, my P.G. lady phoned me, we had a friendly conversation, and in the end she asked me not to call her, she said she would call me and that is how it has been ever since. We had many good conversations and good friends. I almost forgot to mention that the Masonry was again a force in my life that enabled me to overcome whatever roadblock appeared.

In the meantime, I had three encounters with the feminine world. The first two faded away quickly and the third one was a charming Russian doctor that I went to visit in Stavropol, Russia. What a supreme experience in friendship and hospitality it was with my doctor friend and her family. For the past seven years, she has come here, it is wonderful. When I became ill in 2015, she surprised me with a visit last year.

I had a serious fallout with my beautiful granddaughter. I am happy that we reconciled. Today she is the mother of a beautiful baby, my great-granddaughter. Her husband is quite a character. They live here in Kitimat.

And here are mother and daughter:

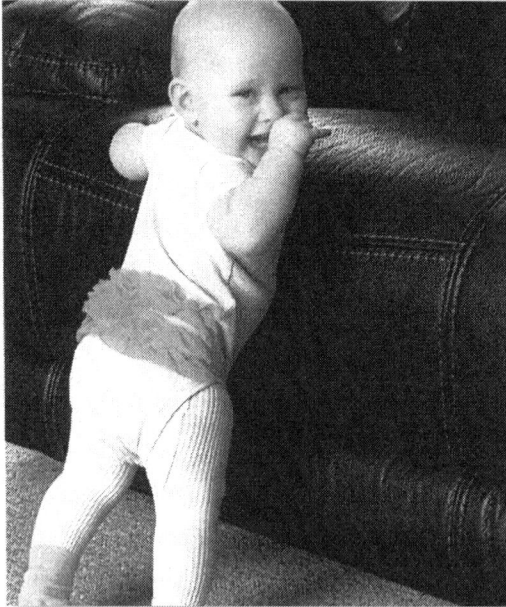

Leon Dumstrey-Soos

From:	Adrienne D [mysticgirl2005@msn.com]
Sent:	February-14-16 8:21 AM
To:	gososo@telus.net
Subject:	Happy Valentines Day , please do not delete just read
Attachments:	IMG_0561.JPG; ATT00004.txt; IMG_0570.JPG; ATT00007.txt

Good morning Bubba

I just want to say there has been to much tragedy for me not to reach out to you. You don't have to answer this, I just want you to read if you could please do that. I feel that you don't have a true knowledge of who I have become and I'd like to introduce myself in hopes that I can maybe put a smile on your face and know I'm not a greedy, lazy, waste of time you once believed me to be.

2012- I graduated from TRU with good grades and a certificate in Support Work. Moved back to Kitimat and felt I was too young to be taken seriously in that profession I returned to the restaurant, as assistant manager and head caterer!

2013- I lived on my own and supported myself with no ones help. I bought a vehicle and invested some of my inheritance from my mom in which I plan to buy a house with one day. I continued to work at restaurant where I became the manager and basically ran the business.

2014- Still managing the restaurant and being introduced in the community as a caterer, I did luncheons for businesses like Enbridge. In this year I also met a man I soon fell in love with.

2015- With my top score credit my partner and I bought a truck, and moved into a house. I continued to work for the restaurant and he worked in the union on site. Being the biggest year yet my partner Cody asked me to marry him and we were told we were expecting. I also learned you were very sick.

2016- Started with a terrible murder that sickens me and I'm very sorry you had to go through this. In this year which will be my 23rd living I plan on giving birth shortly to a little girl. Also marrying the love of my life. But also I know I will lose the first man that I ever loved .... You. As for the rest that's for destiny.

I hope you learned something about me after these many of years not talking. I have no intentions of getting anything from you out of this. All I would like is for when my daughter is born if it's not too late, you could meet and hold your Great-Grand daughter and smile with some last bit of happiness. Nobody deserves to live their last days with the loss,loneliness, and heartbreak you must feel.

I have attached some special pictures of my little family. If you have read this far thank-you for listening. Here's something I hold dear to my heart that you taught me and I never forgot "Dobar dan and laku noc"
Love you
Adrienne Ann

Happy Birthday to you.........

Happy Birthday to you, Happy Birthday
dear Baba, Happy Birthday to you!!!!!!!!!

After all we learned from one another
We took the good with the bad
I hope I remember all those times
To help me with the "darlings" I had...

Happy Birthday Dad!

Lots of love Tania
xxooxx

209

At times in life we needed someone you were there, whether we knew it or not.
When we were happy or sad or just not too hot.
You always knew just what to say or what to do.
Even when you weren't sure yourself, how we'd make it through.

Somedays I think of all the years we've had,
Loving, fighting, laughing, crying...
I'm just glad that you are my DAD!

xxxooxxx

My Family's Demise

Steven, Stephanie, Parker and Declan, the Jeffrey family and I—it is a long story. It was/is a relationship built like a good old brick house, brick by brick. The connection started a long time ago. When my wife got her realtor licence, she joined Johnston & Barkley Realty, a real estate company where Stephanie was a young lady who was employed as a secretary. When my wife sponsored her for a beauty-queen contest in our community, it was the first time I met her, as well as her mother.

Years passed from that day. In the meantime, I become a Mason, and one day Ed took me to Williscroft Street to visit a new candidate, Peter S. Bill McC. was already there. He was the lodge's secretary at the time. Both Ed and Bill helped Peter with the memory work, which is a hugely important part of the Masonic ritual. I was pleasantly surprised to see Peter. I met Peter decades earlier when I started to work at Alcan. It was on the Alcan wharf that I met Peter, who was a supervisor there. I was there for only a week, and that was the last time I saw him until that particular day. Peter had aged; Bill and Ed assisted him in some daily chores, the Masonic way to help a brother.

Steven and Stephanie lived next door to Peter. It happened that between them talking to Steven he had shown interest in Freemasonry. I went with Ed one day to visit Steven and there was Stephanie; what a surprise. Not too long after that, I had a few conversations with Steven regarding Masonry. So, he became a candidate and joined us. I must say he was one candidate with merit and a lot of ability. I took a liking to Steven. Time passed, and they moved to Cable Car. Ed retired so he and Bill were doing a few small jobs. One day I ended up looking at the gazebo they had built for Steven. We had a few beers while Steven and I talked about wine making—Steven quit drinking sometime later—then he took me to show me the house and the property. I also had a landscaping business, so we discussed the situation of the backyard.

It was a difficult piece of property, mostly clay and not properly graded when the previous owner built the house. There was no road access to the back of the property. I made a few proposals to Steven and Stephanie, which they accepted.

By building the second crossing and turning the existing pathway into a passable road, it all turned out good. Some of the work was not done for a very good reason.

Cable Car is about six or seven kilometres away from town. Both of them were engaged in the community and Parker, their first child, had to be transported to school. Sports became an extra effort, particularly in winter, as they were both working. I was and am honoured by always being invited to their home for special occasions. Then, one day, they decided to move into town. They purchased a home at Braun Street. Many bricks of our lives were put together there...

On the home front, a message came from my younger daughter that she was finished with her multicultural boyfriend in the Yukon and she was coming home. As usual, she didn't tell me the whole story. Not only had she lost her value in the home up there by simply not making any requests—she was, in the end, taken advantage of, in my opinion; I was juggling both their homes for rentals—she also informed me that she had met someone else up there and they were getting married, and that I should come up and meet him. Oh my god, I thought! I did go up there and ... surprise! The new boyfriend was a divorced man with five kids. I explained to her that she needed to do something with the place in Kitimat or she will have another loss, as her ex-boyfriend's parents wanted closure on the property.

Then one evening my phone rang. "This is John, Babette died." He was a live-in boyfriend.

"Huh, where is she?" I asked him. He told me he had cremated her! Nice; without telling me beforehand. He said he was sorry. Bull, I thought. I told him I would come down for the funeral, so I informed the girls and we ended up in Penticton. It was an extraordinary occasion. Apparently, she was taken to the hospital in a coma. She was there for three days and then died, and the bastard did not phone me, and that made me suspicious. After the service and funeral, I went over to the office of the lawyer who was the executor, who told me the story, and then I went to the house. It was a mess, save for the master bedroom and en suite. That made me think something was not right. I looked around moved the headboard, and blood came up from under one leg. I called John into the bedroom, closed the door and pointed out the blood, and told him to tell me the story.

"Well, she was in the bathroom and hit her head on the tub and went into a coma."

"Why did you not call me right away?"

"Well, I-I-I..." That confirmed my suspicions. First, he had the house-sale documents prepared with his name on them, then went to the executor who told him to forget about it. There was no body; I could not request an autopsy. I was sure he did her in and I could not prove it.

Both daughters were with me, giving me a hand moving stuff out of the house. There were a few friends of theirs helping. We rented a storage space and a truck, and we made it a speedy job. Considering all of the emotions, all went well. The best part was me keeping my temper cool. A few days later, we all departed back to our homes. I drove the U-Haul that had a trailer with the car on it. On the way, I stopped at Tania's place and unloaded the stuff she wanted, and continued to Kitimat. By the time I arrived at Kitimat, Vesna's new boyfriend arrived with his one daughter, and they were already talking about marriage. I looked up to the heavens. "Please Lord, keep me sane." I could see there would be no long-term solution. As the guy had grown-up daughters, he had a litany of problems.

It is very difficult to move forward, unless I abandon everything and just leave. I could not, as I had many responsibilities and I do not just quit. So as a naive, good father, I simply made a mistake. So, more of his kids came here, and not at his expense. He was clever at manipulating her, so on it went with the wedding. Two years later they divorced, and then the really extreme part of my life began.

First, the mother of my wife died, and she left a nice inheritance for the girls. Tania changed her boyfriend around Christmas time. She left one irresponsible man for another who had a small zoo of exotic animals. Oh boy, big love, big cats—the poor thing was spellbound. Just about the same time, both girls received an inheritance from their grandmother.

It must have been quite a thing for her, parading around with, touching, travelling with and walking with the big cats. The inheritance was quickly spent on vehicles and the new boyfriend's extravaganzas. She sent me a photo with her kitty.

Life in the valley continued surprisingly peacefully. I made several trips to Penticton and visited my mother-in-law and my poor wife's grave. Not too long after, she ended up in the hospital with dementia. She passed away a year later and left a considerable inheritance to my daughters.

Going back and forth, I always stopped in 100 Mile House where Tania lived; the kids were growing. My stops were short, and I was not very inquisitive. It was their lives. I was always wondering where the money came from for all the expensive toys and designer clothing for their son when the daughter was out of picture. Ady (my granddaughter) was not well treated by him; why did the mother do nothing about it? Later, I discovered that he had a grow-op, but my daughter refused to acknowledge it. And that was the last time I saw her. Was she living under threat? I never found out. Probably manipulated. The individual she lived with was a piece of work, I must say, never had any use for him. He was, in my opinion, a social parasite that ruins and destroys other lives. I constantly shook my head in disbelief over why my daughters chose such similar paths in life.

I continued my life, as you see, with enormous burdens. No matter how much care and support I gave, both my daughters—may they rest in peace—sent me beautiful cards acknowledging this and how much they loved me, yet all my efforts to get them off their paths in life were for nought. I remember one time, Tania told me, "Dad, I hate you because you are always right." Years later they both perished.

Writing this, you have no idea how sad and painful it is now that I lost them both. My heart and soul are moaning, groaning, twisting in horrible pain that never ends when these memories appear, with unstoppable tears running.

Then, on March 10, 2007, the second thunder struck bullseye in my family. It was 11 p.m. when the phone rang, and the voice of a male said, "This is Kim, Tania is dead." The way he said it made me think it was a hoax at first. I hung up. Then the phone rang again, and the same caller repeated the message. I thanked him and hung up. I sat on the bedside, trying comprehend what I had heard, then the phone rang for a third time.

"Mr. Dumstrey-Soos, this is Constable Chris Manseau from the 100 Mile House RCMP detachment. Your daughter Tania has been mauled by a tiger and died. My condolences."

"Thank you," I said. We hung up. Then it hit me, and I started to scream at the top of my lungs for quite a while. (I was so grief-stricken, just like this moment as I am writing this. I cannot see the keyboard and I am not sure if I will be able to finish this writing.) When I stopped, I felt cold, remembering cautioning Tania about the danger she was playing with. All in vain; I lost her forever.

Then I phoned my other daughter with the sad news, telling her I would talk to her in the morning. Vesna never uttered a sound. Right after that I phoned my good friends and brothers. Rick was the first one I called because was a lawyer, to give me advice. It was midnight by that time. Just as Rick left, Ed arrived, and stayed with me for a while, then Steven came in the morning. By that time, I think I had stabilized. I started to make plans to go to 100 Mile House as soon as possible. This I confirmed with Vesna and decided to leave the next day.

Leon Dumstrey-Soos

From:	"Tania Dumstrey-Soos" <mtann@shaw.ca>
To:	"Tracy Black" <tracy_black@hsbc.ca>, "The Baba" <gososo@telus.net>, "Nicole Newby" <the3amigos@shaw.ca>; "Michelle Savage" <michellesavage@shaw.ca>
Sent:	November 25, 2006 7:14 PM
Attach:	MeandRaja 001.jpg
Subject:	Emailing: MeandRaja 001

```
Just drop a line to say hi and show you me and
my kitty.
```
The message is ready to be sent with the following file or link attachments:
MeandRaja 001

Note: To protect against computer viruses, e-mail programs may prevent
sending or receiving certain types of file attachments. Check your e-mail
security settings to determine how attachments are handled.

30/01/2007

Tiger warning ignored: SPCA   Page 7 of 9

- Taser report spurs reforms
- Season's first snowfall arrives in Metro Vancouver
- Defence suggests manslaughter at Matasi murder trial

- More Latest News

Tiger warning ignored: SPCA

**An official says the government and RCMP were cautioned about zoo
where woman was fatally mauled**

Miro Cernetig, Vancouver Sun

Published: Saturday, May 12, 2007

For the most part, the tricky job of regulating exotic animals has been left to
cities, which also have been slow to act. In many jurisdictions it is still
permissible to have a tiger in your backyard, at least until the neighbourhood
revolts.

But that is changing. The City of Vancouver -- which has seen recent cases
including a sharp-toothed cayman dropping off a balcony in Kitsilano --
passed a bylaw in February that bans keeping most exotic animals as pets or
selling them.

The SPCA and VHS have spent almost two decades trying to get such a law
introduced on a province-wide basis.

Email to a friend Printer friendly
Font:

- °
- °
- °
- °

http://www.canada.com/vancouversun/news/story.html?id=ba866322-cbe7-460c-a39f-34... 26/11/2007

216

province-wide regulations should be created.

"Clearly we've had a tragic incident," said Bell. "We want to deal with it as quickly as we possibly can."

Aside from the poor living conditions of the Siberian Magic zoo's tigers -- one of which had to have its tail amputated after an injury -- the SPCA's Moriarty said authorities were made aware of the serious threat to the public.

"These cats were housed in 12-foot-by-12-foot pens made of chain-link fence, with a simple padlock," she said. "He admitted that he walked tigers on a leash, that his kids fed them, that he took the tigers out and let members of the public take pictures with the tigers. It was a tragedy waiting to happen."

But why did it?

The reality is that this year, after almost 20 years of urging from the SPCA and VHS, the B.C. provincial government has finally begun reviewing its Wildlife Act with an eye to outlawing such menageries that contain tigers, lions, crocodiles, poisonous snakes and perhaps even elephants.

A permit is only needed to keep an indigenous species in captivity, such as wolves or bears or moose. Exotic pets are left unregulated by the province.

- 1
- 2
- next page

Home   Great home delivery subscription deals here!

Ads by Google

Panic Attacks

- Taser report spurs reforms
- Season's first snowfall arrives in Metro Vancouver
- Defence suggests manslaughter at Matasi murder trial

- More Latest News

Tiger warning ignored: SPCA

An official says the government and RCMP were cautioned about zoo where woman was fatally mauled

Miro Cernetig, Vancouver Sun

Published: Saturday, May 12, 2007

VICTORIA -- Government officials and the RCMP were warned repeatedly for almost two years that a menagerie of tigers and lions at the Siberian Magic private zoo posed a serious danger to the public, the SPCA said Friday.

But despite the warnings and the poor conditions of the animals, no action was taken that might have prevented the death Thursday of Tania Dumstrey-Soos, 32. She was mauled by one of the tigers she was caring for in the private zoo near 100 Mile House.

"This is an absolute tragedy that could and should have been prevented," said Marcie Moriarty, who heads investigations for the SPCA into cruelty to animals.

A photo taken during a B. C. SPCA investigation in 2006 shows a cage at Siberian Magic. The SPCA was unable to find a new home for the tigers, one of which subsequently mauled and killed Tania Dumstrey- Soos.

B.C. SPCA handout

☐Email to a friend☐Printer friendly
Font:

- *
- *
- *
- *

☐ BOOKMARK ▪ ⌨ ♔.

"We were made aware of the dangers in 2005. We served five violations-of-animal-welfare orders, the last in January 2007. We informed the regional district, the RCMP and [provincial] conservation officers."

B.C. Environment Minister Barry Penner was also given a written warning more than a year ago about the dangers at the Siberian Magic zoo. He also was told its operator, Kim Carlton, was taking his tigers to malls and did not have suitable cages to prevent escapes.

"This is in our opinion a disaster waiting to happen," said a Dec. 1, 2006 letter from the Vancouver Humane Society (VHS), which was accompanied by video footage.

Humane society spokesman Peter Fricker said there was no response from the minister. Penner also was not available Friday for comment. Nor would the RCMP comment on the case.

However, after resisting years of lobbying from the SPCA and VHS to regulate the booming exotic animal industry, Thursday's death has prompted the provincial government to consider taking action.

Agriculture Minister Pat Bell said the rise of exotic animals in captivity is an emerging phenomenon that was left to regional districts to manage. He said he will be meeting with Penner next week to review the mauling and consider if

---

Sinoski, Vancouver Sun, Vancouver Sun

Published: Saturday, May 12, 2007

Tania Dumstrey-Soos clutched a cell phone as she lay near death outside the cage where she had just been attacked by a male Bengal tiger.

She told her fiance Kim Carlton that she loved him. The former extreme fighter replied that he loved her too as he frantically raced home to Siberian Magic, his exotic animal zoo near 100 Mile House.

Emergency crews arrived at the Bridge Lake zoo about 9 p.m. Thursday to find family members desperately trying to revive an unconscious Dumstrey-Soos.

☐Email to a friend☐Printer friendly
Font:

- *
- *
- *
- *

☐ BOOKMARK ▪ ⌨ ♔.

One of her own children witnessed the fatal attack and at least two of Carlton's children were at the scene.

"She was laying beside the cage when she was on the ground and she was saying that the cat had swiped at her," said Scott Nelson, Dumstrey-Soos' employer and mayor of Williams Lake, who spoke with Carlton Friday.

"Basically [Carlton] said that they had exchanged 'I love yous' back and forth and she had passed out before the ambulance got there."

Dumstrey-Soos had been saying good night to the tigers, as she did every night, said Nelson. "She went down to pet the animal, [but] the tiger grabbed her by the leg."

Emergency crews transferred her to 100 Mile Hospital where she was pronounced dead.

The attack by the Bengal tiger named Gangus, one of three in Carlton's zoo, follows warnings by the Vancouver Humane Society that the facility was a danger to the public. The B.C. government responded Friday, saying it will review the mauling and consider whether provincewide regulations on exotic animals are needed.

RCMP Const. Annie Linteau said the tiger reached from inside the cage and attacked the woman as she stood outside. All three tigers and other animals remained in the private zoo late Friday as the investigation by 100 Mile House RCMP continued.

The BC Coroners Service has been notified and an autopsy is scheduled to determine the cause of death. The provincial Conservation Officer Service and the SPCA are also assisting in the investigation, police said.

Nelson said Carlton was at home Friday with the couple's five children -- three of his own and two of hers, aged 14 and six.

"They're horrified at what's happened," he said.

Nelson employed Dumstrey-Soos as a sales representative and office administrator for the Cariboo Advisor newspaper.

"I can tell you that Tania was a great lady and she worked hard for us," Nelson said.

"Tania was just extraordinary and bubbly and positive," he continued.

Nelson said Dumstrey-Soos had been involved for some time with Carlton's animals. "She loved those animals, absolutely."

Nelson would not comment on the safety of the attraction, except to say: "It's well set up."

But there has been controversy about Carlton and his zoo.

For almost a decade Carlton and his collection of exotic animals -- in particular a tiger he used to take on mall tours across western Canada -- have

---

The SPCA, which finds itself underfunded, is limited in what it can do to police exotic animals. Under current animal-welfare laws it may seize an animal only when it is proven the animal is being denied food, water or medical care, or is being beaten, said Fricker.

As well, there's the difficult problem of what to do with a 350-lb. tiger that needs a better home. The SPCA spent thousands of dollars trying to find new lodging for the tigers at the Siberian Magic zoo, even asking the Calgary Zoo to adopt them. It found no takers.

"There are just so many tigers in captivity already nobody has space," said Moriarty.

Most people don't know it, but while tigers grow rarer in the jungles of Asia, North America is actually awash in them. Tigers are one of the favourite animals of the exotic-animal industry which has emerged as a $1-billion worldwide business.

While it is almost impossible to bring exotic animals across the Canadian border today because of international treaties that protect endangered wildlife, it's actually not difficult to buy a creature of the world's jungles. That is because many of the animals were brought in before such restrictions and have been bred in captivity.

Large cats, such as tigers, have proven to be easier than most to breed. Tigers and lions can be bought for a few hundred dollars as adorable cubs. In the United States it is estimated that there are now more than 10,000 tigers and lions kept by private individuals and private zoos. Nobody knows how many tigers are kept in B.C., but the SPCA estimates there are likely more than a dozen.

mcernetig@png.canwest.com

• previous page

TODAY'S WEATHER
CLOUDY
23 °C
4 Day Forecast | Traffic

"Big bottom line:
The scale going up is getting me d

Saturday, April 19, 2008 | Today's Toronto Star

PHOTOS VIDEO COLUMNISTS BLOGS

thestar.com

☑ Search thestar
Advanced Search |

HOME NEWS COMMENT BUSINESS SPORTS ENTERTAINMENT LIVING TRAVEL WHEELS HEALTH

Toronto & GTA | Ontario | Canada | World | Comics | Contests | Crosswords | Horoscopes | Lotteries |

Tiger kills woman in B.C

May 11, 2007 08:15 PM

CANADIAN PRESS

✉ Email story
🖨 Print
☐ ☐ ☐ Choose text size
✎ Report typo or correction

🔖 BOOKMARK

100 MILE HOUSE, B.C. – A 32-year-old woman was mauled to
death by a captive tiger at an exotic animal farm in the B.C.
Interior while one of her kids and her fiance's two children
witnessed the terrifying attack.

The woman even spoke with her fiance and owner of the farm, Kim
Carlton, by cell phone as she lay dying, her employer said in an
interview.

"Before she passed away Kim did say that he did have a chance to talk to Tanya," said Scott Nelson,
who employed Tanya Dumstrey-Soos as a receptionist and saleswoman at the 100 Mile House
Advisor newspaper.

"He said the two were able to say they loved each other and he was obviously horrified."

Nelson, who is also the mayor of Williams Lake, B.C., said Dumstrey-Soos and Carlton had recently
become engaged to be married.

It was thought the cat began clawing at the woman's dress as she stood outside its cage.

Const. Annie Linteau of the RCMP's E Division said a number of children witnessed the attack and "at
least one of the children belonged to her."

She said it's too early to say if anyone could face charges.

Nelson said he believed two of the children were Carlton's kids – Dakota, 12, and 15-year-old
Kodiak.

"We were obviously horrified, more horrified that the young kids saw it, that they were there and
obviously our hearts are with them."

He described it as a bizarre, freak accident. He said he spoke to Carlton about what happened.

"He told me Gangus was the cat. He didn't think the tiger had bit her. It's that she had a dress on
and she was standing there and he was playing with the dress and grabbed her legs.

"She was standing outside the cage and talking to Gangus, the cat swatted at the legs."

He said Gangus was the only one of the three tigers that wasn't declawed.

The incident had the provincial government promising to look into the regulations that allow private
citizens to keep such animals. The SPCA is calling for legislation to ban the practice.

Agriculture Minister Pat Bell said he will work with other authorities to determine if there is the need
for legislative or regulatory change, and in the event that there is I will be moving forward
expediently to ensure that those changes are made."

Regional coroner Bruce Chamberlayne said Dumstrey-Soos was taken about 40 kilometres to hospital
in 100 Mile House after the attack but couldn't be revived.

Chamberlayne said witnesses would be interviewed but it would be up to the investigating coroner to
decide whether any of the kids would be involved.

"The youngsters, of course, would be very, very disturbed and traumatized by the event so we would
proceed very, very carefully in talking with the children."

The farm where Dumstrey-Soos was attacked is called Siberian Magic. Carlton puts on exotic animal
and magic shows there as well as selling services such as photos with the big cats.

RCMP said all the animals remained secured on the premises, about 40 kilometres east of 100 Mile
House. Among the animals at the farm are three tigers, a lion and a lemur.

Siberian Magic's website invites people to visit the Bridge Lake, B.C., facility to experience "the
wonderful worlds of magic and exotic animals."

"Visit our animals up close and personal. Capture the memories and have your photo taken with our
amazing Siberian tiger, Kisa, or our African lion, Sarmoti, as well as many other wonderful animals."

The site claims the company educates people about exotic animals in a "safe and enjoyable way."

But Marcie Moriarty, general manager of cruelty investigations for the SPCA, said the facility is a
"public safety catastrophe."

"The tigers are being kept in 12-by-12-foot chain-link enclosures with a mere padlock on the
enclosure. The animal owner had admitted to walking the tigers, his kids feed them.

"This could all have been avoided with provincial legislation that bans the keeping of exotics by
private citizens."

She said Carlton has been investigated by the SPCA since November 2005 when he moved his tigers
to the 100 Mile House area.

After notifying regional authorities about their concerns, the SPCA tried for months to seize the
animals but there wasn't any room at any facility to take the exotic animals, Moriarty said.

"We contacted the Calgary Zoo to see if they had space and the sad fact is we came up with
absolutely no way to seize and move the tigers so we were stuck with simply making orders and
recommendations," Moriarty said.

She said the SPCA provided an order to Carlton setting out the Canadian Association of Zoos and Aquariums standards for keeping the animals.

"The use of exotic animals in entertainment is simply playing with fire," Moriarty said.

Peter Fricker, a spokesman for the Vancouver Humane Society, said the group visited Carlton's company last year because of concerns about the animals' small enclosures.

In a Dec. 1, 2006 letter and DVD about the facilities to the local manager of conservation officer service, the society also raised alarm bells about public safety.

"There is not adequate fencing to protect the public from these wild and potentially dangerous animals," said the letter that was copied to Environment Minister Barry Penner.

"As well, the animals are being taken into public places including schools and malls in which the public, including small children, is encouraged to not only get in close proximity but also to engage in touching and other activities," the letter continued.

"This, in our opinion, is a disaster waiting to happen."

The Environment Ministry has not responded to the letter, Fricker said.

Erin Kincaid, event manager for the Bearfoot Bistro in Whistler, B.C., said the restaurant had considered having one of the tigers at an annual masquerade event in November 2005.

But there was such an outcry from the community and animal-rights groups that the restaurant quickly decided to not have a tiger at its circus-themed show that year.

"We were just unfamiliar with the fact that there were so many people that felt so strongly against it," Kincaid said.

Kincaid said she felt sick when told about a tiger mauling a woman to death.

"More than anything my heart goes out to the tiger. I really hope that the tiger doesn't end up having to pay for this because this is not the tiger's fault at all. I truly believe that it's how they keep them."

Leon Dumstrey-Soos
33 Banyay, Kitimat, BC V8C 2P5
Phone: 632-6755 / 632-1304

February 6, 2008

Andrew Yang

CBC/Early Edition Vancouver B.C.

Hi Andrew.

Re: ICBC Harassment & Victimization of Deceased

This is the follow up to our conversation on Friday, February 1, 2008 in regards to the matter of ICBC's harassment and victimization of y Deceased daughter Tania, her children, sister and myself.

Right after the death of my daughter, I informed ICBC at the office in Kitimat, of the fact, May 11, 2007, as well as Scotiabank and the Royal Bank in 100 Mile House to freeze all accounts as required by law. When I arrived in 100 Mile House, on the advise of my lawyer, I asked Mr. K. Carlton (my deceased daughter's boyfriend at the time) to surrender her vehicles into storage. I chose the local Ford dealer, and to give me the registrations an license plates. Mr. Carlton was not co-operative.

When I, as closest living relative (until court process is completed) asked ICBC to cancel the insurance, they refused, as I was not able to surrender the license plates. In fact, they continued insurance because of the monthly payment plan arranged prior to Tania's death, and allowed driving privileges to her boyfriend in spite of the owner being deceased, the bank account being frozen and the estate taking over the handling of the assets. In fact, through this action, ICBC put in jeopardy public safety and the estate's property and continued with further victimization of my family.

In the past nine months Estate Lawyers (Wozney & Co. in Kitimat) and myself have tried to contact someone above the regular bureaucrats in customer service/collections of ICBC – without success and always the same answer. No plates, no cancellation.

I am enclosing a copy of the one last letter from ICBC, which to me, as the father of the deceased daughter, is extremely offensive, insensitive and a demonstration of the incompetence of ICBC.

ICBC in their own right have allowed the usage of a deceased person's property, possible damage and loss of value of the same and endangering public safety as the owner had no more control and the estate was refused their cooperation and protection. Scandalous!

How can ICBC operate so under the Ministry of Public Safety when their action/policies undermine PUBLIC SAFETY that ICBC represents?? There is something terribly wrong. Their letter demonstrates one thing only – to collect premiums from the deceased person and her heirs (children) regardless and unscrupulously. This is revolting!!

Thank you,

Leon Dumstrey-Soos

Ps:As I told you yesterday (Feb 5/08),for some miraculous reason ICBC offered to NIL this account.When I asked for the written apology from ICBC,individual could not give one as the authorization on the subject came from higher up without offering any apology to my family.that they have harassed for nine month..Shame!Shame for their lack of civilized ethics.

Coppy to Minister of public safety

Robin Austin- MLA Skeena-

Chrm. Of ICBC

Leo_ _OS

From: "Leon Dumstrey-Soos" <gososo@telus.net>
To:
Sent: April 9, 2008 2:51 PM
ICBC /Delphia Johnstone Your letter from March 20/08

Dear Madam,

I do sincerely like to thank you on your sympathy expressed in re my daughters Death.Which occurred on May 10/07.

Further to your letter,I am deeply disappointed and very concerned :

That,ICBC did not find necessary to apologize

That,You,ICBC failed - deliberately in my opinion-to address the concerns in my letter.

That,Yours and ICBC.s lack of understanding that the DEAD PERSON can not communicate, accept the fact in an INTELLIGENT way,leaves me speechless.

That,You,ICBC failed to address the INTEGRITY of your customer,MY DAUGHTER,Yours,ICBC integrity.You addressed as paramount,I strongly reject this attitude.Does anyone in the ICBC cares to take dictionary and read the meaning of the word?I am an immigrant and English is my second language, never the less I made an effort to find the definition of the same: INTEGRITY-Behaviour in accordance with strict code of values;moral,honesty..-.

That,ICBCs "INTERNAL WORKFLOW ISSUES" -as a BUSINESS- can not be put on to the CUSTOMER as a BURDEN or an ISSUE. (Just as this a case is going on for almost a year without any significant changes,your letter and add to it THE RECENT SCANDAL in ICBC does not assure me in improvements and my confidence in Institution of ICBC).In recent years,in how many similar cases have ICBC served the public as incompetently ?

That,You, ICBC failed to understand the reason for me paying the insurance on O82JLJ! Simply ,I did it out of the my respect -INTEGRITY-to the DECEASED who was totally and insensitively victimized by the ICBC.Culture,where I was born respect their dead!. Where I asked for help and assistance you denied me! Interestingly,ICBC "Payment Plan Default Invoice",defines exactly what you can/could do,or could have done,second line:"Seize your vehicle plates.CANCEL YOUR INSURANCE etc.."!! Does any one in ICBC realize how much -in case of my family and who knows how many others-ignorance,arrogance,incompetence and victimization may have been eliminated by acting upon- CLEARLY-on the rules of policy that ICBC has written for themselves in the first place.

Sadly,ICBC with the Ministry that Governs it- as a public Institutions that

09/04/2008

222

govern and are responsible for the PUBLIC SAFETY ON OUR ROADS-has failed and
has deteriorated to the point of THE SCANDAL. In my opinion ICBC
MONOPOLY protected by the poor POLITICAL CLOAK, completely lost its
INTEGRITY in serving the public.
Thank you.

Leon Dumstre-SooS
33 Banyay Str
Kitimat BC V8C 2P5
250-632-6755

--
No virus found in this incoming message.
Checked by AVG.
Version: 7.5.519 / Virus Database: 269.22.10/1367 - Release Date: 09/04/2008 7:10 AM

09/04/2008

ICBC   building trust. driving confidence.

March 20, 2008

Mr. Leon Dumstrey-Soos
33 Banyay Avenue
Kitimat BC, V8C 2P5

Dear Mr. Dumstrey-Soos:

RE: Ford F250 pick-up truck, plate 4585KR
       Ford Explorer, plate 082JLJ

I am responding to your letter received February 6, 2008, addressed to Mr. Andrew
Yang at CBC Early Edition, and copied to the Insurance Corporation of British
Columbia (ICBC). I apologize for the delay in my response.

I extend my deepest condolences for the loss of your daughter. I appreciate that it
has been a difficult time for you and your family.

With respect to your daughter's two vehicle policies, they could not be cancelled
without return of the licence plates. Each ICBC insurance policy corresponds with a
particular licence plate number and the plates must be turned in to cancel the
insurance. This is to protect the integrity of our insurance system and maintain the
very low rate of uninsured drivers in this province. A licence plate with an
unexpired sticker is counted on to carry Basic compulsory insurance, including Third
Party Legal Liability coverage. We would not want to see a situation where
insurance is cancelled without the driver's knowledge while the driver continues to
operate the vehicle with the licence plates and a current sticker.

Both of your daughter's policies were on a monthly payment plan. When the
payments stopped, due to an internal workflow issue, the status for one of the
policies was not updated. When you were initially contacted, it was about the Ford
Explorer, policy 082JLJ, only. You paid the outstanding amount in July of 2007.

There was a delay in updating the payment plan status of the policy for the pick-up
truck, plate 4585KR, and you were not notified of its status until January of 2008.
The delay in notifying you of the status of this policy's payment plan was
recognized and the amount outstanding was written off at that time.

/2

151 West Esplanade | North Vancouver | British Columbia | V7M 3H9

ATTN: MR.
ANDREW YANG
EARLY EDITION

BRITISH
COLUMBIA

February 21, 2008

NOV 28 '21
- FEB 21
3 MOS
TO REF-

Mr. Leon Dumstrey-Soos
33 Banyay Street
Kitimat BC V8C 2P5

Dear Mr. Dumstrey-Soos:

I am responding to your November 28, 2007 letter regarding the regulation of exotic animals. I would like to convey my sincere condolences on the tragic loss of your daughter. I also would like to apologize for the delay in my reply.

At this time, there is no federal or provincial licensing component to own exotic animals; however, I understand the Ministry of Environment is considering making changes to the *Wildlife Act*. As such, I have taken the liberty of forwarding a copy of your letter to the Honourable Barry Penner, Minister of Environment, for his consideration.

The BC SPCA has posted a Submission to the BC *Wildlife Act* Review Project on their website: http://spca.bc.ca/WildlifeAct/SubmissionPackage/BC%20SPCA_Wildlife%20Act_Executive%20%20Summary.pdf.

An executive summary of their recommendations can also be viewed by visiting the following website address: http://spca.bc.ca/WildlifeAct/SubmissionPackage/BC%20SPCA_Wildlife%20%20Act_Submission.pdf.

Tigers and most exotic animals are on the Convention on International Trade in Endangered Species (CITES) lists and trade is restricted internationally; however, once the animals are in the country there is no legislation governing the keeping of these animals. Some municipal governments may enact legislation regarding the keeping of exotic animals, but they are few and far between and in my experience lack any significant enforcement.

...../2

Ministry of
Public Safety
and Solicitor General

Office of the Minister

Mailing Address:
PO Box 9053 Stn Prov Govt
Victoria BC V8W 9E2

Mr. Leon Dumstrey-Soos
Page 2

As I am sure you are aware, the BC SPCA will investigate any allegations of cruelty to animals and, where founded, will forward briefs to Crown Counsel. In those situations where there are concerns for public safety, either police and/or bylaw enforcement are advised, all of which I understand was done in this particular case.

I appreciate that you have taken the time to share your views with me.

Yours truly,

John Les
Solicitor General

pc: The Honourable Gordon Campbell
       The Honourable Barry Penner
       The Honourable Wally Oppal
       The Honourable Pat Bell
       His Worship Scott Nelson
       Ms. Maureen Pinkney
       Ms. Laura Dewar
       Ms. Marcie Moriarty

This is the part of my life that I completely break up writing about. Because of that I am enclosing all the important correspondence pertaining to the subject. For the past four hours I have been trying to complete this page. Emotions are immense and uncontrollable. I just sit, stunned and staring at what I wrote with tears pouring out of my eyes.

I am petrified to think what will happen when it's time to write about the demise of my angel child Vesna.

Upon my arrival at 100 Mile House, there was a gathering of friends and relatives—some sixty people—interviews with the RCMP—my officer was Chris Manseau—and a meeting with the Coroner, Laura D. What a lady, and what support I got from her and all present. I went to check on Tania's children and then on to the funeral home.

I stopped at the condo where the children were. Adrienne was there with the children of Tania's new man, who claimed that she was his fiancé. Media was everywhere. I asked them not to bother me. As I was standing there—there were some strange characters around—a young man approached me, saying, "I am Kim; I am sorry." I thanked him and asked him if he could tell me what happened, so we went to the side of the condo to talk. I also asked him to surrender the keys and registration for the two vehicles, as he was not the registered owner, so we went to the ICBC office. A person there told us that he had the right to drive the cars. For the second time, I pointed out to her that Tania was dead, but she declined to comment, and accordingly Kim refused to surrender the vehicles.

And this is where a two-year battle with this useless institution began. I'd like to thank Amanda, the manager of Envision Insurance in Kitimat. My letters to that invisible bureaucrat are enclosed. ICBC would not cancel the insurance unless the plates were surrendered. How does a dead person return something? I considered the vehicles stolen. It took over a year for ICBC to cooperate after I contacted ICBC (see enclosed letters).

The state of another vehicle that was financed by the Bank of Nova Scotia was swiftly resolved. I will never be able to express enough appreciation to the Bank of Nova Scotia for their compassion and charitable deed. Thank you!

The Regional District of 100 Mile House, the Chair and members that served at the time, committed an unforgivable act of total irresponsibility by public servants in not paying serious attention to the provincial SPCA two years prior to this grisly occurrence, who said that the Exotic Animal Zoo's shelters in Green Lake were "a disaster in waiting." If they changed the building code so that all the cages were to be fastened to a solid surface—wood or concrete—three readings later (three months) they would have a bylaw in place and could enforce it. Perhaps Tania would live today. They failed in their duty!

On the day of the reception there were three groups (in my opinion hostile to each other, particularly past and present boyfriends). The atmosphere was pretty charged, so I asked the RCMP detachment for assistance. They were more than forthcoming.

In the end, I bailed one of her vehicles out from the local dealer. Her daughter decided to come with us (Vesna was there with her husband Jason). I drove home to Kitimat with Tania's ashes with me on the front seat, and we had a long conversation. For the first time, my daughter was the one listening...

I decided to take over the executorship of her estate. It was a process that lasted for two years. In the meantime, I looked after the house and the rentals. Tania's daughter ended up with friends as her caretakers, and I had very little contact.

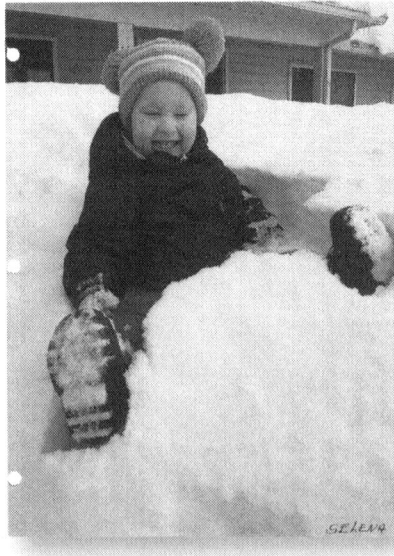

SELENA

Through all this time, Steven and his family were behind me. Steven promised to be with me when the time came to put Tania to rest.

Tania had desired to be buried next to her mom, who was put to rest in Penticton. There was only one plot left which my mother-in-law has given to me, and now I had given it my daughter. Off we went to Penticton where the service was arranged.

Her sister and daughter declined to come along. I was deeply hurt, and I cried all the way. At the cemetery in Penticton I could not let go of Tania's urn. I was trying to place her into her eternal resting place. I was numb, frozen, without emotions and tears. Now as I write this, all I feel is what should have happened then. I am in such pain and tears are pouring out of me. Oh my god, I am hurting so badly, please help me to conclude this. I think this is the hardest thing, to put the dead body of your child into the grave. No one will ever understand it unless you experience the nightmare yourself. Thirty-three years old, beautiful, smart and dead.

Adrienne graduated. I made a great effort in trying to get her into a college or university that she agreed on. I negotiated for her financing for the duration of her studies. I also had a scholarship that I had been paying into since she was seven—a good chunk of money. I also had her mother's car repaired, so she was perfectly set up. She left for Thompson University. At Christmas she came back. I asked her when she was going back. "No, I am not going, I fell in love." My heart shrank. I left, and we did not have contact for about three years. One day, surprise, a letter came from her to which I replied with a phone call, where I was told that an apology goes both ways. I said OK. Communication and peace were established. She was married, got pregnant and gave birth to a beautiful baby, Selena.

A few days ago, she phoned and told me that her marriage is over—oh my god, I thought. There was conversation for a while which lead nowhere.

Leon Dumstrey-Soos

From:	"Richard Foster" <rfoster@oxfordscientificfilms.tv>
To:	<goscoso@telus.net>
Sent:	July 8, 2010 9:37 AM
Subject:	Oxford Scientific Films

Dear Leon,

Thank you kindly for your time on the phone earlier today; I greatly appreciate you speaking to me when I contacted you so out of the blue. We would really like the opportunity to tell Tanya's story to raise awareness of the lax animal control laws and the danger these animals present even to those confident in handling them.

The series we are making for Discovery Animal Planet is called 'Fatal Attractions' and it is about human-animal relations, what drives people to keep such animals as pets and where the boundaries can become blurred – putting owners, friends and the public at risk. We are not intending to sensationalise any part of Tanya's story or focus solely upon the attack. We are also, as I said before, very interested in getting to know Tanya's personality and character and the spirited nature you described so lovingly.

You are very welcome to visit our own company website to view some of the excellent programmes we have made in the past (www.oxfordscientificfilms.tv) and I would particularly like to point you in the direction of our Bafta and Emmy-award winning film 'Africa's Witch Children' which highlighted the plight of many Nigerian children branded as Witches and outcast from their homes and communities.

My Director would like to speak with you in the coming weeks and, if it is still alright with you, will call one morning about the same time as today to explain what they hope to achieve with this film and how Tanya's story and your views will fit into the piece. I understand your anger and frustration with the system that has let you and your family down and I will be speaking to some of the officials such as Barry Penner to ask them why they acted so slowly in this instance.

Please don't hesitate to contact me should you have any questions regarding the series or any of the above – my details are outlined below.

Thank you once again for your time and honesty,

Take Care,

Richard
Richard Foster
Oxford Scientific Films
47 Marylebone Lane
London W1U 2NT

T: +44(0)20 7317 1356
F: +44(0)20 7317 1331
M: +44(0)7736 323 344
www.oxfordscientificfilms.tv

Oxford Scientific Films Limited - Registered in England & Wales No. 6777063 Registered Office: 4 new Burer Square, London W1U 2NT

Disclaimer: This email may be confidential and/or privileged. If you are not the intended recipient of this email, you must not disclose or use the information contained in it. Please notify the sender and delete this document if you have received it in error. We do not guarantee this email is error or virus free. If this is a commercial electronic message under the Spam Act, you can unsubscribe by return email to the sender with "unsubscribe" in the subject line.

children branded as Witches and outcast from their homes and communities.

My Director would like to speak with you in the coming weeks and, if it is still alright with you, will call one morning about the same time as today to explain what they hope to achieve with this film and how Tanya's story and your views will fit into the piece. I understand your anger and frustration with the system that has let you and your family down and I will be speaking to some of the officials such as Barry Penner to ask them why they acted so slowly in this instance.

Please don't hesitate to contact me should you have any questions regarding the series or any of the above – my details are outlined below.

Thank you once again for your time and honesty,

Take Care,

Richard
Richard Foster
Oxford Scientific Films
47 Marylebone Lane
London W1U 2NT

T: +44(0)20 7317 1356
F: +44(0)20 7317 1331
M: +44(0)7736 323 344
www.oxfordscientificfilms.tv

Oxford Scientific Films Limited - Registered in England & Wales No. 6777063 Registered Office: 4 new Burer Square, London W1U 2NT

Disclaimer: This email may be confidential and/or privileged. If you are not the intended recipient of this email, you must not disclose or use the information contained in it. Please notify the sender and delete this document if you have received it in error. We do not guarantee this email is error or virus free. If this is a commercial electronic message under the Spam Act, you can unsubscribe by return email to the sender with "unsubscribe" in the subject line.

Internal Virus Database is out-of-date.
Checked by AVG.
Version: 7.5.560 / Virus Database: 270.12.26/2116 - Release Date: 15/05/2009 6:16 AM

My efforts then turned towards the provincial government to change legislation on the housing of exotic animals. By joining forces with the BCSPCA and the CBC, and Environment Minister Hon. Barry Penner, an amendment was made to the wildlife act by the minister in April 2008.

Then in July 2008, a surprise arrived in the form of a phone call from Oxford Scientific Films, asking about doing a documentary on Tania's tragedy. An agreement was made, and the film crew arrived under the leadership of Miss Anna Thomson, the project's director, in the fall of 2008. It is a half-hour documentary, and it took a week to complete the project with Vesna and me as major participants. See photos; what a bunch of people.

LEON DUMSTREY-SOOS

Leon Dumstrey-Soos

From: "Leon Dumstrey-Soos" <gososo@telus.net>
To: <news@pgcitizen.ca>
Cc: <gososo@telus.net>
Sent: April 6, 2008 12:15 PM
Subject: Death of my daughter Tania Dumstrey-SooS article by Kathy Travers March 31/08

To the Editor.
Dear sir,
First I would like to thank Ms. Travers and BCSPCA in their efforts on the
subject.Also this is my first attempt and my family to brake the tormenting
silence to the public and believe me is not an easy task.
I am 76 years old immigrant,56 years ago I came here to rebuild my
life,build my dream my family and to escape from the wars,oppression and
injustice.I was embraced into my new homeland with the trust to
authorities.Suddenly my dream , dream of my grandchildren,and my family is
shuttered,as well as that trust for the Authorities,Life of my
family -particularly of Tania's two children- her sisters and mine, has been
severely interrupted,as we PAID THE PRICE IN LIFE of my family member for
the ignorance,arrogance and incompetence of those Authorities that we
trusted in.WE have been victimized!
I have no words to express the loss,pain and emotional anguish that my
family suffered over this tragedy.My daughters two children have been
traumatized and will be life long VICTIMS of this grizzly and senseless
occurrence.Particularly my six year grandson,who spent last moments with his
mother,while tying -in vein-to pull her away from her horrible demise,
watching her being literally eaten alive.... I know ,and I understand this,
as it reminds me of the similar occurrence in my life in WWII where my
brother and I, as a young boys-9 and 10-tried to prevent the rape of our
mother by the group of the invading soldiers... we were severely
beaten....one never forgets ,NEVER!

CROWNS decline to proceed in the Court with the submissions of BCSPCA and
the Police , despite the fact that the HAZARD has been established, is
unbelievable!
This is not acceptable in CIVILIZED SOCIETY!We can not continue to have
dangerous animals -"EXOTIC" wild or "WILD"- in less secure environment.Do we
need another fatality to prove the point?Do we need more children to be
traumatized?What is the benefit of maintaining the status quo?What other
than lethargy is preventing more then specific
legislation accompanied by severe penalties?Why is the PROVINCIAL CORONERS
OFFICE silent?Why is there no "INQUEST"?Why does THE LAW OF THE LAND not
offer the COURTESY to my family?

We have FAILURE OF JUSTICE here!

LET US NOT FORGET,yes ,there was not an Provincial Legislation in place
Yet the FACT IS, that nothing in the world PREVENTED LOCAL GOVERNMENT-be
that Municipal or REGIONAL to implement TIMELY AND RESPONSIBLY LOCAL.

06/04/2008

230

LEGISLATION that may have-as BISCAY indicated-prevented this tragedy.

In closing,again,I applaud to BCSPCA and their supporters in their valiant effort on the issue,however on behave of my family and myself I condemn and hold responsible all those that through their ignorance and incompetence have collectively contributed to our immense and immeasurable loss.

Please note that anyone wishing to make a contribution towards the education fund of my grandchildren forward it to:
Tania Dumstrey-SooS Children Education Fund BANKof NOVA SCOTIA 201 City Centre Kitimat BC V8C 1T6.
Thank you.

Leon Dumstrey-SooS
33 Banyay str.
Kitimat BC V8C 2P5
250-632-6755

--
No virus found in this incoming message.
Checked by AVG.
Version: 7.5.519 / Virus Database: 269.22.8/1362 - Release Date: 06/04/2008 11:12 AM

06/04/2008

BRITISH COLUMBIA
The Best Place on Earth

NEWS RELEASE

For Immediate Release
2008ENV0040-000548
April 16, 2008

Ministry of Environment

NEW PROTECTION FOR WILDLIFE AND THE PUBLIC

VICTORIA – The Environmental (Species and Public Protection) Amendment Act, introduced today by Environment Minister Barry Penner, makes amendments to the Wildlife Act and the Environmental Management Act (EMA).

The Wildlife Act, the legislative foundation for the interaction of people and wildlife in B.C. going back to the 1800s, has not had a major rewrite in 25 years. Since that time, new issues have arisen in the management of wildlife.

"These amendments to the Wildlife Act will allow us to fill in regulatory gaps for managing alien species, such as snakes and tigers, and help us protect both the public and native wildlife," said Penner. "We are also increasing maximum fines and penalties for poaching to up to $250,000 and two years in jail, sending a clear signal that we won't tolerate illegal hunting."

Amendments to the Wildlife Act will add new authority to regulate ownership of harmful alien species and double fines for wildlife violations. In addition, park rangers will be given greater enforcement power, while new provisions will govern the feeding of wildlife, hunting rules, and the guide outfitting industry.

"We're pleased that the amendments to the Wildlife Act include increased penalties for those who choose to flaunt the regulations," said Patti MacAhonic, executive director of the B.C. Wildlife Federation. "Stiffening the fines and penalties will act as a deterrent by sending a message to would-be offenders that there's a high price to pay for their misdeeds."

The legislation introduced today provides authority to address the possessing, breeding, release, trafficking, shipping or transportation of alien species such as tigers and venomous snakes and other species that are potentially hazardous to public safety or native wildlife. Under the amendments, the minister will be able to prohibit or regulate the keeping of listed alien species, making it an offence to acquire, possess or sell them, except as authorized in regulation. Up until now, the government of B.C. has not had authority to take such measures with respect to alien species because they do not fall under the definition of "wildlife" in the act.

"Giving the environment minister the authority under the act to regulate exotic species that could be considered a threat to public safety is a valuable tool," said Sara Dubois, manager of Wildlife Services for the B.C. Society for the Prevention of Cruelty to Animals. "It can be used by our officers, who have sometimes in the past found themselves at a loss in dealing with situations involving dangerous exotic animals."

Park rangers will have increased authority to monitor hunting and fishing activities to ensure those activities are being done in accordance with the Wildlife Act.

-more-

- 2 -

The legislation authorizes the environment minister to make regulations that restrict the feeding and attracting of certain wildlife in specific areas. This will make it easier for the ministry to deal with wildlife feeding problems where and when they arise, and to enhance public safety.

In addition to these amendments to the Wildlife Act, the Environmental (Species and Public Protection) Amendment Act also amends sections of the Environmental Management Act to clarify the scope of the government's authority concerning spill response and cost recovery, and to improve general regulation-making powers for results-based regulations and minister's codes of practice.

For all the details on this and other new legislation, please visit:
http://www.leg.bc.ca/38th4th/votes/progress-of-bills.htm

-30-

1 backgrounder(s) attached.

Media   Kate Thompson
contact: Media Manager
           Ministry of Environment
           250 953-4577

For more information on government services or to subscribe to the Province's news feeds using RSS, visit the Province's website at www.gov.bc.ca.

After Tania's documentary was completed, I returned to Kitimat. Golfing season soon ended. There were rumours of Alcan being taken over by RTA. After Tania's death, I did not pursue much work. Rumours of Alcan modernization became reality. The community started to bubble without significant benefit. A large camp was created. Many homes were bought on speculation. I sold my home and the remainder of our properties and moved into an apartment. I came to an age where a home to my liking would require quite a lot of expense.

Steven, Stephanie and family moved to Fort McMurray. I missed them tremendously. I became really close with Steven, not only as a friend and brother, but I consider him a son. They are all doing good; knowing Stephanie, it all depended on her determination, which she always had in abundance, to manage and keep the family intact. What wonderful boys they have, and how they progressed. An open-minded relationship. Reminds me of my uncle: ever-ready for consultation. Everything is transmitted in soft-spoken words. Sometimes they firm up, but they are effective, because of enormous care, love and trust. What a family they are! Parker and Declan are turning into young gentlemen. A pair of young giants in every aspect of life, and as male specimens. It is wonderful to watch them.

My partner has moved from Vancouver to Vancouver Island. His daughter Erin tragically passed away. Vesna divorced, and shortly after moved away to, of all places, 100 Mile House. Later I found out that she promised her sister she would look after her son. I could never understand my daughter's decision. I visited them several times, and I have noticed that she was cleverly manipulated. She refused to talk about it.

At home, I disposed of the rest of our properties and also sold my house and moved into an apartment building next door. Then there was a trip to Mexico, my favourite place on Earth. It was a bash.

When I returned it was still winter, and I met the doctor lady from Russia. We started to communicate, which turned into a seven-year long-distance relationship. A very nice person. She visited here several times. She was an ear specialist, and I tried to get her here as such, but unfortunately the system prevented her from being a contributing individual of high capacity to our society. The same thing happened some sixty years ago when schooling was rejected here in B.C.; I was told to start at grade six or seven.

In May, I went to a Shrine ceremonial in Edmonton, where I connected with my godchild, Nicole. It was a memorable visit. There was a beautiful parade, banquet and barbeque at Nicole's.

It is amazing how the mysterious hand that directs the traffic of our lives puts us together, sooner or later. This chapter I am dedicating to my very good friend Gus, an Austrian chef who has a beautiful restaurant in the nearby community of Terrace. Visually, we knew each other from when my family came for dinners there, or from when I used to stop for a beer in his pub some forty years ago.

In the early seventies, when we had the laundromat and dry-cleaning store, we leased a one-bedroom apartment right behind it on Broughton Street, on the seventeenth floor of a high-rise. My partner Art and I took turns looking after the store. In the two years of living there I never went into the rec room or swimming pool in the basement of the building, yet Art did and there he met the Gus. We talked about how strange that was.

I used to come to Terrace often for golf, still do. One day some fifteen years ago, I came to play and there was Gus, Mike and Freddy. I had not seen Mike for quite some time, not since our soccer games in Kitimat. Fred I knew through many golf tournaments, and Gus was naturally visible. That day they were a man short, so I asked to join them. And so, from that day on Gus and I grew closer and closer.

As time went on, I got to know his wife. Gus was also a tennis fanatic. He has a beautiful home with a tennis court in the backyard, with many participants on the weekends. His wife, Heli, an Australian lady, did not participate much due to fragile health. Yet Gus was a perpetual human machine: go, go, go all the time. I am the same way; that is where my nickname comes from: Gogo, which later became my Shrine clown name. I am twenty years Gus' senior.

There were/are many happy garden hours spent; Gus was an unbelievable host/chef. They had an older corgi by the name of Bunyip. As he aged, they got another young one, a girl, Fuji; what a special canine person she became. Heli was getting on for the worse. The phone rang one October three years ago; Gus was on the phone saying Heli died. It was 1:30 a.m.; I quickly got out of bed, and forty minutes later I was at his door. He was pleased, I could see. He was also shaken, telling me what happened. Heli was cremated, and next January Gus took her to Australia and put her to rest there. I babysat the home and the dogs.

For some time, my friend complained about his left knee, which had been repaired. When he came back from Australia in February, he recuperated after a busy fall and ongoing frustrations with those unwilling to contribute to society. We have the relationship of two human sponges absorbing the ongoing crap of each other's lives. Gus was very successful; he is not a giver-upper no matter how tough it gets. He has some other health issues. He gets upset with me because I care. He had a wonderful visit from his sister Hilde and her husband Werner. Wonderful people. Did a lot of golfing and had lots of fun; Gus as usual puts up a feast. What a marvel of a chef he is; you have to watch him in action. All that push, push had its consequences.

We are certainly looking forward to the new season. Gus is quite unhappy with his knee repair, because the doctor that did it kind of brushed it off, when Gus recently visited him with concerns over the knee, he said he will have to redo it, as therapy did not bring enough mobility to the joint. Apparently, a fatty deposit creates the discomfort which apparently should be simple to remove. Also, good to hear he put the business on the block. I wish him luck!

PRIME MINISTER AND PREMIERS OF CANADA

Recently the B.C. Government announced increases in minimum wage.

Also you have indicated that some changes in Social assistance will be forthcoming. ie. recipients will have to do some work and receive less.

When one closely observes the two new approaches of government to so called fairness and social justice, 'Social' is omitted as well as Justice.

Example: A single person with one dependant on social assistance receives approximately $900.00 per month (correct me if I'm wrong) plus other assistance money if needs are justified. Same person working on minimum wage, 160 hrs. per month, earns $1,120.00 but pays $141.00 for taxes, $22.59 for CPP, and $33.60 for UI, which leaves this person $922.81. This person will not receive any other assistance money as

the person on Social Assistance will. In reality it has to be paid all out of his own pocket, yet he or she is working and contributing to the society. Actually government is penalizing him/her for working for the same money or less than that of one on Social Assistance, who makes nocontributions.

If it is the government's intent to bring the two groups closer on the basis of dollars received then I believe it to be socially immoral - 'antisocialistic' period, particularly if the welfare recipients have

advantage by receiving more money than working minimum wage people.

It is sad to see that the bureaucrats who design and create these programs are totally distant from real social justice as well as politicians, except for their own pocket or agenda reasons. They will not deliberately design programs without taxing people. One cannot be a socialist without understanding it, and act and work like one; with compassion.

Had the government and its bureaucracy on the issue acted as a true and loyal socialist (if there are any left) then I believe one would probably propose and firmly declare: (if you want people to work rather than be on Social Assistance) Minimum wage workers should not be taxed for two years or longer (pay for only UI and CPP) in order that they may economically reinstate themselves and rebuild their lives.

This would, I believe, benefit the government as well as the economy in general. All that needs is political will, and social justice, not just in rhetoric but also in deed.

I strongly believe that this proposal would put many to work, improve their social and health standards, (as work always does), and greatly improve the economy and reduce health costs. Their tax contribution

will be collected by their spending for their livelihood needs.

As you see, Dear Minister, nothing else will work unless you give poor and disadvantaged people, that want to work, a real break and do not discriminate against them.

Thank you!

Yours truly

2

In the fall of 2014, my daughter Vesna bought a beautiful home in 100 Mile House overlooking Horse Lake. I went to visit and helped out with various things, and before I left, I suggested to her that it would be financially better for her if I moved there, and it would give me something to do. She was not interested at that point. I was surprised; early in the year 2015 my daughter had accepted my invitation to visit Croatia and meet family and relatives there. I was particularly keen to meet my two nieces, Tea, her husband Theo, and Mom and Dad. Maya and Sergio and son Marin in Pula; Eva and her husband Igor; children Sara and Rok;

Mom and Dad: Mario and Jana in Ljubljana, Slovenia, all of about the same age, thinking perhaps they may create a loving enjoyable future together. Branko, Mirjana, Natasha and Luka—friends in Zagreb. As a matter of fact, my hopes were fulfilled! We had a fantastic time; Vesna was ecstatic. They all made plans for a next-year visit that never came. Then two harsh tragedies struck. I was diagnosed with terminal cancer, and then a true horror, the news delivered by an super-nice RCMP officer, Todd Wiebe: Vesna has been murdered. Oh my god! I have to stop writing for a while; nothing but tears. Tomorrow is March 18, 2018, the memorial service for them. How I miss their call ... "How are you, my papa?" I miss my girls. There are no words for it

How it all began: At the end of May 2015, I returned from a holiday with my daughter Vesna. On June 15th, I joined my golf buddies in Terrace: Mike, Freddy and Gus. Walking off the 18th tee, I suddenly felt horrible pain in my left-side rib cage, which made me fall to my knees. My companions were very concerned. A short while after, I recovered, and they helped me up. I attributed the experience to being out of shape after not playing for about a month. A week later, I started to have slight discomfort in my right hip and lower back. There were sleepless nights due to the severe restlessness of my legs, a torturous experience. Again, I thought I was overdoing it in golf. By the end of July, I started to have more severe pains in different parts of my body; regular painkillers were prescribed but they did not register. I also noticed that I was losing weight rapidly (fifty-six lbs total in three and a half months.) The pains became regular, sudden, viciously excruciating. When an attack occurred, it would just throw me to the ground. I would be in agony for several minutes, and then it would stop. My friend Ed was attending me most of the time, taking me to the hospital for painkiller injections and back.

Dr. Kay solved the problem of my restless legs! Then, out of curiosity, I went on the Internet to research the subject, and I read reports from the Mayo Clinic: "indication of cancer." Oh Boy!

In February 2016, I was to move in with my daughter Vesna in 100 Mile House; I never told her what was going on. I slowly packed, with Ed helping.

The bone cancer pains I experienced—I could only think about middle-ages torture in inquisition chambers. Ed found me staring down from my balcony a few times. I said to him, "You know, Ed, I have no power to get over this. If I could jump over [I am on the third floor], with my luck I would probably just break an arm and hurt myself some more." We laughed!

I was at the point of committing suicide. Twice I could not find my gun clip. Looking down into the barrel of my rifle, it was not to be. Dr. Kay prescribed twelve-hour painkiller injections that worked like a charm. Then she made an urgent requisition for a scan. The result was not favourable. When I was done, the nurse came back with tears in her eyes (I knew the lady), saying, "I am so sorry, Leon," and walked out. I got up, and while I was dressing, I looked up at the screen; it looked like a lit cross. I said a short, silent prayer realizing what was happening. The question was, how long? So, I had to wait for the oncologist report, which came a few days later and the verdict was eight months to a year to live—a hell of a prospect!

The day when I was presented with the diagnosis, Dr. Kay, Dr. Lombard and Dr. Carstens were facing me with serious faces, and I thanked them for the report and said, "Of all the options I have—if any—there will be no chemotherapy or radiation administered to me."

They said in chorus, "We agree, these are not the options for you. What we are here for is to improve your quality of life in the best way possible." I thanked them.

While I was debating my options, Dr. Kay prescribed me hydro-morphine, starting with 3 mg twice daily and then upping to 6 mg in the morning plus 6 mg in the evening, 12 mg total. Boy, this was enough to kill a horse. It surely improved my quality of life and enabled me to play golf with no pain period, and to get a fantastic sleep. Everyone just shook their heads. Dr. Kay pleaded with me—God bless her—every day to take a gamble on hormone therapy. I said, "Doctor, what kind of gambling table is this that demands nothing less than your life as a stake, where my chances are practically zero."?

"It is something new in cancer treatment; you will be dealt from a new deck. Like in anything else, at least you have a chance," she said.

I questioned whether it was too late, and finally I gave in. Once I agreed to gamble on the hormone therapy, I went immediately to the Prince George Cancer Clinic in November 2015 to see Dr. Miller, where I was informed that my PSA (prostate-specific antigen) was 2700!

Dr. Miller said to me, "Mr. Dumstrey-Soos, no one lives with their PSA being so high."

"Well, Doctor, in that case, consider me passing through saying goodbye!" (I am an optimist and very humorous by nature.) After a lengthy conversation about my options, including castration, I said not a chance. Dr. Miller laughed! I was prescribed Bicalutamide tablets for the two weeks prior to my first hormone injection, which was to be on February 19, 2016, and will be repeated every three months thereafter for the rest of my life. Giving me all the instructions, she said, "Please stop at the registration on the way out and pick up your papers."

Before I thanked her—some super lady doctor she is—I asked her what hormone therapy consists of. "Synthetic female hormones," she answered...

"Oh boy," I said to her. "I will have a new girl or woman or who knows what else induced into my body by syringe and then contained within my body every three months." Oh my god, what is there yet to come? Having a woman living inside of you. On the positive side, no dates, no marriage, no expensive shoes, jewellery, vacations, cars, mortgage, etc. This is awesome; they will not be all over me, they will roam inside of me. Then I thought about getting one every three months. I will end up with an all-inclusive self-contained harem. We had a good laugh. Mama Mia, little did I know what was coming.

Stopping at the registration, a very attractive nurse asked me, "Mr. Dumstrey-Soos, I have the names of all your medications except the hormone one; do you know the name?"

Dr. Miller did not give me any names, so thinking quickly I looked up at her name tag and said with a serious face, "I think the name is Sarah." She was about to write it down, and at that moment everyone in her office burst into laughter, including Sarah.

Regardless of all that was happening, my condition started to improve and my appetite came back, as did my weight. My life went on less my only child. Two months later, I was free of morphine, and in May I was playing golf. Late Summer, I had an appointment with Dr. Miller and I had a scan, two years after the original one. I was horizontal; there was a scan operator, Dr. Miller and an oncologist. All I heard was, "Unbelievable ... miracle..." so I asked what was going on, and if I could have a look. There was not a single black spot on my skeleton.

Dr. Miller said smiling, "The only thing we cannot see is the soft spots. Wow, not a trace of anything, it is a miracle! I will see you in three months on Skype."

Today, almost three years from when it began in June 2015, I decided to write the true story of my miraculous survival from horrible terminal bone cancer. I am an eighty-six-year-old Kitimat resident and, before I continue, I would like to express my utmost thanks to my family physicians: Dr. Sabina Kay; who with gentle but firm persistence urged me not to give up and then took immediate action; her office staff, for always accommodating me and assisting me; the radiology department of Mills Memorial Hospital in Terrace, for their compassion while I had the scan; Dr. Lombard and Dr. Kay, who, when the radiologist report that stated multiple metastatic activities involving both axial and appendicular skeleton terminal—bone cancer—came, announcing eight months to a year to live, were open and direct, and when I asked for no radiation or chemo therapy they agreed. Thank you to the nursing staff of the Kitimat General Hospital, and the emergency department that administered my pain injections.

Once Dr. Sabina Kay convinced me to take a chance on hormone therapy—"It is a gamble and you have nothing to lose"—the gamble worked, I would say, 95%! There is science, and I had a chance. There is hope, and there are consequences.

Finally, a special thank you to Dr. Stacey Miller and the staff of the cancer clinic in Prince George, the Cancer Lodge staff, and the Cancer Car drivers (many are my brother Masons). I am now one and a half years past my second death sentence. Again, thanks to all, to the One above especially and to the rest of you here on Earth!

Today, March 18, 2018, was a memorial Mass for my family. Thank you to all those parishioners for the attention and kindness that they gave me.

In May and June 2018, I again went through serious check-ups after Dr. S Miller expressed concerns over possible transgressions on my inner components, because the hormone therapy booster has some shortfall effect on hormone therapy. On June 7, Dr. S. Miller and I had a Skype conference, and she explained the upcoming changes in medication to me: there will be two that will be administered by another oncology specialist who I would be referred to, so in tandem with Dr. S. Kay they ordered an urgent scan on my inner parts and another bone scan.

Scan on my inner engine parts reported clear—another miracle!

The bone scan showed:

"There is interval development of focal uptake at the left SI joint region in keeping with new metastatic lesion here. The remaining appearances are otherwise stable with no evidence of disease progression identified elsewhere. Stable scattered degenerative changes."

Wow, after thirty-six months, another battle won! I am anxiously awaiting a conference on July 5 with Dr. Richards, who has already contacted me.

In Loving Memory

Tania Babette Dumstrey-Soos
September 25, 1974 - May 10, 2007

Vesna Lea Dumstrey-Soos
March 7, 1978 - January 4, 2016

A memorial Mass will be held Sunday, March 18 at 10am at Christ the King Catholic Church in Kitimat.

In June 2012, horrible news came from Fort McMurray: Steven, my brother, my son, got hit by a truck driven by a drunk driver. He was unloading his golf clubs at the curb in front of his house. He was struck from behind and pinned against the rear bumper of his truck. Steven was most seriously injured. The lower part of his body was totally mangled, and he went into a coma. He ended up in an Edmonton hospital due to the severity of his external and internal injuries. The doctors induced the coma in order to do multiple surgeries. I am remembering our first conversation after coming out of coma; Steven's voice sounded strange, like someone coming back from the other side.

Oh boy, with a new job just started, now Steven is battling for his life in the process of buying a new home; furniture from Kitimat was in transit, kids had to get to school. Stephanie, Steven's wife, stepped into this nightmare with unmovable determination, poise and character, fearfully fighting for her husband's life and the preservation of family's future. Courage and sacrifice to preserve her love, her motherhood and honour and pride as a wife and mother and as a woman. You may only read about it in fiction, but this was something else, something above all imagination, a total war against death and the abyss. A war on many fronts, mental and physical. If there ever was a mother, woman and lady in shining armour and of a strong faith, she is the one sitting today in her rocking chair with a smile on her face. A veteran mother and wife who came out of this horrible nightmare stronger, as her husband recovered and her two boys progressed under her almost angelic protection. Her wise council was always available to them in a soft, firm voice. This is the short story of a tragedy that ended up as a miracle with many rewards.

I returned from the Prince George cancer clinic armed with a new medication called Bicalutamide. I took them for fourteen days. When I took the first pill, it had some side effects. I felt dizzy. No wonder, with all the medications I was taking! Or, the strong effect of the feminine gender, I think.

On the 8th of December 2015, I went back to see Dr. Miller. Strangely, I felt good. When asked how my sex life was, I answered "zero." There was satisfaction on Dr. Miller's face as she said, "Therapy has started to work, I think; we will wait a while longer for the gamble to pay off." Nice, doctor. While my manhood is assassinated by synthetic female hormones, medical science is celebrating. What a conditional trade: sex for life. The only good thing is that I am eighty-five and my desires are lesser; thank you Dr. Miller for dealing me a lucky hand. The gamble paid off. We had a good laugh!

By the 11th of December 2015, I was back home in Kitimat. My loss of fifty-six pounds was very noticeable; I was skinny. I am six feet tall.

One day I went to Terrace to see my good friend Gus, who had not seen me for a while, and when I arrived, he said, "Holy smoke, you are skinny. I was wondering what that noise was as you came into the house. Do you realize that you rattle while walking?" More laughter. I spent Christmas and New Year's with Gus.

On Christmas Eve, Vesna called: "Dad, could you come earlier?" I never told her what was going on with me.

"Sorry, sweetie, I am still packing." I will never know if I would have prevented her demise or if both of us would have ended up dead. Somehow, I feel it is my burden—who knows?

All my pains were gone. On the 8th of December, Dr. Kay administered the first hormone injection of Zoladex. Now the joy of my gamble was about to start. We also discussed the possible elimination of hydro-morphine.

On the second of January, I returned home. On the fourth of January, the horrible news came: the murder of my daughter Vesna. This is/was my 9/11.

My appetite was strong. I remember throughout all my life that no matter how sick I was I could eat. I spent most of my time next to the fridge. About fourteen days after the injection I was slowly experiencing a strange transformation. Changes I could not understand at first, so I made an appointment with Dr. Kay and I explained what was happening. With a mysterious expression on her face and a smile, she casually said, "Oh, nothing serious, you are having menopause." What, are you serious? "Nothing new, we women all go through it," Dr. Kay said casually, "and now you know what we women go through. But Doctor, I am not a woman! She just smiled. "Just wait, there will be more to come." And it sure did!

It took about six months for the female demon to settle. I ripped off a few of my PJs and pulled off the curtain rod trying to open the window. I walked through my balcony screen door. Boy, I was possessed by something vicious. It felt like bad renters were wrecking my place. They sure were, this time inside of me. Heat flashes made me putt a one-footer off the green. It totally destroyed my game, amongst other things. Maybe luck made me have menopause before I got menstruation. Who knows? There is a reason for everything, I think. The hair disappeared from my armpits, ears and nose. Other parts went from gray to black to blonde to red. My vision changes constantly. Just two weeks ago I got another new pair of glasses. Today, after the injection, I resorted to the oldest pair in my vision arsenal.

Nightmares, oh my. The other night I dreamed about being pregnant in the delivery room, spread eagle, a doctor holding the baby's head, screaming, "How will we get this one out?" At that moment I woke up in panic and totally wrecked my bedroom. After a while, I calmed down and sat on the bed, laughing hysterically and thinking, *What would have happened if the voice suddenly said push, push, push!?* I tell you...

Misplacing my coffee cup in the morning was the order of the day. Pouring orange juice not milk into my coffee, then putting them both into the fridge after running around my apartment naked wiping sweat off and looking for a long time for my coffee...

How many mornings in the past two years did I look into the bathroom mirror and say to that person, "Who the heck are you?" And no wonder, by now, after seven injections, almost half of my body has a new, soft, tender skin—good Lord, just like a teenage girl. What else will happen in the next seven?

There is also a phenomenal shrinkage you-know-where; it will definitely require circumcision. I better stop as it will drive you all nuts reading this stuff.

Menopause. One may think women suffer, and that may be true, but I can tell you one thing: these seven women living in me made sure that my suffering was ultimate. Simply take any symptom and multiply it by seven.

Just think, I am going to Europe on April 4, 2018. Today is March 19, and my seventh beauty has invaded my body. I said to Dr. Kay that this girl and the others will have a free ride to Croatia. I think these women are in the right time and place. Oh boy, how lucky can you get!

I read some statistics on terminal bone cancer and they were not very encouraging. 1% survives one year. Today I am entering my third year after the diagnosis in 2015; I am truly a miracle. So, I humbly answer in an unusual way when asked how I am. I always politely answer, "I feel that I am a girly-boy and I am shitty-well, thank you." And the saga goes on!

Leon Dumstrey-Soos

Subject: FW: Is there a Chance for Rational thinking?

From: Leon Dumstrey-Soos [mailto:gososo@telus.net]
Sent: January-09-14 6:33 PM
To: 'Leane Dalgleish'; 'letters@calgaryherald.com'; 'Premier Christy Clark'; 'pm@pm.gc.ca'
Subject: Is there a Chance for Rational thinking?

To the Editor

The other day I watched the news from Kamloops BC and there was Provincial "DEBT CLOCK" indicator showing 60+ Billions and ticking..I am sure it is quite bit more!
Shocking!
Add to this a continuous opposition of various kind to any/all the major projects(OIL-GAS-MINING-Site C, that are by now 10-20 years to late) ,that does not in my opinion take into consideration/consult 160.000 hungry children(recent report on CBC), poor, elderly, unemployed, where 20% 16-25 years of age are unemployable being not sufficiently educated and/or qualified (CBC in 2013), housing shortage, cost of living ,Land claims, health care, education, roads, bridges, transportation, grants, welfare and the list goes on! Wow!
Who and how will we pay for all this and when if -no projects no jobs no TAXES are there? Government itself indicated that most of the projects will be on line in 10 years from now! What between now and then? 100 Billion debt!! There will be not much left to tax!

There is a small country in the Western Europe by the name of NORWAY,1/3 of BC and almost same population and landscape. For most part since WWII it had/has Coalition Governments of Left or Right. They are quietly pumping oil- with all Parties WORKING TOGETHER- found in North Atlantic for past 40 years. They created "10 OIL COMMANDMENTS" by which they regulate their OIL success. Perhaps one of the best policies on the subject in the world. They have approved over 40 more exploration permits. All major players participating. They believe that Oil to them is an temporary WIND FALL therefore they have created a huge "OIL PENSION FUND" of ONE TRILLION DOLLARS for the future RAINY DAYS, paid by oil income. Unemployment is at 3% or less, average salary $6,000.00 plus. All Social Issues have High Priority! Yes it is easy when you can afford it!

The real secret of their success is in changing SOCIALIST POLICY from WEALTH REDISTRIBUTION to WEALTH CREATION and SHARING!
To note: FUND represents $150.000.00(Euro$) for every man, woman and child!! AND WE in BC are in the hole for $14,130.00 for every Citizen and going deeper every second!!

Perhaps is the time For British Columbians that all of us start to WORK TOGETHER, think rationally not emotionally and look at least 50 years ahead- our GRAND CHILDREN- as by that time most of the present "SELF" will not have flesh on their bones! Let us create some WEALTH in meantime!

Those that oppose and criticize issues they completely do not understand only undermine their own credibility!

Happy New Year!

Ps: Today is March 2018-03- Not too long ago Norway announce that heir NATONAL HERRTAGE FUND reached ONE TRILLION EURO$!!!..country with almost the same population as BC , but most Importantly they have politicians with the brains!

1

Here I am, three days after receiving my seventh girlfriend in synthetic hormone shape. I tell you, this one sure is driving me nuts while I try to sit behind my keyboard and type the tragedy of my life at the same time, to no avail.

I can feel a horrendous struggle coming up next. I buried most of my family. I have no words to say, I shed so many tears, I feel it will take a superhuman effort to finish this book. I am constantly crying in my heart for my angel child while attempting to write the last pages of this tragic life story. Dear Lord, have mercy on me, please...

No one will ever know or understand the grief and pain I go through every day, the agony I am in, the immense loss I suffered by these tragic and grisly occurrences that destroyed the lives of my two beautiful daughters, and seriously damaging my inner existence.

The sentence uttered by RCMP officer Todd Wiebe on January 4, 2016 on the phone was, "Mr. Dumstrey–Soos, your daughter Vesna has been murdered. My condolences." I thanked him, and the phone went dead. I somehow immediately knew who did it.

I think I went very angry. Taking 12 mg of hydro-morphine had some effect on my reaction; everything went into a spin, and when it stopped

I screamed and screamed in helpless rage. I remember sitting down, moaning like a badly wounded horse. I have heard the sound many times; it is awful to listen to.

Then the phone rang again and there was Vesna's boss, Debbie S., saying the same thing and offering me condolences. Then I realized it was true. A while later I phoned Rick, then Ed and Gus. Rick W. came pretty quick, who again as a friend gave me all the instructions I needed. Then the ugly, drawn-out, sad, emotional process started. I was in so much personal turmoil, anguish, anxiety and grief, and totally submerged by the enormous emotional weight of the compounded pain, that at times it became so unbearable that my friends became concerned for my safety.

The RCMP apprehended the murderer three days later in the Kamloops area. The trial has been postponed several times due to the murderer changing his lawyer, thus stalling the process. It will probably start in September or October 2018. It is an ordeal of enormous mental effort and stress to prepare myself, then nothing happens. Back off, wait and regroup—it is like climbing a slippery slope barefoot!

The murderer has been charged with first-degree murder! The murder was cruel, merciless and gruesome, inflicted for a long period of time—nine hours. I hope I live until the trial to see and hear the evidence and sentencing that will finally bring closure on this horrific tragedy and story.

I arranged the cremation with a local funeral home in 100 Mile House where Vesna's body was returned after the autopsy that was done in Kamloops. In the meantime, I think morphine kept me sane! I walked like I was in a trance; nothing made sense. Ed, and my Dr. Kay in particular, stayed close so that I did not do something stupid. I have not seen the coroner's report as promised. Oh boy!

RCMP victim services officer Leisl. K. urged me to make a victim's statement.

My friend Ed was returning from his trip to the Okanagan, so I asked him to pick up Vesna's remains in 100 Mile House and bring her to Kitimat for internment. At the same time, I arranged for a niche in the Kitimat cemetery mausoleum.

The service and internment was held on April 16, 2016 in Christ the King Church—my pride. Some five hundred people participated: relatives, friends and citizens. Thank you all!

I asked Vesna's boss Debbie if she knew someone to take the care of the house. She directed me to Mr. Wayne W., a real estate agent in 100 Mile House. What a gentleman, what a professional, what a man. I contacted him on the phone. What help he provided—priceless. I instructed him to change the locks, which he did. I recommended him later to the public trustee.

Neither Rick nor I could undertake the position of estate executor, so all was placed into the hands of a governmental institution called "public trustee," that provided me with the protocol of the institution. Yet the progress was slow and confusing and disorderly. I do not think that the person in charge of the public trustee's office could understand their own guidelines. It was an example of the utmost incompetence and created some serious breaches of privacy.

Between January 8 and August 1, I waited for the public trustee's contractor to clean the house. After packing up several boxes, they were transported to their warehouse in Burnaby. Later in July, the public trustee's office asked me what I would like to do with them. I asked them to please send them to me in Kitimat. I think the shipment arrived by mid-July, as I was informed at the same time that the house had been cleaned. I started to unpack the boxes, and upon checking the warehouse packing slip I noticed that two boxes belonged to someone else, some family from Vancouver. I was so upset I could not stop shaking. Ed took me to the Emergency. Dr. Kay arrived shortly and gave me a sedative to calm me down.

I informed the public trustee of the security and privacy breach, and the irresponsible disclosure of private property in their trust by their own warehouse, who in turn suggested I "destroy it if it does not belong to your daughter." Would you believe this? I was furious!

I asked the public trustee to let me in the house, so I could take care of my daughter's spiritual room. I drove to 100 Mile House and arrived on August 1. My good Dr. Kay ensured that I had the medications needed for all potential emergencies. Mr. Walker was my contact to let me into the house.

Then a shock after I entered the house: everything was as the investigators had left it—scattered, thrown around, not packed or cleaned as I was informed it would be by the public trustee's office. Scandalous! Offensive! In all fairness, when one who supposedly acts on behalf of the public trust creates so much confusion and unnecessary grief, then collects a fee for the service and all other things pertaining to the case from the estate of the deceased and accomplishes very little, their fee should be returned back to the estate.

As I walked through the house in a state of extreme silent rage, a few friends were present and helped me to pack Vesna's spiritual room. Debbie and Mayra, the RCMP victim service's officer, had worried looks on their faces, as they knew my health condition. While they were packing, I went downstairs to the laundry room—the murder scene location—and helplessly I kneeled and started to cry and pray. After a while I returned to finish packing. I thanked Debbie, Mayra and Wayne for the help and drove 1000 km strait to Kitimat. Fury gave me endurance. I was home at 7 a.m. the next day. All the way I was thinking about what to do next. Finally, I decided—after seeing the incompetence of the authorities—to return to 100 Mile House and finish the removal of all the Vesna's belongings and clean up.

I sent a letter to the public trustee informing them of my intention, and asked for access to the house, which was granted to me. I made a call to Vesna's friend Trevor in Williams Lake to organize a U-Haul and to help on the coming weekend. I arrived in Williams Lake on the 5th of August and stopped at Trevor's to confirm that the arrangement was in place. It was, so we made a date for the next day at 9 a.m. at Vesna's home. Then I drove to 100 Mile House and checked with Wayne for the key, and then checked into a motel.

At 9 a.m., we started with eight people. Trevor and some boys he brought were on time, and he brought a 24-foot U-Haul, and we filled it. There was an appointed representative from the public trustee who was supposed to take inventory of what we are taking. I asked the person how much she was getting paid for her effort. "$45 per hour," she said.

Oh! How easy estate money is spent by those not responsible. Everyone was listening. "Being that this is money from my daughter, I ask you to work with the others as I am taking full responsibility for everything taken. For that kind of the wage you can agree with me or leave, please," I said. She helped.

Then I divided the group and instructed them what to do and how. It was easy for me, one of my businesses in the past—we had three others—was a property management and complete building maintenance company. Being that this was the place of the gruesome murder, I did not want any of the contents, so I asked Trevor if he would like all the stuff—except what was granted to the individuals when they approached me—because I was sure Vesna would have wanted it that way. Trevor was surprised, I think, and accepted it. I was sure I was doing the right thing and I thanked him happily. By 3 p.m., we were finished.

I went straight home, thanking everyone. When I came back to Kitimat, I wrote a letter to the public trustee outlining what had transpired.

The estate process continued to drag its feet for about two years. The house was sold, and all liabilities satisfied. The final statement is not completed due to a technological breakdown, I was told. That was close to six months ago now...

I remember the words of President Reagan: "Your worst nightmare begins when there is a knock on your door, you open it and the persons standing outside say, 'We are here from government, we are here to help you.'" Right!

And it is a nerve-racking game waiting for the trial. I am dead tired and exhausted. Thank you all for reading this.

Appendix

In Loving Memory of

Vesna Lea Dumstrey-Soos

March 7, 1978 to January 4, 2016

Vesna was born in Kitimat, BC on March 7, 1978. She tragically died on January 4, 2016 in 100 Mile House, BC.

Vesna is survived by her father Leon Dumstrey-Soos, niece Adrienne Dumstrey-Soos of Kitimat, BC, nephew Nicholas Martel of 100 Mile House, related families Premate, Brecevich-Maretich, SooS of Croatia and Hungary; Rešetar and Sever of Slovenia; Andersons of Alberta; Sugimoto, Spanevello and Harrison of Vancouver Island, BC; Neiffer of Vancouver, BC; Striker's of Terrace, Vancouver and Qualicum Beach, BC; Henning's of Stuttgart Germany; the Germuths, Corinne Scott and J. Monaghan of Kitimat.

Dear friends Dr. Alevtina Larskaya of Stavropol, Russia; Misha and Marina Bocharow of Moscow, Russia; Sasha and Lena Bocharow of Surgut, Russia; Vladimir Bocharov of Stavropol, Russia; Mirjana Franjkovic and Branko Supe of Zagreb, Croatia.

A special thank you to Debbie Scott and colleagues of the Cedar Crest Society in 100 Mile House, where she was employed as a Child Development Consultant, and Margaret Warcup and colleagues at Kitimat Child Development Centre for their memorials, kindness and compassion demonstrated for Vesna and condolences offered to me.

My old friends Janice Newman, Ed and Tim Martin, Rick Wozney, Bill Hickman, Paul Brais, Chris Rigoni, Ken Miniffie, Bill and Sheila Eynon, Don and Sheila Reid, Barbara and Ken Campbell of Kitimat; Norm and Leonilda McRitchie and Olga Khayne of Vancouver.

Gus Gerdei, Lyle Harvey, Mike Brady, Fred Lewis and Jim Riding of Terrace, BC who stood by and gave/offered me support during an extreme trial in my life.

Thank you to the Nobles of the Gizeh Temple in Vancouver, BC, Companions of the Kalum Chapter Terrace, BC and all the Brethren of the Kitimat Lodge #169.

A service for Vesna will be held at a later date at Christ the King Church in Kitimat, of which timely notice will be posted.

Vesna will be immensely missed by many. May she rest in peace.

EXPERIENCES that which is called death, with NO EXCEPTION. YOU'VE all accepted that one a long time ago. SPIRIT, which is WHO WE REALLY ARE, or SOURCE, is ETERNAL. So what death MUST BE is a CHANGING of the PERSPECTIVE of that ETERNAL SPIRIT. If I AM standing in MY PHYSICAL BODY and AM CONSCIOUSLY CONNECTED to that ETERNAL SPIRIT, then I'M ETERNAL in NATURE and I NEED NOT EVER again FEAR any ENDEDNESS because, from that PERSPECTIVE I UNDERSTAND that there is NOT any of THAT!!!

ABRAHAM

Emailed from Vesna just before she died.

Leon Dumstrey-Soos

Subject: Victim Impact Statement -

Victim's name: Leon Dumstrey-Soos

Accused Person's name: Mike Martel

Police file number: 2016 E-19 100 Mile House B. C.

To the Honorable Court

Firstly, thank you for allowing me to present my Victim Impact Statement. The grizzly senseless murder of Vesna Dumstrey-Soos my daughter along with her pet dog affected me in so many ways.

As an 85 year old father, my daughter's wish for me was to spend my last years with her. We were planning my move from Kitimat, BC to 100 Mile House, BC for the end of February 2016. Then just before Christmas 2015 I was diagnosed with terminal bone cancer which in itself was devastating news for me and my daughter.

Then on January 4th 2016 I was informed by the RCMP of the tragic senseless murder of my daughter, which together with my health issue, was mentally and physically catastrophic for me.

I have no words to express the loss of my daughter or how after this tragedy to be a normal functioning person as a grandfather, great grandfather, friend or contributing citizen.

The loss of my daughter, by this senseless occurrence, has caused me immense pain, emotional anguish and the trauma, for the rest of my life.

My sleep through the night is constantly interrupted by the nightmares of this horrendous crime. I just sit up and cry and cry just as now while I am writing this. I cannot stop remembering or constantly thinking of this crime, it plays over and over in my mind, day and night. No matter what I do I start to cry, and this is emotionally draining and devastating and stop me from moving past and get on with my day.

I am emotionally drained most days as I go through them. I consider it having a good moment when I do not break into tears at some point and just simply cry.

My emotions are all over the map, from highs to ultimate lows. I am exhausted from these constant emotional changes and mood swings from happy to utter sadness and despair. Before the grizzly murder of my daughter I had a pretty good Idea where I was going in my life, I was emotionally balanced regardless of my health. I had a clear vision of my short future. Now these intense emotions bring constant uncertainty in my days and

1

fill my heart and soul with pain and despair. I am tired, very tired, from this mental torture every night before I go to sleep and every morning when I wake up, sitting on the edge of my bed as memories of this grizzly occurrence flood over me and I wonder how to start my day.

There is not enough time today or words to describe to you or the court how this senseless murder of my daughter has and continues to truly affect me emotionally.

It is difficult to put into words the true extent of the emotional damage that I continue to suffer and live with daily as a direct result of this senseless crime. I will never know the true extent of emotional damage that I have sustained and have to live with every moment for the rest of my life.

This is not the life I wanted for myself and my daughter Vesna a life that is filled with immense emotional pain and uncertainty caused by the senseless murder of my daughter.

This horrific heinous occurrence will leave deep and painful scars in me all my family members, relatives and our friends for all the time to come.

Thank you your Honour

Leon Dumstrey-Soos

Dear Leon

This poem came from an older Kitimat newspaper that was written

For Kitimat residents who have lost a child.

I hope it brings you peace and my prayers are with you.

"I'll lend you for a little time a child of mine," he said.
For you to love while she lives, and mourn for when she's
dead. It may be three or seven years, or maybe thirty-
seven, But will you, till I call her back, take care of her for
me? She'll bring her charms to gladden you, and shall her
stay be brief, You'll have her lovely memories as solace
for your grief. I cannot promise she will stay, since all
from Earth return, But there are lessons taught down
there I want this child to learn. I've looked the wide
world over, and in my search for teachers true, and from
the throngs that crowd life's lanes, I have selected you.
Now will you give her love, nor think the labour vain,
Nor hate me when I come to call to take her back again.
I fancied that I heard them say: "Dear Lord Thy Will Be
Done." For all the joy the child shall bring, the risk of
grief we'll run. We'll shelter her with tenderness, we'll
love her while we may, And for the happiness we've
known, forever grateful stay. But shall the angels call for
her, much sooner than we've planned, We'll brave the
bitter grief that comes, and try to understand.

Note tear smudges

Leon Dumstrey-Soos

From:	Leon Dumstrey-Soos [gososo@telus.net]
Sent:	August-01-16 2:47 PM
To:	'Read, Christine'
Cc:	'Wayne Walker'
Subject:	Estate of late Vesna Dumstrey-Soos File # 103590/5090775

Dear Ms. Reid

Just to bring you up to date. I have packed Vesna's Spiritual Room however emotions of my grieve had an immense effect on me, so I have not completed the intended task for other Items that I and my Granddaughter wanted. I have booked my flight for this coming weekend to complete this.

Sincerely

Leon Dumstrey-Soos

Leon Dumstrey-Soos

Subject:	FW: Estate of late Vesna Dumstrey-Soos File # 103590/5090775

From: Leon Dumstrey-Soos [mailto:gososo@telus.net]
Sent: August-08-16 9:49 PM
To: 'Read, Christine'
Subject: RE: Estate of late Vesna Dumstrey-Soos File # 103590/5090775

Dear Ms. Reid

This morning I arrived home and had some difficulty with my computer. So here we go:

The last weekend In 100 MH was probably most testing emotionally, physically and mentally for me and Vasna's Friends who helped in packing. Believe there were many tears shed in every room.

I arrived on Friday Aug 5th and was contacted by the Lady that you authorized to let me in to the house. Then I met with Mr. Walker and ask him as I was very tired and emotional not to meet her till next day-Sat. Aug 6 at 8.30 am at the house.

(Before that I asked Mr. Walker to arrange for the dumpster to be placed at the house. I also arranged for the U-Haul (20ft) , pick up and crew of 5 , besides myself, Vesna's close colleague from her office and your Rep. Total 8 people

I arrived after 8am on Aug 6th and your Lady Rep shortly after.. When we entered house she told that she has to record all Items to be taken. I said it is too late for this now as the people and the vehicle are available only for one day I took photos of every room and that should be sufficient . I am taking full responsibility.

Crew with U-Haul came at 9 am. We emptied the house by 3pm.

Only Items stayed there- my decision it is I believe better selling feature - fridge, stove dishwasher ,washer and dryer. Some Left over building material gas and wood stove in Garage . Garden tools in the shed.

Please note - I Donated :

To Vesna's Work Place number of pictures, children's books and plants that survived.

I donated to your Rep. For her children's group all water colors and Halloween costumes and stuff. Also I have given to her all household cleaning materials ,tools and Vac cleaner. And some lumber in the back of the house

As we made quite a mess I have instructed your Rep. Her company :

To clean the house throughout.

To wash rec. room and garage floor.

Her husband to touch up door jamb in bdrm. #2 and door in bdrm # 3

Two chips on stairwell wall

1

When the family photos, albums and jewellery were packed , on my visit to the house I found some photos left behind. Who were those people? What standards , qualifications and instructions they had/got and from whom.

When your warehouse in Burnaby send to me nine boxes of family photos, albums and jewellery, I discovered two boxes belonged to the family from Duncan Vancouver Island. When I pointed this out to Ms. Reid she questioned my ability to recognize my family belongings. What a insult!

I was in very unpleasant situation due to the fact that Ms. Reid committed serious error and compromised your/her office by breach of privacy and confidentiality.

I returned the boxes back to your Burnaby warehouse at my expense. To date Ms. Reid did not confirm receiving them .

I asked for copy of Court Order that confirms her to be Administrator to the above Estate. No answer!

I asked for the house to be listed . No answer?

There is evidence that she was bullying local contractor.

In closing: All the above is indicative of not very confident performance of Ms Reid . This Estate is not complicated to resolve so I ask you to resolve this situation as soon as possible and as I have lost confidence in Ms. Reid. Appoint new officer in her stead please if you think it will be necessary.

If I have inadvertently offended Ms Reid, I sincerely apologize, my only wish is to get closure on this issue so I can get out of this horrible nightmare.

Sincerely

Leon Dumstrey-Soos
#309-34 Banyay str.
Kitimat BC
V8C 2P7
Ph: 250 632 6755
e-m gososo#telus.net

Leon Dumstrey-Soos

From:	Leon Dumstrey-Soos [gososo@telus.net]
Sent:	July-18-16 10:24 PM
To:	'Read, Christine'
Subject:	Estate of Vesna Lea Dumstrey-SooS file#103590/5090775

Dear Madam,

Firstly thank you again for boxes with the photos etc. I apologize for the emotional phone call, unfortunately when the boxes arrived anything to do with my daughters is very hard on me.

In your last communication you inquired about my health, thank you The therapy for my terminal Cancer sometimes has strange effect. I have good and not so good days. I hope this matter with the estate will be soon over so I can distance myself from this nightmare as it has lot influence on my well being. Please help me!

Best Regards

Leon Dumstrey-Soos

From: Leon Dumstrey-Soos [mailto:gososo@telus.net]
Sent: July-20-16 10:32 PM
To: Read, Christine
Subject: Estate of late Vesna Dumstrey-Soos Re; Boxes send from your warehouse by Mr. Hurd

Dear Madam
Please note that after examining the contents of the boxes send, two of them did not contain anything related to our families. I have prepared boxes to be returned to your warehouse in Burnaby. Box 7 of 9 shipped #7767 0348 0890 and box of 9 shipped #7767 0348 1636.

Also I have been notified by Mr. Walker to remove items from the Vesna's Spirit Room. I will attend to this matter before this coming weekend.

Best Regards

Leon Dumstrey-Soos

Leon Dumstrey-Soos

To: Leon Dumstrey-Soos
Subject: RE: Estate of late Vesna Dumstrey-Soos Re; Boxes send from your warehouse by Mr. Hurd

From: Leon Dumstrey-Soos [mailto:gososo@telus.net]
Sent: July-21-16 11:35 AM
To: 'Read, Christine'
Subject: RE: Estate of late Vesna Dumstrey-Soos Re; Boxes send from your warehouse by Mr. Hurd

Dear Ms. Reid

Boxes in question are definitely not Vesna's, they contain some important memorabilia of Carter family. I will send them back at my expense.

Further I spoke today again to Mr. Walker and all is set for the next weekend as Mr. Martel is picking tools for his brother this weekend. Thank you

Leon

From: Read, Christine [mailto:CRead@Trustee.bc.ca]
Sent: July-21-16 7:26 AM
To: Leon Dumstrey-Soos
Subject: RE: Estate of late Vesna Dumstrey-Soos Re; Boxes send from your warehouse by Mr. Hurd

Mr. Dumstrey-Soos,

Please do not return these boxes. If you don't wish to have these items of Vesna's, we will simply dispose of them as they will not yield anything in auction. This would be an unnecessary added expense to the estate. Unless you are suggesting that these boxes were not Vesna's belongings?

I am glad that you are finally able to attend the residence and have Vesna's Spirit Room cleared out. Please note, if there was any other items (one's that you have mentioned to me before) that you wish to have we would ask that you pick those items up at that time. After you have left the residence the remainder of the house will be sent to auction and/or disposed as we prepare the house for listing.

We are still waiting for probate to be issued. I will notify you when this has been completed.

Christine Read | Estate Administrator
Estates and Personal Trust Department | Public Guardian and Trustee
700 – 808 West Hastings Street | Vancouver BC V6C 3L3
T: 604.660.0956 | F: 604.660-0964 | cread@trustee.bc.ca | www.trustee.bc.ca

1

Leon Dumstrey-Soos

From:	Leon Dumstrey-Soos [gososo@telus.net]
Sent:	July-21-16 12:07 PM
To:	'Read, Christine'
Subject:	RE: Estate of late Vesna Dumstrey-Soos Re: Boxes send from your warehouse by Mr. Hurd

Correction - the name is Clarke from Duncan BC, sorry for error. Leon

From: Read, Christine [mailto:CRead@Trustee.bc.ca]
Sent: July-21-16 7:26 AM
To: Leon Dumstrey-Soos
Subject: RE: Estate of late Vesna Dumstrey-Soos Re; Boxes send from your warehouse by Mr. Hurd

Mr. Dumstrey-Soos,

Please do not return these boxes. If you don't wish to have these items of Vesna's, we will simply dispose of them as they will not yield anything in auction. This would be an unnecessary added expense to the estate. Unless you are suggesting that these boxes were not Vesna's belongings?

I am glad that you are finally able to attend the residence and have Vesna's Spirit Room cleared out. Please note, if there was any other items (one's that you have mentioned to me before) that you wish to have we would ask that you pick those items up at that time. After you have left the residence the remainder of the house will be sent to auction and/or disposed as we prepare the house for listing.

We are still waiting for probate to be issued. I will notify you when this has been completed.

Christine Read | Estate Administrator
Estates and Personal Trust Department | Public Guardian and Trustee
700 – 808 West Hastings Street | Vancouver BC V6C 3L3
T: 604.660.0956 | F: 604.660.0964 | cread@trustee.bc.ca | www.trustee.bc.ca

From: Leon Dumstrey-Soos [mailto:gososo@telus.net]
Sent: July-20-16 10:32 PM
To: Read, Christine
Subject: Estate of late Vesna Dumstrey-Soos Re; Boxes send from your warehouse by Mr. Hurd

Dear Madam
Please note that after examining the contents of the boxes send, two of them did not contain anything related to our families. I have prepared boxes to be returned to your warehouse in Burnaby. Box 7 of 9 shipped #7767 0348 0890 and box of 9 shipped #7767 0348 1636.

Also I have been notified by Mr. Walker to remove items from the Vesna's Spirit Room. I will attend to this matter before this coming weekend.

Best Regards

Leon Dumstrey-Soos

From:	Leon Dumstrey-Soos [gososo@telus.net]
Sent:	August-10-16 8:17 PM
To:	'Read, Christine'
Cc:	'Wayne Walker'
Subject:	RE: Estate of late Vesna Dumstrey-Soos File # 103590/5090775

Dear Ms. Reid

It have been two excruciating weekends for all involved and I am somewhat relieved that we are done.

As of today house is empty cleaned and prepared for listing and I ask for your support in following:

That you issue an authorization for listing soon as possible for Mr. Wayne Walker Realtor/ Royal LaPage 100 Mile house BC

That due to the tragedy that occurred on the premises all proposals to be dealt with/at discretion of Mr. Walker.

That I ask to have final say in acceptance/rejection on any offer/proposal.

Best Regards

Leon Dumstrey-Soos

From: Read, Christine [mailto:CRead@Trustee.bc.ca]
Sent: August-05-16 8:08 AM
To: Leon Dumstrey-Soos
Cc: 'Wayne Walker'; Kwan, Isabel
Subject: RE: Estate of late Vesna Dumstrey Soos File # 103590/5090775

Hi Leon,

I am glad that you have had the opportunity to pack up Vesna's Spiritual Room. Please make sure that you have taken everything you are wanting from the house on this last visit (including the items that you have mentioned to me before, as I haven't had them packaged up). After you leave on this final visit the entire house will be cleared out in preparation for listing. I hope you have safe travels on this journey.

Christine Read | Estate Administrator
Estates and Personal Trust Department | Public Guardian and Trustee
700 – 808 West Hastings Street | Vancouver BC V6C 3L3
T: 604.660.0956 | F: 604.660.0964 | cread@trustee.bc.ca | www.trustee.bc.ca

From: Leon Dumstrey-Soos [mailto:gososo@telus.net]
Sent: August-01-16 2:47 PM
To: Read, Christine

Leon Dumstrey-Soos

To:	Ms. Aiila Viitanen Regional Manager Public Trustee BC
Cc:	Ms. C. Reid
Subject:	Estate of late Vesna Dumstrey-Soos File # 103590/5090775

Dear Madam

I am contacting you regarding my concerns how the estate of my murdered daughter has been conducted by Public Trustee Administrator Ms. C. Reid.

I am not pleased that the business of the my daughters estate has not been conducted in an transparent and *more* efficient fashion.

I have not received regular updates what Ms. Reid actions have been taken, accomplished and not accomplished. I believe I deserve this courtesy.

I am an 85 old father who prior to my daughter's death was diagnosed with terminal cancer. *Bone*

Unfortunately I lost two grown daughters to tragic death . I suffer immensely every moment every day in every aspect that occurs in their afterlife, which compounds and contributes more and more to my emotional and health stress.

In case of my older daughter Tania I was executor of her estate. There were two children and her Will. My Public Trustee Officer was lady by the name Ms. Nadine Valin.
Her guidance and support was exceptional. In her absence there was always a contact person.

Now with the estate of my murdered younger daughter Vesna due to my health I asked Public Trustee office to appoint the administrator. Which is Ms. C Reid. After 6 months situation is totally the opposite from my previous experience with Ms Valin. Have the Statutes and Regulations of Public Trustee Office changed so much?

Poor communication with the Ms Reid is just adding more emotional stress to my person. She has no right to treat me in such an arrogant manner.

It appears that in past six month Ms. Reid took power trip over my daughters grave. I am very concerned , angered, surprised and saddened by the lack of support and empathy as I have not unlimited time left to work/wait with Ms .Reid . With her lack of communication, good effort and compassion for my condition I am led to believe that she is stalling and incurring extra expenses to the estate.

I am concerned ,to date I never got any information what is/was going on . Why?

For example:

When I came to pack my Daughter's Spiritual room (6 mos. later) outside landscape was neglected and inside house was a mess.

The truck was missing/taken from garage. To date I do not know who took it and why? *By Ms Reid Orew.*

When the family photos, albums and jewellery were packed , on my visit to the house I found some photos left behind. Who were those people? What standards , qualifications and instructions they had/got and from whom.

1

when I printed also to McRew

When your warehouse in Burnaby send to me nine boxes of photos, albums and jewellery, I discovered two boxes belonged to the family from Duncan Vancouver Island. Ms Reid questioned my ability to recognize my family belongings. What a insult! I was in very unpleasant situation due to the fact that Ms. Reid committed serious error and compromised your/her office by breach of privacy and confidentiality.

I returned the boxes back to your Burnaby warehouse at my expense. To date Ms. Reid did not confirm receiving them .

I asked for copy of Court Order that confirms her to be Administrator to the above Estate. No answer!

I asked for the house to be listed . No answer?

There is evidence that she was bullying local contractor.

In closing: All the above is indicative of not very confident performance of Ms Reid . This Estate is not complicated to resolve so I ask you to resolve this situation as soon as possible and as I have lost confidence in Ms. Reid, appoint new officer in her stead please

If I have inadvertenly offended Ms Reid, I sincerely apologize, my only wish is to get clossure on this issue so i can get out of this horrible nightmare. *and ou with my life what I have left of*

Sincerely

Leon Dumstrey-Soos

THIS IS THE LETTER OF ACCUSERS BROTHER

Leon Dumstrey-Soos

From:	Rob Martel [rob.martel@telus.net]
Sent:	June-10-16 4.06 PM
To:	'Leon Dumstrey-Soos'
Subject:	message

Leon,

I just heard your message. Thanks so much for reaching out and thinking of us.

I was trying to make it up for a couple days to see mom/dad on monday, however with Ryans graduation barbeque next weekend I need to take care of house issues first. I talk to them everyday now, and they need help more than ever so its hard not to make it up. I will pass along your hello and well wishes.

I think we are all struggling in our various ways. We have been trying to balance giving him space and showing him boundaries/rules for moving on.
It sure has been testing at times. We know what he has gone through for his limited 15 years of his life has been traumatic to say the least and yet he grieves and knows there is nothing from that now, and is leaving him in a bad state of depression at times. We are doing what we can to get him out of the house. He works out and eats well. We kept one of the boats for now, and have gone out a few times, which he also seems to enjoy doing.
Other than some of Ryans lacrosse games and family/friend functions we have where he does participate, he holds close to himself.
We just had a deep conversation with him in regards to his attitude slipping again and trying to get him to move forward a bit again. It was very emotional for us all, and was the first time I've seen him break down like that. We are backing off now again, for a bit so everyone can catch their breath but are trying hard to 'correct' what has been a very bad pattern his last years lately.

Anyways, I just wanted to give you a quick update and as always feel free to call or write. I am going to try and lean on Bev and possibly Adrienne to perhaps help with some time with them too, to see if that helps at all. I am not letting him go back to 100 Mile to see his friends at this point as we have got past some of those habits I hope.

take care,

Rob
ps- I will think of you next sunday and hold a special thought/prayer for everyone too.

1

263

HER MAJESTY THE QUEEN

AGAINST

Michael Edward Martel

STATEMENT OF FACTS AND ADMISSIONS

PURSUANT to the provisions of Section 655 of the Criminal Code of Canada, MICHAEL EDWARD MARTEL and his counsel admit the following facts and make the following admissions for the purpose of dispensing with proof thereof:

1. Vesna Dumstrey-Soos ("Dumstrey-Soos") was a 37 year old woman residing at 6053 Norman Road, 100 Mile House, British Columbia (the "Norman House") on January 3, 2016.

2. Dumstrey-Soos and the accused Michael Martel ("Martel") had been in a common law relationship in 2015, residing together at the Norman House with Martel's son Nick Martel ("Nick"). Nick was Dumstrey-Soos' nephew.

3. In the latter part of 2015, the common law relationship ended and Martel and Nick moved to 6531 Valhalla Road, 100 Mile House, British Columbia (the "Valhalla House"), where they were residing together on January 3, 2016. The Valhalla House is less than one mile from the Norman House.

4. Dumstrey-Soos began a relationship with another man, Trevor Todorowich ("Todorowich") in December of 2015. Todorowich resided in Williams Lake, British Columbia at the time.

5. On or about December 19, 2015 Martel became aware that Dumstrey-Soos was seeing another man.

6. After spending time with Todorowich over Christmas and New Year's in Williams Lake, Dumstrey-Soos returned to the Norman House on January 2, 2016.

7. Martel was seen at the Norman House on January 3, 2016 at approximately 4:30 PM. Dumstrey-Soos and Martel were the only persons at the Norman House at the time and Dumstrey-Soos was observed to be alive and well. Martel was observed to be sober and upset after his visit with Dumstrey-Soos.

8. Martel attended the Valhalla House at approximately 5:00 PM on January 3 after visiting with Dumstrey-Soos, where he had dinner with Nick.

9. Martel returned to the Norman House sometime after 9:00 PM on January 3, 2016. Dumstrey-Soos was at home playing a video game with Todorowich (who was in Williams Lake) at the time. She was dressed in pyjama pants, a tank top and sweater.

10. Martel entered the Norman House and shortly thereafter physically attacked Dumstrey-Soos in and around the laundry room of the Norman House.

11. The attack was unprovoked as that term is defined under section 232(1) of the Criminal Code.

12. Martel struck Dumstrey-Soos multiple times on the back of the head with a wooden implement approximately 2-3 inches in diameter and approximately one foot in length ("Fish Bonker"). The blows caused extensive lacerations over Dumstrey-Soos' entire scalp and multiple skull fractures. Dumstrey-Soos' hands were fractured as a result of her attempting to protect her head from the blows from the Fish Bonker.

13. Blood staining and pieces of hair and scalp ripped from the head of Dumstrey-Soos were located in various locations in the laundry room, evincing a violent struggle. Attached as Exhibit "A" are photographs of the laundry room where Dumstrey-Soos' body was located.

14. After Martel had assaulted Dumstrey-Soos with the Fish Bonker, he bound her hands behind her back with Tuck Tape. He then pulled the sweater she was wearing over her head and wrapped the sweater multiple times with Tuck Tape, securing Dumstrey-Soos' sweater around her head and face.

15. Martel then procured a .22 calibre rifle and shot Dumstrey-Soos in the head and face four times through the sweater and tape. Martel shot Dumstrey-Soos in the left eye, the mouth, the top of the head and the back of the head.

16. When Martel assaulted and shot Dumstrey-Soos he meant to cause her death and in fact did cause her death. Martel possessed the necessary legal intention to murder Dumstry-Soos.

17. Dumstrey-Soos died as a direct result of the injuries described above inflicted upon her by Martel. Attached as Exhibit "B" is the Autopsy Report prepared by Dr. Lisa Steele dated January 12, 2017. Attached as Exhibit "C" are the photographs taken at the autopsy of Dumstrey-Soos.

18. Martel shot the dog he shared with Dumstry-Soos in the head with the same .22 calibre rifle, leaving the dog's dead body in the bathroom adjacent to the laundry room.

19. Martel texted the following messages to Dumstrey-Soos' phone between 4:50 and 5:25 AM on January 4, 2016: "Sorry baby for what I did can't live without you"; "Forgive me god"; and "I love you...can't live without you".

20. Martel returned to the Valhalla House at approximately 6:00 AM on January 4, 2016. At some point, he shot and killed his two cats with the same .22 calibre rifle he had used to shoot Dumstrey-Soos with.

21. Martel left the Valhalla House at approximately 10:00 AM on January 4, 2016 after changing his clothes, leaving the clothing saturated with Dumstrey-Soos' blood in his bedroom. Martel took the .22 calibre rifle that he used in the killing with him.

22. After leaving the Valhalla House, Martel then attended the 100 Mile House transfer station, where he dumped a load of garbage. Nothing of evidential value was located at the dump site after a subsequent search.

23. Martel then attended a local convenience store at approximately 11:20 AM and purchased a piece of pizza and a soft drink.

24. Martel then fled to Kamloops. He checked into a motel in Kamloops at approximately 2:00 PM without advising anyone of his whereabouts. Over the course of the day on January 4, 2016 Martel withdrew $2,340.00 from his bank account. When he was arrested two days later, Martel did not have any cash on his person.

25. Martel turned himself into the police at approximately 2:00 PM on Wednesday, January 6, 2016. Before turning himself in, Martel disposed of the firearm he had used to shoot Dumstrey-Soos with. That firearm has never been recovered.

DATED at Vancouver, the Province of British Columbia, this 11th day of January, 2019.

Kristy Neurauter
Counsel for Michael Edward Martel

DATED at Prince George, the Province of British Columbia, this 11th day of January, 2019.

Richard Fernyhough
Crown Counsel